THE TIME OF YOUR LIFE

To see into the life of things and at the same time to take our proper place in the scheme of things are complementary goals. Understanding the natural rhythms of life as we live them is nothing more or less than what every farmer and naturalist strives for. Those of us who live in urban centers can bring our attention to bear on time and how we experience it. Living in a manner consistent with finding the right times to perform the proper actions can become a way of life, one filled with the most exciting challenges.

Charting the Times of Your Life is like a road map to your yearly life, one which can help navigate the perilous currents and savage pitfalls of existence. The highest goal must not only be understanding our seasonal life here on Earth but also living it—fully, deeply, intelligently—and enjoying it well.

Also by Gary Goldschneider

The Secret Language of Birthdays

The Secret Language of Relationships

The Secret Language of Destiny

CHARTING THE
⋆ TIMES ⋆
OF YOUR LIFE

GARY GOLDSCHNEIDER

Previously published as *The Astrology of Time*

POCKET BOOKS
New York London Toronto Sydney

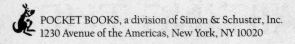 POCKET BOOKS, a division of Simon & Schuster, Inc.
1230 Avenue of the Americas, New York, NY 10020

Library of Congress Cataloging-in-Publication Data
Goldschneider, Gary.
    [Astrology of time]
    Charting the times of your life: an astrological guide to days, weeks, and seasons /
  Gary Goldschneider.—1st Pocket Books trade pbk. ed.
        p.   cm.
    Originally published: The astrology of time. New York: Atria, 2002.
    1. Astrology. I. Title.

BF1708. 1. G6 2005
133.5—dc22   2004051064

ISBN: 0-7434-5693-9
       0-7434-6049-9 (Pbk)

First Pocket Books trade paperback edition January 2005

10 9 8 7 6 5 4 3 2 1

For information regarding special discounts for bulk purchases, please contact
Simon & Schuster Special Sales at 1-800-456-6798 or
business@simonandschuster.com.

Originally published in hardcover in 2002 as *The Astrology of Time*

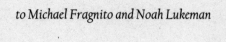

to Michael Fragnito and Noah Lukeman

ACKNOWLEDGMENTS

First I would like to thank my publisher, Judith Curr, for having the vision to issue this unusual book. To my editor at Atria, Brenda Copeland, who brought the book to fruition with great sensitivity and precision: many thanks; also to Peter Christensen.

I would also like to thank my personal editor, Sara Goldschneider, who somehow found time in her busy life to exercise her excellent professional skills.

To Michael Fragnito goes the credit for suggesting that I write this book in the first place.

To Noah Lukeman, my literary agent, much gratitude for formulating the structure of the book and being my representative and friend.

Thanks to Aron Goldschneider, who first got me thinking about the days themselves. Of course, I thank my dear wife, Berthe Meijer, who kept me happy and healthy and furnished (with love) the culinary fuel that powered the savage beast.

Nègremont, France
June 28, 2002

CONTENTS

PREFACE

Things turn out best when they happen at the right moment.

We all know the feeling when things are going well, when we are moving in the right direction, on target, like an arrow heading straight for the bull's-eye. At times like these it seems as if we are being carried along by the flow of events and don't have to struggle to control them. We feel confident and strong. Convinced of the rightness of our actions and the circumstances surrounding them, we feel ready to undertake almost anything. We are secure in our dealings with others. We are able to shoulder responsibilities and complete tasks that would have seemed impossible only a day earlier.

We might find, for example, that a misunderstanding with a close friend, once a source of contention, seems simply and suddenly to have resolved itself. Or we might make a series of telephone calls and find that we are able to reach people immediately and communicate with them effectively. We might even find that our routine seems somehow easier, as a parking space miraculously opens up and a long-awaited check arrives— both on the same day. Life seems easy during times such as these.

But what about those periods when nothing goes right? If things turn out best when they happen at the right moment, does it mean that taking action at the wrong time can spell disaster? Will nothing turn out right if the timing is wrong—no matter what we do? Sometimes it seems like it. Instead of feeling capable and confident we feel anxious and upset. When we no longer trust ourselves, our positions seem unsure. Routine issues are suddenly more complex, and the simplest tasks are no longer simple. At work, our attempts to contact an associate on a routine matter go awry, and several unfavorable e-mails hit our desk, one after another. At home, a child wakes repeatedly throughout the night and a pet makes its demands at just the wrong moment. We pick the wrong time to bring up a certain subject with a friend and he reacts badly. Misunderstanding, chaos, and frustration swirl around us. No matter what we attempt it just turns out wrong.

Are we really justified in assuming that each second, minute, or hour is equal to every other? Or does each unit of time have its own character, its own inherent essence, which makes it distinct from every other one? What if there were qualitative as well as quantitative differences in time? What if the quality of time were just as important as the quantity of it? Could it be that the characteristics of a moment in time—that is, its *rightness* for certain actions, its *feel*—are just as important as the actual length of that moment? If that were true, then rather than trying to give ourselves more hours in each day, we could concern ourselves with raising the temporal quality of our experiences. Our whole outlook on life could change.

Look at time itself. We know two types of time: objective and subjective time, what the Greeks called *chronos* and *kairos*. *Chronos* is objective and quantitative and is usually thought of as *how much time*. *Kairos* is subjective and is thought of as *what kind of time*. The world of western science and technology is based squarely on objective time. Mathematical equations, which describe chemical or electronic processes, deal in precise numbers of seconds, milliseconds, or microseconds, so objectivity is a must. On the other hand, metaphysical, spiritual, or religious matters deal with subjective time, what some might call "God's time." We use a combination of *chronos* and *kairos* in everyday life, but more and more we are interested in quality time, which is one very important aspect of *kairos*.

So, how does time affect what happens both in the universe and in everyday life, and how does it affect the theories of personology, astrology, and other so-called occult disciplines? Think of synchronicity, one of the most important concepts introduced to the world by the Swiss psychiatrist and philosopher Carl Gustav Jung. Jung taught us that a central principle of synchronicity is that events that happen at or around the same time share the qualities of that moment. As he pointed out, there is a whole class of events that just can't be explained by causality; that is, by the laws of cause-and-effect. Why does *this* seemingly random event happen at precisely the same moment that *that* seemingly random event occurs? It's a question we all ask from time to time. Jung thought of synchronicity as psychological in nature and sought to find a correspondence between the psychological state of the observer and the event that occurs. But what if this correspondence were embedded in the very nature of time itself?

Perhaps coincidences are directly related to subjective time—to *kairos*—and even based on the workings of this type of time. When two events happen to occur at the same significant moment in time, the same *kairotic moment*, it means that they are powerfully related to each other. More than that, though, our perception of this connection, our surprise at a seemingly miraculous occurrence, can burst into our consciousness and lead us to believe we have witnessed a miracle. Thus, once we become tuned in to the workings of time, we can see that life is filled with miraculous coincidences that happen all the time, not just once in a lifetime. Understanding the qualitative nature of time, *kairos*, we can learn how to grasp the right moments, and even how to make them work for us in daily life. We begin to live life in a better way, one that produces more beneficial results.

We all need to realize that synchronistic effects can lead to increased understanding, influence our thinking, and even determine the actions we take in the future. Traditionally, however, we are taught to be suspicious of synchronicity and meaningful coincidence, and to base our thoughts on rational analysis and causality.

While synchronicity stresses the importance of two events happening at the same moment in time, causality teaches that things happen according to the laws of cause and effect: When I hit a ball with a bat, causing it to fly into a window and break the glass, I say quite simply that "I broke the window." But why did I manage to hit the ball at just that moment? And of all the places the ball could have gone, why did it go in the unluckiest direction?

The question of hitting the ball at the right or wrong moment is of more interest to someone who thinks according to the principles of *kairos* and synchronicity than it is to someone who thinks of analysis and causality. Of course we can say that the velocity of the ball, the angle of the bat, and the impact of the swing all combined to send the ball flying through the window. But that still doesn't explain the lucky or unlucky aspects of a moment that produces a winning home run for one person and a broken window for another—why one person becomes a hero and another a chump.

An interesting anecdote, perhaps apocryphal, is told about Jung and Freud having a conversation. Freud was telling Jung about a dream he had about a black bird. At the moment Freud described the dream, a great clatter occurred as a large black bird smashed against the window. Freud was obviously shaken by the coincidence but, ever rational, tried to dismiss it as something trivial. Seeing such a confirmation of his theory of synchronicity burst in on his archrival, Jung, however, was thrilled.

Synchronicity says that instead of things happening causally (event A producing event B producing event C), they actually happen simultaneously and share the qualities of the moment. Instead of measuring the seconds and minutes between events, we become more interested in looking at their shared qualities; namely, what they have in common as a result of their happening at the right time. So, in fact, synchronicity is not just two things happening simultaneously, but two things happening simultaneously *at a significant moment in time.* Once we begin thinking of things happening at significant moments, our way of looking at the world changes, and with it the way we live our lives. The quality of time, rather than its quantity, becomes the determining factor.

When a person is born his birthday can be placed in personology's Grand Cycle of Life. That Grand Cycle is made up of three interlocking circles involving the zodiac, the person's age, and the season of the year. Therefore, each birthday has three important frames of reference. For example, if a person is born on April 7 he is an Aries, the first sign of the zodiac. One aspect of his personality is that he is childlike, as he corresponds to approximately age five in his energy level. Also, he is born in the early spring, at the beginning of the personological year. These facts are synchronous with each other; i.e., they refer to the same point in time. When an astrologer draws up his birth chart, synchronicity is at work. He is presented with a diagram of the planets in certain signs at the moment he was born. In this way, at least, astrology and personology are similar, in that they both rely on the principles of synchronicity.

However, this is also where the two disciplines diverge. Personology establishes its twelve cusps firmly on natural earth cycles and on the types of people traditionally born at certain times of the year. Astrology, on the other hand, derives its twelve signs from heavenly constellations of stars. Astrology is based on the birth chart and applies that chart to upcoming events and important days in order to give advice and guidance. The outcome of buying and selling stocks, romances, and business meetings can all be predicted according to your birth chart, and you may even receive advice that tells how the result can be altered. Both disciplines can be used as a guide to daily living, but whereas astrology is celestial and theoretical in orientation, personology is more earthy and pragmatic.

Personology seeks to understand a person and the event he is facing on different terms from astrology. Gone are the technicalities of planetary squares and trines, degrees of the zodiac, place and time of birth, and all the rest of it. In their place only the birthday and day of the event are used. The person born on April 7 learns that he is an Aries II, born in the Week of Success and on the Day of Enthusiastic Belief, and that he has come into this lifetime with very youthful energies that can remain with him for life. That as a springtime person he is an initiator, going through life enthusiastically starting many projects and finishing very few. That he understands the world best through the faculty of intuition.

Each of us is born on a day that exhibits objective characteristics. At the same time, we live the days of the year, which themselves carry their own energy. When the energy of our own particular birthday collides with that of any day, week, month, or season of the year, we may experience a gratifying or unsatisfying result, which in turn can manifest itself as success or failure, joy or disappointment, pleasure or pain. That we all have good days and bad days is general knowledge, but based on the astrology of time we can anticipate year after year which seasons will be favorable or unfavorable. Could this possibly be true? Do we even subconsciously expect events to turn out a certain way if they occur on a specific day?

Let's return to our April 7 person. During the springtime, the season in which he was born, the quality of intuition that is his birthright is in full flower. This could be the best time of year for him. But what happens during the fall and winter, when the faculties of sensation and thought are dominant? Will this be an uncomfortable time for him or one in which he does not traditionally do well? On the other hand, how do people born in the fall deal with springtime energies? Specific answers will be given in the four main sections of this book, but suffice it to say that challenges are learning experiences as well, and that being comfortable with the time of the year in which we were born may not be the be-all and end-all.

We are often attracted not only to people born in an opposite astro-logical sign and in another season of the year but to times of the year quite different from the ones in which we ourselves are born. Although these energies are radically different from our own, we are able to interact with and learn from them. During some periods in our lives we want things to go easily so we can gain emotional satisfaction or pleasure; at others we look for challenge, and we need to grow by battering through obstacles, solving problems, and overcoming difficulties.

As this book will explain, personology enables us to establish certain objective criteria about different times of the year, as hard as this may be to believe. But think of it. Wasn't the development of the calendar in human history precisely such an undertaking? The times of planting and harvest, of the first or last frosts, the longest and shortest days, as well as the ones on which the lengths of days and nights were equal, were of utmost importance. Even our ancestors recognized that seasons are good and bad for certain activities.

For modern city dwellers, who seem irrevocably cut off from the nat-ural cycles of the seasons, rediscovering the natural rhythms of life and tuning in to them can become a very exciting endeavor. Indeed, these sea-sonal cycles slumber within every one of us, exerting their subtle influences deep within, most often outside of our awareness of them. Much of the research on SAD, seasonal affective disorder, has shown how biochemical reactions to lack of light in the dark days of winter may cause or contribute to depression and other psychological disorders.

In contrast to astrology, psychology, and sociology, the personological approach to life urges us to understand our birthday, or indeed any given day, deeply and thoroughly before going on to examine other facts about our birth. By stressing the importance of finding our place in the yearly cycle we can begin to look at the world, ourselves, and others in a new way, perhaps eventually coming to live in harmony with our world instead of battling against it.

The whole question of the relationships among personology, astrology, synchronicity, and time itself, particularly the time of *kairos*, is a fascinating one. But it is in the living out of these concepts, in experiencing and coming to grips with them in everyday life, that the most gratifying rewards can be found. Sharing a telepathic experience with a friend, for example, can touch us to the core of our being. A chance happening, such as the meeting of a former acquaintance or lover after the passage of many years, can teach a great deal about how life works and lead us to think at a deeper level about whether there is such a thing as coincidence at all. In fact, perhaps coincidence is the highest law of the universe rather than just the meaningless accident we are taught it to be by older and "wiser" minds than ours.

I am often asked what my own personal philosophy is. I usually answer: "I believe that we live in a universe of chance, punctuated by miracles and ruled by God." In a sense, no individual action occurs by chance, because everything occurs by chance, and it is in the strange coincidence of these chance happenings that true miracles occur, more often than we think, if only we were open to perceiving them. Epiphanies can occur once in a lifetime or every minute, according to our perceptions of them. It has been argued by Aldous Huxley in *The Doors of Perception* that every event, past, present, and future, that has ever occurred should be available to us at any moment, but that these doors are closed by parents, teachers, and indeed by us ourselves in order to keep our sanity. But why not open those doors just a crack, work with those marvelous energies, and gradually open them wider, allowing a kind of superconscious awareness in all of us, at the very least at certain important moments in our lives.

To see into the life of things and at the same time to take our proper place in the scheme of things are complementary goals. Understanding the natural rhythms of life and at the same time living them is nothing more or less than what every farmer and naturalist strives for. Those of us who live in urban centers can bring our attention to bear on time and how we experience it. Living in a manner consonant with finding the right times to perform the proper actions can become a way of life, one filled with the most exciting challenges. *Charting the Times of Your Life* is like a road map to your yearly life, one which can help navigate the perilous currents and savage pitfalls of existence. The highest goal must not only be understanding our seasonal life here on Earth but also living it—fully, deeply, intelligently—and enjoying it as well.

Time present and time past
Are both perhaps present in time future,
And time future contained in time past.

—T. S. Eliot

Go ahead. Make my day.

—Clint Eastwood

THE PERSONOLOGY OF TIME

Personology theory is decidedly Earth-oriented. Its yearly rhythms are always the same, endlessly repeating the cycles of progressively longer and shorter days, demarcated by the way stations of the two solstices and two equinoxes. These are the basic facts of life as we humans have experienced it, from prehistoric times right up to the present. The earth is of course alive, and it is Mother Gaia's cycles and rhythms that we are forced to live. Perhaps Earth is not our original home, but in adjusting to it we have internalized its conditions into our very DNA.

Astrology, on the other hand, deals with the stars from whence we came. We know that primitive man was fascinated by the shape of the constellations in the night sky and that, almost from the beginning of time, societies around the world formulated the signs of the zodiac that we know as the basis of astrology. Mapping out the movement of the planets through the signs and making predictions about people's lives and future events based on planetary transits (and the aspects they formed with each other) became the task of the astrologer. Perhaps astrologers are simply occupied with mapping out the course of our lives as planetary beings. And perhaps our fascination with planetary cycles is nothing less than the transference of our longing to return to our true home.

Personology is not opposed to astrology in any way. In fact, it is derived from it. Personology incorporates the human aspect of astrology into a system based on many other disciplines: biography, psychology, numerology, tarot, medicine, and even music. Every human activity finds its place in personology, including forming relationships.

It is precisely this derivation from human experience here on Earth that allows personology to become a kind of practical guide to living. Personology is related not only to astrology but to human psychology as well. But where the psychological study of personality is more focused on the individual and his or her problems (and, in the last fifty years, concentrated more on social interaction and genetic influences), personology relates the individual to natural cycles. By putting men, women, and children into a comprehensive world picture, the theory of personology can help explain humans as cosmic beings. Personology is vital and dynamic. It takes psychology out of the clinic and into the real world by positioning humans in the world of nature.

So personology draws on both psychological and astrological theories and research, and in essence yokes them together at common points. However, by combining these principles, personology has evolved into a separate and distinct discipline. It has formed its own set of basic parameters by structuring the year in a cross formed by the solstices and equinoxes, and in so doing has thrown a whole new light on the human condition.

Personology regards the lengthening and shortening of days and nights, accompanied by the yearly rhythm of seasonal change, to be the basic facts of mankind's existence here on Earth. For thousands, indeed millions, of years, mankind and its ancestors have lived this rhythm until it is bound up in our biological structure. Although mankind traditionally has ordered the year astrologically, personology points out that it is not the celestial constellations or signs, but the cusps between them, that in fact have more relevance to our daily life. The two solstices and two equinoxes, which are the way stations of the year, demarcate the beginning and end of each of the four seasons. Furthermore, these four pivotal points of the year are astrological cusps, or transitional areas, between pairs of adjacent signs. Spring begins on the Pisces-Aries cusp (March 19–24), summer on the Gemini-Cancer cusp (June 19–24), fall on the Virgo-Libra cusp (September 19–24), and winter on the Sagittarius-

Capricorn cusp (December 19–25), in the northern hemisphere. These fixed points have stayed constant.

In the process of building the personology theory, I gave names to these four power points, namely, the Cusp of Rebirth, the Cusp of Magic, the Cusp of Beauty, and the Cusp of Prophecy. I derived these names from the natures of the people born during those times and, once established, I named the other eight cusps. Finally, I gave titles to the thirty-six "weeks," or periods between each cusp (beginning with Aries I, Aries II, and Aries III, and ending with Pisces I, Pisces II, and Pisces III). Ultimately, every day of the year was named, giving the present-day format of personology (seasons, signs, weeks, and days, in increasing order of specificity).

Thus certain signs, cusps, and other periods of time have names that identify, classify, and, to a certain extent, explain personalities. This is the basis of personology: the psychology of personality. However, having named these time periods and described the kinds of people born in them, I stopped there. It didn't occur to me to go one step further to realize that in describing the kind of people born on a given day I was also describing the energy of the day itself.

My son Aron, editor of *The Secret Language of Birthdays*, shocked me one day years ago by posing a very straightforward question, one he had obviously been thinking about for a long time. He asked me cautiously whether it had ever occurred to me that it might be possible to describe not only the energies of the people born on a given day but the energy of the day itself. Surprised, I replied that I hadn't thought about it and, putting it out of my mind, turned to the next task at hand. Yet his question returned repeatedly years later and began to haunt me.

For a long time it had seemed necessary only to name, classify, and categorize the different kinds of personalities. But once all three of my books had been published and sold, reviewed and assimilated, I felt free to contemplate my son's question, to move on and broaden the theory of personology and its applications, and to consider other, perhaps larger, concerns, such as time itself. Thus, the study of the astrology of time has led me to deepen personology theory with reference to the energies of the seasons, months, weeks, and days themselves, and at the same time to show how this theory can be used in everyday life.

Why is it necessary to bring an interesting and perhaps amusing cosmology such as personology out of the realm of the theoretical? And could applying it in our lives really effect important changes? If the last one hundred years have taught us anything, it has been the importance of perception, of bringing our points of view and thoughts to bear on changing reality. So what of our perception and understanding of time? Isn't that important too? The answer, of course, is a resounding *yes*. Living the seasons and fully understanding our connections to Earth's rhythms can open us up to the most fundamental and firmly established principles of our existence. And if changing our orientations (our thinking) can have immediate and practical consequences on the way we view our lives, then understanding the seasons and the astrology of time can have immediate and practical consequences on the way we live them.

TO EVERYTHING A SEASON

The cycles and natural rhythms of the cosmos are determining factors in our daily lives. The moon—Earth's satellite—influences earthly events, such as the tides and the female menstrual cycle, with its waxings and wanings. It can even hold sway over our psychological state—which explains the unfortunate label *lunatic*. We live our lives according to the sun's light, with diurnal variations of day and night determining our waking and sleeping patterns. And of course the phenomenon of the seasons themselves is due to the interaction of the sun and Earth.

Astrology has long taught us that the position of the planets in our solar system influences every aspect of our lives. Many cultures bear this out. Churches historically pointed upward in Eastern Europe and soared to the sky in the medieval cathedrals of Western Europe so that heavenly energies could be directly conveyed from God to the worshiper, through the crown chakra, or top of the head. Western customs symbolized the heavenly grace bestowed on human beings with the monarch's crown and the halo behind the head of every depicted saint. The Russian tradition signified this direct streaming of energy by pouring a basket filled with small gold coins over the head of the new czar at his coronation. Our modern skyscrapers may be marvels of innovation and engineering, yet they also serve as powerful symbols of our attempt to reach out and make contact with cosmic forces and conduct their energies back to earth. Perhaps we are reaching out to God?

As soon as we accept how cosmic and earthly energies are related to each other, our whole outlook on life changes. We begin to see our daily world as the midpoint between the macrocosm of space and its galaxies and the microcosm of molecules and atoms. Our lives are only one level of the life around us and within us. During the Middle Ages it was widely believed that each level of existence was connected to the next, that an invisible chain was formed between animals, humanity, the spirits, the angels, and finally, God. This theory, known as the Great Chain of Being, affected everyday life in the most practical of ways. It permeated religion, of course, but also government, the arts, architecture, medicine, and romance. People felt secure and knew they were part of a bigger plan. Even though they suffered terribly from disease, war, and pestilence, they had few doubts about their place in the universe.

The loss of this orientation, stemming from the rise of rational thought and technology, is at once the triumph and tragedy of the Western world. The rise of science in the West did much to eliminate certain diseases and resulted in man having a greater influence over his environment. But, at the same time, we lost our place in the universe and our connection with natural phenomena and cycles. By attempting to control and subdue nature, we have lost contact with it. By ignoring the connection between nature and ourselves, we continue to destroy each other and our own environment.

The Grand Cycle of Life relies on the interconnectedness of the life of man and woman, the cycles of the seasons, and a band of heavenly con-stellations around the earth (what we call the zodiac). A great belt of stars, the zodiac stimulated even the earliest civilizations with its patterns. The configurations made by the night stars have long prompted watchers to connect the dots and create huge symbolic figures—Sagittarius the Archer, Taurus the Bull, Pisces the Fish, and so forth—that are now con-sidered archetypes of human nature and behavior. Indicative of humanity's long-standing obsession with the night sky, with its stars and planets, these archetypes also came to represent elements of history, religion, nat-ural phenomena, psychology—and in fact became a projection of human life itself.

All planets, as well as the sun and the moon, travel through each constellation in turn. That's why, when viewed from the earth, the positions of each planet may be seen in any given sign and why the position of the planets relative to each other can also be viewed and studied. As investigation into the stars became more sophisticated, the amount of time needed for each planet to travel once around the zodiac circle became apparent. Four everyday concepts we often take for granted—the day, the month, the year, and the lifetime—are really derived from cosmic cycles. The day is the period when the earth turns once on its axis relative to the sun; the month is the time it takes the moon to revolve once around the earth; the year is the time needed for the earth to complete one orbit around the sun; and the lifetime is approximately the time it takes the planet Uranus to complete one revolution around the sun.

Embedded in the celestial cycle of the year is the cycle of the seasons. Connected to the seasonal nature of the zodiac signs, the seasons are, quite naturally, connected with the celestial cycle itself.

Spring signs: Aries, Taurus, Gemini
Summer signs: Cancer, Leo, Virgo
Fall signs: Libra, Scorpio, Sagittarius
Winter signs: Capricorn, Aquarius, Pisces

And just as there is a connection between the celestial and the earthly cycles, the cycle of man's life from birth to death is also tethered to the seasons. Traditionally considered a straight line, this progression of life is considered a cyclical one by personology and is divided into seven-year periods, each of which corresponds to an astrological sign and to a season of the year, as follows:

Birth to age 7—Aries—early spring
Age 7 to 14—Taurus—midspring
Age 14 to 21—Gemini—late spring
Age 21 to 28—Cancer—early summer
Age 28 to 35—Leo—midsummer

Age 35 to 42—Virgo—late summer
Age 42 to 49—Libra—early fall
Age 49 to 56—Scorpio—midfall
Age 56 to 63—Sagittarius—late fall
Age 63 to 70—Capricorn—early winter
Age 70 to 77—Aquarius—midwinter
Age 77 to 84—Pisces—late winter

Now the big question arises: How do I live my life according to this system? Is it even desirable to do so? Before answering this question, it is necessary to make one important observation. The Western philosopher Immanuel Kant believed that we create the world every time we look at it, in terms of space, time, and causality, even though, in actuality, we don't really know what is out there. This is just another way of saying that to someone who looks at the world through rose-colored glasses, everything always appears good, and that a pessimist expects the worst each day and usually gets it.

Kant's theories will not say anything new to those readers who believe in the concepts of visualization and self-fulfilling prophecies. What we think and say has a tremendous influence on what happens to us in our lives. To return to the issue of living life personologically, let us assume that human beings could come to believe in the basic principles of personology or in another spiritual, humanistic discipline that stresses the theme "as above, so below." This belief is a primary principle of esoteric thought, a principle that was taught by many philosophers the world over in every period of recorded history. Hermetic philosophers, the Greeks, the Egyptians, the Babylonians, the Jews, the Sufis, and medieval Christians all related the heavens to the earth, higher spiritual thought to earthly existence, God's world to man's world. Basically, this belief means that the cycles and natural rhythms of the cosmos are determining factors in our daily lives. Personology, as a modern discipline, bases itself squarely on the principle "as above, so below" and thus reveals itself as a contemporary discipline partially based on traditional metaphysical thought.

Assuming that we could come to believe in the basic principles of personology or in another spiritual, humanistic discipline that stresses this esoteric theme, the consequences of just this act of belief could be startling. If we could learn to respect Nature at a high level of commitment, we would be less willing to pollute the earth and deplete its natural resources. We would stop killing off whole living species, genetically altering the food we grow, and changing global weather patterns through the burning of fossil fuels. On a personal level we could begin to live our daily lives, pursue our careers, form our relationships, and indulge in leisure-time activities with our connection to earthly and cosmic cycles in mind, respectful of the laws of the universe and the position we occupy in the hierarchy of things.

To live in harmony with Nature and its cycles would create a new basis for civilized life. We need to recognize and respect the importance of natural phenomena and their links not only to mankind's existence but also to the life of the universe itself. Even the order of the stars and the natural beauty of the heavenly zodiac are there to remind us of the magnificence of Nature's life. We would do well to bear this in mind as we move to fulfill our spiritual destinies.

Spring

Spring! After the cold, dark days of winter the word arouses such joy. It summons up visions of hillsides bursting into bloom, of trees and shrubs gently unfolding their new greenery, of newborn lambs bleating and fresh smells abounding. City parks are also in leaf and the lovely smells of spring in the air put a skip in the step of even the most cynical urban residents. Spring fever takes hold of our romantic sensibilities, making infatuation or falling in love almost inevitable. Life becomes more spontaneous, and we have more energy and interest to launch new projects and endeavors. Spring gives us a chance to start afresh and holds a new promise for each day. As day follows night, so does spring inexorably follow winter, allowing us to start anew with a clean slate. Tomorrow is another day; spring begins another year.

When March 21 rolls around the weather is often wild and unpredictable. This turbulence is an important part of what spring is really about; unfortunately, so many of us are eagerly awaiting the sunshine that we feel that spring hasn't arrived until the weather turns warm and sunny and it's almost summer.

In reality, spring is not only unpredictable but also quite violent, particularly in countries like Russia, Canada, and the United States, where the melting ice transforms tiny streams into torrents of raging water. A profusion of growth in the plant world takes place in early spring, and this growth is mirrored by an explosion in the insect population. Animals who have been struggling to survive or have been dormant for many months now wake up and come to life. And of course all of these natural phenomena, including the lengthening of the days and a general warming trend, are reflected in the psyches of the human inhabitants of our planet.

Those born in the spring, so-called springtime people, are initiators or start-uppers. Springtime people excel at starting new projects. They are the best people to rely on for developing new ideas or endeavors. Because they often have acute faculties of intuition, those born in the spring are most productive when following their hunches. Frequently impulsive, springtime people expend their energy in quick bursts and inspire those around them with their enthusiasm. Not necessarily in it for the long haul, they keep moving forward so that they can begin yet another endeavor and they tend to leave their projects for summer and fall people to bring to fruition. Springtime people often leave a trail of unfinished projects behind them.

However, it's important to address more than the personalities of people born in the spring—we also must address the nature of springtime endeavors themselves. During spring we become once again engaged in spending more time outdoors. This is the time for running, jumping, climbing, and laughing. Optimism abounds, accompanied by the abundance of energy needed to get jobs done. People take great pleasure in family outings, picnics, hikes in the woods or mountains, and excursions of all kinds. A hunger to make the most of the time between the past dark and cold days and the coming hot and humid ones, to once more emerge into full-blown activity takes hold of many of us.

Personology teaches us that the yearly cycle of nature coincides with the cycles of human life and of the zodiac. Springtime therefore not only symbolizes the first twenty-one years of human life, but also the first three signs of the zodiac: Aries, Taurus, and Gemini. Turning first to the human development from birth to the end of the teenage years, we find a bewildering process of growth and differentiation, not unlike the development of organic life in nature during the springtime. Often a time of violent change, both the season and the corresponding period of human development are irrepressibly caught up in the processes of initiation, of bursting energies, and of behavior guided by the fiery forces of will, which struggles against any attempts to hold it down or back.

Likewise, events occurring in the signs of Aries, Taurus, and Gemini happen quickly and often unexpectedly. Those born under these signs benefit from contact with stable and responsible personalities who can ground their creative impulses. The signs of Aries, Taurus, and Gemini state as their mottoes "I am," "I have," and "I communicate." We see the Aries child putting his roots down in the sign of Taurus and learning the value of communication in Gemini. Thus the progress or evolution from one sign to the next mirrors that in nature and in human development.

The Spring Personology Periods:
March 21 to June 21

The Weeks

The season of spring lasts from the spring equinox of March 21 until the summer solstice of June 21. It is composed of the three astrological signs of Aries (March 21–April 20), Taurus (April 21–May 21), and Gemini (May 22–June 21). This first quarter of the year is further subdivided in personology into the following "weeks" or personology periods:

Pisces-Aries Cusp: The Cusp of Rebirth (March 19–24)
Aries I: The Week of Curiosity (March 25–April 2)
Aries II: The Week of Success (April 3–10)
Aries III: The Week of Social Betterment (April 11–18)
Aries-Taurus Cusp: The Cusp of Power (April 19–24)
Taurus I: The Week of Manifestation (April 25–May 2)
Taurus II: The Week of Study (May 3–10)
Taurus III: The Week of Nature (May 11–18)
Taurus-Gemini Cusp: The Cusp of Energy (May 19–24)
Gemini I: The Week of Freedom (May 25–June 2)
Gemini II: The Week of Communication (June 3–10)
Gemini III: The Week of Exploration (June 11–18)
Gemini-Cancer Cusp: The Cusp of Magic (June 19–24)

The Cusps

The spring quadrant is given structure by the cusps between the astrological signs. At the beginning of spring we have the spring equinox, known in personology as the Cusp of Rebirth, which distinguishes it from other seasons. At the end of spring there is the summer solstice, the Cusp of Magic. At monthly intervals between these two important points we find the Cusp of Power (between Aries and Taurus) and the Cusp of Energy (between the signs of Taurus and Gemini). These four cusps: Rebirth, Power, Energy, and Magic help characterize the season of spring as fully as the signs of Aries, Taurus, and Gemini, but in a more human sense. This is because we are no longer referring to the abstract formations of stars in the heavenly constellations but rather to life as it is lived here on Earth. By bringing the frame of reference closer, we better relate it to our daily existence.

✳

The Cusp of Rebirth

MARCH 19–24

The Cusp of Rebirth corresponds with the advent of the spring equinox in the northern hemisphere. Thus, this six-day period is the quintessential start-up point in the whole year. The best time to launch new projects, the Cusp of Rebirth favors all new beginnings, especially those that are motivated by pure impulses, unfettered with calculation and preconceived notions. Once under way, projects begun at this time move on by themselves with unstoppable energy.

The faculty of intuition is stronger in the spring than at any other time of the year. This means that we should not get bogged down in any of the other faculties: emotion, sensation, or thought. Now is not the time to worry or carefully plan things out, or to wallow in sensuous or cloying feelings. The spark of impulsiveness must be kept alive, for it will not be available at any other time in the year in such an untrammeled form. Joining intuition and impulse together can result in an irresistible force, allowing us to move mountains.

Traditionally a time in which we begin our spring cleaning and make household repairs, the warm weather also ushers spring fever into our lives. Spring promotes all sorts of romantic advances, sexual or otherwise. As the sap begins to run in trees, so does our blood begin to run warm again after a long freeze. As we search for new companions or objects of desire, fantasy and love begin to develop in the strangest ways. Chance meetings abound at this time, throwing the most unexpected combinations of potential partners together in the oddest of circumstances. Awkwardness is common during this period, for everything is so new that there are few precedents or habitual modes of behavior to rely on.

As springtime can be a catalyst in the onset of violent events, the flood of human emotions that is released at this time can cause ordinary happenings to turn violent too. Special care must be taken to avoid being alone with someone who has been showing signs of instability. Such meetings are better negotiated in a public place, where social control can be operative. Moreover, our own passions must be expressed, but also mastered. In this way frustration will be avoided and the energy put to better use, particularly for the benefit of others.

The greatest danger on the Cusp of Rebirth, of course, is that spiraling energies will spin out of control. The damage caused by such volatile forces can be considerable. However, it is usually of the type that can also mend quickly, in the physical and emotional spheres. In addition, it may be necessary for old habits to be destroyed, and such destruction can prove ultimately to have a positive, even liberating, result. Relationships that have failed to evolve may have to be discarded, painful as the process may be. In this week, an old relationship can be quickly replaced with a new one. Jealousy and possessiveness have little power in this week, compared to the strong need for personal expression. Like the process of birth itself, from which the cusp takes its name, going backward is detrimental; the only way to go is forward.

The Personology of People Born on the Cusp of Rebirth

Those born on this cusp are not easy to handle. Extremely direct and out-spoken, they are not overly concerned with what others think about their often aggressive attitudes. They usually tend to get their way through their insistence that they are correct. Because of the more sensitive and watery nature of Pisces and the dynamic and fiery temperament of Aries, these individuals embody an odd mix of the faculties of feeling and intuition. Not fond of being criticized or analyzed, Pisces-Aries people feel that with regard to themselves, they are what they are; take it or leave it.

Annual Events That Occur on the Cusp of Rebirth

March 21: Day for the Elimination of Racial Discrimination
    Spring Equinox: day and night are equal in length
March 23: Liberty Day

Major Historical Events That Have Happened on the Cusp of Rebirth

March 19, 1932: Sydney Harbor Bridge opened in Australia
March 20, 1815: Napoleon returns from exile on island of Elba
March 21, 1871: Bismarck opens first parliament of German Reich
March 22, 1919: First international airline service established
March 23, 1919: Mussolini's Fascist party established
March 24, 1603: Elizabethan Age ends with death of Elizabeth I of England

Famous People Born on the Cusp of Rebirth

Spike Lee, Bruce Willis, Ruth Page, William Shatner, Joan Crawford, Johann Sebastian Bach, Holly Hunter, Philip Roth, Glenn Close, Gary Oldman, Akira Kurosawa, Chaka Khan, William Jennings Bryan, George Benson, Pat Bradley, Ingrid Kristiansen, Matthew Broderick, Sergey Diaghilev, Fanny Farmer, Wyatt Earp

Birthdays Especially Affected on the Cusp of Rebirth

If you are born on the Cusp of Rebirth (March 19–24), the Cusp of Oscillation (July 19–25), or the Cusp of Revolution (November 19–24) your energies blend well with those of this week. Results should be obtained with little effort on your part.

Cusp of Rebirth people will be free to express the full force of their initiative and intuition. Cusp of Oscillation people can capitalize on their love of adventure and excitement. Cusp of Revolution people will find their feisty nature rewarded in beginning new endeavors.

If you are born on the Cusp of Magic (June 19–24), the Cusp of Beauty (September 19–24), or the Cusp of Prophecy (December 19–25) you will face problems and challenges during this week. You will have to work harder to achieve your goals.

Cusp of Magic people have to learn to keep their emotions under control and remain objective. Cusp of Beauty people may need to sacrifice some of their love of pleasure in order to get the ball rolling. Cusp of Prophecy people should try to be more open and spontaneous.

✹

The Week of Curiosity

MARCH 25–APRIL 2

During this week we must follow our drive to explore and investigate everything around us. Curiosity may have killed the cat, but we all know that we often get nowhere without it. Testing our surroundings is not only a way to get ahead, but also to evaluate whether the bridge we are crossing is strong enough to support our weight. The primal energy of the preceding week (the Cusp of Rebirth) is tempered here by a cautious demeanor, rather than manifesting as a headlong rush. Although the drive in the Week of Curiosity is just as strong, it is more purposeful.

Probably the most difficult task to attempt during this week is to get to know ourselves in a meditative or self-critical fashion. Yet some introspection will take us a long way here. Reflection can even become a constant companion of action, allowing us to evaluate and appreciate a dynamic experience as it is being undertaken. In this way, the need for action can be expressed but in a more thoughtful fashion.

The other side of curiosity—observation—is also important in this week. Indeed, there will be times during which our purposes are better served by watching rather than doing. By putting the emphasis on observing how something is done, we can prepare ourselves for new experiences in the future.

Be careful. If undue value is placed on action during the Week of Curiosity, depression may be experienced in quite severe forms. Such depression may result when things do not seem to be happening with any speed or regularity. Remember: Our own quiescent states mimic the nonhappening in the immediate environment. Also, since depression is frequently nothing more than anger kept deep down inside, the disappointment which results from lack of action must be mastered. This requires some philosophical detachment and a real belief that tomorrow is another day, bringing with it new hope.

Playfulness is especially favored during this week. Not only formal games, sports, and friendly competition of all types, but a playful attitude expressed in our daily lives. Light banter in our speech or a slight skip in our step conveys to others a lighthearted attitude which can be particularly persuasive and nonthreatening. By keeping our view on life light, we will succeed far better during this time than by forcing things or smashing obstacles aside.

Because of the childlike energies of the Week of Curiosity, our own inner child must be acknowledged and valued. This is not the right time to expect seasoned experience and wisdom from others or ourselves, but rather to appreciate innocence, simplicity, and even naïveté. By valuing untutored or untried energies and emotions, we can come in contact with some of the most basic areas of human existence. A fresh, uncomplicated approach to life is especially favored now. With it will come a direct and new appreciation of all the many wonders of life, as if experienced for the first time.

The Personology of People Born in the Week of Curiosity

Childlike, those born in this week prefer a straightforward approach to life. Yet, although they demand that others be straight with them, they may exhibit highly complex behavior and struggle with their deep feelings. Nothing can bother people born in the Week of Curiosity more than being misunderstood or having their words twisted or misinterpreted. Because of their extreme honesty, they find it difficult to dissemble or engage in underhanded activities. Their nobility impresses others and usually endears them to friends and foes alike. Although quick to be irritated or angered, they are also quick to forgive. The quietude of their nature may only be apparent to those who know them well, and they do not reveal their true self easily to others.

Annual Events That Occur During the Week of Curiosity

April 1: April Fool's Day
April 2: International Children's Book Day

Major Historical Events That Have Happened During the Week of Curiosity

March 25, 1957: European Common Market established
March 26, 1979: Israel and Egypt sign peace agreement
March 27, 1899: First international radio transmission
March 28, 1917: Founding of Women's Army Auxiliary Corps (WAAC)
March 29, 1886: Coca-Cola first goes on sale
March 30, 1981: Assassination attempt on Ronald Reagan
March 31, 1889: Eiffel Tower opened in Paris
April 1, 1945: U.S. forces invade Iwo Jima
April 2, 1860: First Italian Parliament convenes

Famous People Born During the Week of Curiosity

Al Gore, Sandra Day O'Connor, Quentin Tarantino, Mariah Carey, Arturo Toscanini, Diana Ross, Hans Christian Andersen, Vincent van Gogh, Aretha Franklin, Nikolay Gogol, Astrud Gilberto, Leonard Nimoy, Alec Guinness, St. Teresa de Avila, Toshiro Mifune, Liz Claiborne, Cesar Chavez, Sergey Rachmaninoff, Camille Paglia, Robert Frost

Birthdays Especially Affected During the Week of Curiosity

If you are born in the Week of Curiosity (March 25–April 2), the Week of Passion (July 26–August 2), or the Week of Independence (November 25–December 2) your energies blend well with those of this week. Results should be obtained with little effort on your part.

Week of Curiosity people can give full rein to their playfulness and be appreciated for their childlike demeanor. Week of Passion people will be admired for their honesty and straightforwardness. Week of Independence people bring a fresh, new approach to the projects in which they are involved.

If you are born in the Week of Empathy (June 25–July 2), the Week of Perfection (September 25–October 2), or the Week of Rule (December 26–January 2) you will face problems and challenges during this week. You will have to work harder to achieve your goals.

Week of Empathy people must be aware of getting bogged down in heavy, complex emotional states. Week of Perfection people should let up in their critical attitudes and take things as they come. Week of Rule people could work on being less bossy and lightening up a bit.

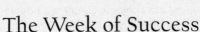

The Week of Success

APRIL 3—APRIL 10

Those who wish for success during this week will need to place themselves at the center of all that is going on around them. Bear in mind, however, that stardom is not the destiny of every human being during this time. Many quiet or unassuming individuals can well advance their cause by making sure that their work is indispensable to others. This can be accomplished by playing an important, even central, role in the activities of family or professional or social organizations. Now is not the time to be shy or retiring, but to stand up for ourselves and what we believe in.

This may very well be the first week since the cold, dark days of winter when we finally leave our sheltered cocoons and emerge fully into the blazing light of recognition. This is not egotism nor unbridled conceit, but rather the firm demand that we and our work be taken seriously. To count, to matter, to be important to others is the message of this week. Of course, appreciation is involved, for without this many weaker souls may fail to exhibit the courage necessary for their personal and career success.

Success has, of course, many meanings. For most it means worldly success, often measured in terms of status, power, or money. But there is also personal success, which cannot be measured in material wealth. This kind of self-realization is often the result of years of patient work, either a struggle for self-knowledge or the fruition of a private passion or hobby. The Week of Success favors the culmination of such endeavors, accompanied by their revelation for all the world to see.

Spiritual success can be measured by the yardstick of devotion, and often by the overcoming of indulgent, addictive, or other self-destructive tendencies. Those in search of high spiritual ideals may also succeed in achieving a level of understanding or acceptance not available to them before. Submission and service, not often recognized as high ideals by a society obsessed with status, may finally be achieved, and along with them a negation of purely egoistic drives. This in no way keeps such individuals from developing a healthy ego commensurate with personal health and development.

The image of a shining star is apt for this week. Inspirational in nature, such energy urges others in the vicinity to also radiate their light outward for all to see. Such energy is indeed contagious, and can lead a group or even a community to rise to the occasion and exhibit the very best they are capable of doing. In this way, the Week of Success can apply to groups as well as to individuals, although its energies usually commence with the success of one enlightened member. Incidentally, failures are also highly possible in this week but should be viewed in the most positive light. Even attempts at success which have temporarily gone astray should be understood, reorganized, and then attempted again at a later and more propitious date.

The Personology of People Born in the Week of Success

Even people born during this week who are not cut out for stardom love to be at the center of what is going on, whether in a family, social, or professional setting. Although solitude attracts them, they will not tolerate being ignored for very long. Actually, they often keep quiet because they do not believe in telling others how great they are, but hope to demonstrate their power with deeds rather than words. Making themselves indispensable to any group of which they are a part, they guarantee a good amount of social interaction for themselves. Thus, although strongly individualistic in orientation, they are very sensitive to the attitudes of others.

Annual Events That Occur During the Week of Success

April 6: National Tartan Day
April 7: World Health Day
April 9: Appomattox Day
        Holocaust Remembrance Day
April 10: Salvation Army Founders Day

Major Historical Events That Have Happened During the Week of Success

April 3, 1922: Joseph Stalin appointed head of Communist party

April 4, 1968: Martin Luther King, Jr., assassinated

April 5, 1794: Revolutionary French leader Danton guillotined

April 6, 1917: United States enters World War I

April 7, 1906: Mount Vesuvius erupts

April 8, 1838: Transatlantic steamship service inaugurated

April 9, 1865: Lee surrenders to Grant at Appomattox

April 10, 1912: *Titanic* sets sail on ill-fated voyage

Famous People Born During the Week of Success

Eddie Murphy, Billie Holiday, Francis Ford Coppola, Marguerite Duras, Harry Houdini, Carmen McRae, Ravi Shankar, Maya Angelou, Colin Powell, Muddy Waters, John Madden, Jane Goodall, Gregory Peck, Betty Ford, Marsha Mason, Marlon Brando, Merle Haggard, Mary Pickford, Steven Seagal, Paul Robeson

Birthdays Especially Affected During the Week of Success

If you are born in the Week of Success (April 3–10), the Week of Challenge (August 3–10), or the Week of Originality (December 3–10) your energies blend well with those of this week. Results should be obtained with little effort on your part.

Week of Success people will shine and enjoy being at center stage. Week of Challenge people can exert the full force of their personalities in striving for high goals in their professional lives. Week of Originality people bring their own unique vision to any project in which they participate.

If you are born in the Week of Unconventionality (July 3–10), the Week of Socialization (October 3–10), or the Week of Determination (January 3–9) you will face problems and challenges during this week. You will have to work harder to achieve your goals.

Week of Unconventionality people may arouse antagonisms from those who fail to appreciate their unusual ideas; therefore, they should explain themselves fully. Week of Socialization people should put their people skills to use and avoid passivity and procrastination. Week of Determination people are so driven to succeed that they may very well stress themselves out; they should learn to relax a bit more.

✳

The Week of Social Betterment

APRIL 11–18

This is the time to renew our efforts toward improving the lot of those in our immediate surroundings. This means not only working to help individuals but also groups, particularly those that have dedicated themselves to community service. A growing realization that we are all here to serve, indeed that service may be the highest spiritual activity of all, will bring individuals far in their quest for enlightenment.

Strong leadership and pioneering energies also abound in this week; consequently we should not shirk the responsibilities placed on our shoulders when it comes to taking charge of a family or other social group. Such energies do not imply dictatorial powers, but on the contrary, a positive kind of leadership which can be exerted by any member of the group exercising his or her own strengths and particular area of expertise. Here being a good leader implies being a good follower and team player as well.

In the Week of Social Betterment we acknowledge the equality of our fellow human beings and forge bonds with them based on deeply human values. A curious blend of reform and tradition manifests in this week. We look to the past for an affirmation of traditional values and toward the future in order to better the living standards of those around us. Religion and spirituality may assume a more important role for us in this week, inspiring us to move further toward increasing individual effort and group consciousness.

The forward thrust of the energies of this week urge individuals and groups to break out of established limitations, push beyond borders, and go where no man or woman has gone before. A true pioneering spirit pervades the Week of Social Betterment and with it a courageous and fearless attitude. In turning campaigns into crusades, groups must be careful not to discriminate against other groups or individual voices of dissent. Intolerance must give way to increased acceptance.

Another danger is that those outside our sphere may be suspicious of such inspirational movements and decline to be led at all. The promulgation of ideas, no matter how selfless or idealistic, may be seen nonetheless as propaganda, and therefore mistrusted or ignored. Crucial to our interactions with such intractable people will be listening to their views with an open mind rather than seeking only to convert them to a dogmatic point of view. Only when a real curiosity or hunger appears on their part can they come in search of new principles. In the long run, trying to force beliefs on another only arouses resentment, leading ultimately to rejection.

Setting up organizational structures at this time may lead to the founding of groups which can continue to function throughout the year, or for many years to come. Therefore, we must think long-term in our planning. Those capable of hanging in there and serving selflessly over the long haul should be sought out for administrative and maintenance roles. Thus, the actual initiators of such projects will be free to move on to new endeavors.

The Personology of People Born in the Week of Social Betterment

Those born in the Week of Social Betterment are often do-gooders who gain great satisfaction from helping others. Although Aries is thought of as a self-centered sign, Aries IIIs are idealists devoted to the betterment of mankind in general, and of their own social or family group in particular.

Yet, because of their positive attitudes they may become quite intolerant of weaker souls who simply need to complain. Born leaders, these pioneers will strike out fearlessly in the direction of any important goal that seems morally justified to them. For those who follow, they must be prepared to give uncompromising devotion to the cause.

Annual Events That Occur During the Week of Social Betterment

April 13: International Special Librarians Day
         National D.A.R.E. Day
April 15: Income Tax and Accountants Day
April 16: School Librarians Day
April 18: Paul Revere Day

Major Historical Events That Have Happened During the Week of Social Betterment

April 11, 1945: First Nazi concentration camp liberated (Buchenwald)
April 12, 1861: Firing on Fort Sumter begins American Civil War
April 13, 1742: Handel's *Messiah* premieres in Dublin
April 14, 1865: Abraham Lincoln assassinated
April 15, 1912: Sinking of *Titanic*
April 16, 1917: Lenin returns to Russia after Swiss exile
April 17, 1961: Bay of Pigs invasion in Cuba routed
April 18, 1775: Paul Revere's ride
April 18, 1906: San Francisco earthquake

Famous People Born During the Week of Social Betterment

Leonardo da Vinci, Charlie Chaplin, Ethel Kennedy, Thomas Jefferson, Bessie Smith, David Letterman, Nikita Khrushchev, Garry Kasparov, Loretta Lynn, Tama Janowitz, Scott Turow, Ellen Barkin, J. P. Morgan, Samuel Beckett, Isak Dinesen, Dennis Banks, Oleg Cassini, Anne M. Sullivan, John Gielgud, Henry James

Birthdays Especially Affected During the Week of Social Betterment

If you are born in the Week of Social Betterment (April 11–18), the Week of Leadership (August 11–18), or the Week of Expansiveness (December 11–18) your energies blend well with those of this week. Results should be obtained with little effort on your part.

Week of Social Betterment people will feel free to implement their visions to improve the lives of those around them. Week of Leadership people can bring their prodigious energies to bear on leading others in their struggle for justice. Week of Expansiveness people see the big picture and must maintain their idealistic aspirations.

If you are born in the Week of Persuasion (July 11–18), the Week of Theater (October 11–18), or the Week of Dominance (January 10–16) you will face problems and challenges during this week. You will have to work harder to achieve your goals.

Week of Persuasion people must be careful not to overwhelm those around them and give others a chance to express themselves. Week of Theater people must rein in their exuberance a bit, so as not to antagonize others. Week of Dominance people should learn to function as an ordinary member of the group without becoming too bossy.

✷

The Cusp of Power

APRIL 19–24

One of the strongest weeks of the year, the Cusp of Power carries with it many opportunities, but there are also great perils attendant to the misuse of overbearing strength. We have all seen the devastation that can result from the unbridled use of power or from the runaway energies of a large object rolling swiftly in the wrong direction.

One of the tricks in working with the powerful energies of this cusp is learning to let things happen. It is vital to guide the force already latent within the flow of life. By trying to control such forces unduly we not only inhibit them but also expend unnecessary energy ourselves. Another helpful rule is to allow others to make their important contribution, and to be a good coordinator or manager of group efforts rather than a dictator. Dictatorship ultimately invites rebellion, thus creating a whole new set of problems for the one in charge.

Diplomacy and compromise are essential during this week. It is important to remember that Newton's Third Law of Motion applies to life as well as to physics: For every action, there is an equal and opposite reaction. Constantly forging ahead without consideration for the feelings of others will itself create obstacles. There are certainly enough of these in life without creating more for oneself.

If there is a lesson to be learned during this week it is certainly that giving up or sharing power may be the most potent thing one can do— and, going even further, realizing that the greatest power is love itself. In addition, the real strength of everyday acts of kindness cannot be underestimated.

The use of the faculty of intuition that was so appropriate to the preceding weeks is here tempered by the faculty of sensation. With the advent of the Cusp of Power we can begin to sharpen and indulge our physical senses and become more comfortable with our bodies. Now is a favorable time for culinary endeavors and for comfortable, convivial get-togethers around the table. Whether Easter and Passover occur in the preceding week or in this one, the growing abundance of life and the demise of dark and freezing winter days can at last be celebrated.

Moreover, the idealism of the first weeks of spring now become tempered by practical considerations. Spring cleaning gets under way in earnest, and with it all sorts of painting and fix-up projects. Not only is this an auspicious time to begin major building projects, but also to establish small businesses, companies, and artistic organizations. Such endeavors can take off rapidly and come to have a life of their own, like the springtime energies of growing plants and trees.

Abundance is certainly characteristic of the Cusp of Power. With so much available, we might wonder whether giving it away or using it up are the only options. However, saving is also possible, indeed essential, if future endeavors are to be given the impetus they need. In the spiritual sense, saving can also imply going inside ourselves from time to time, and through meditation and self-awareness becoming more able to intelligently guide our efforts.

The Personology of People Born on the Cusp of Power

Those born on this cusp make no bones about it. They like to be in control, are used to being listened to, and often wear down their opponents in the long run. Making their presence felt comes as second nature to these rugged individualists. Since they regard themselves as valuable or even indispensable to both professional and family groups, they honestly believe they are entitled to the best life has to offer. Anyone who tries to deny them the fruits of their labor is in for a rough ride. Perhaps the most important lesson power cusp people must learn is that the greatest power is love, and that giving up control in favor of sharing and acceptance will take them further in the long run.

Annual Events That Occur on the Cusp of Power

April 21: John Muir Day
April 22: Earth Day
April 24: Secretaries Day

Major Historical Events That Have Happened on the Cusp of Power

April 19, 1775: First battle of the Revolutionary War
April 20, 1657: Admiral Blake destroys Spanish fleet in Santa Cruz Bay
April 21, 1960: Brasília dedicated as Brazil's capital city
April 22, 1915: Germans first use poison gas against British troops
April 23, 1879: Shakespeare memorial theater opens in Stratford-upon-
    Avon on the day presumed to be his birth- and death day.
April 24, 1916: Rebellion of Irish nationalists in Dublin

Famous People Born on the Cusp of Power

William Shakespeare, Catherine the Great, Vladimir Lenin, Queen Elizabeth II, Jack Nicholson, Sergey Prokofiev, Shirley MacLaine, Barbra Streisand, John Muir, Patti LuPone, Willem de Kooning, Shirley Temple Black, Adolf Hitler, Daniel Day-Lewis, Paloma Picasso, Catherine de Médicis, Richard M. Daley, Lionel Hampton, Joan Miró, Jessica Lange

Birthdays Especially Affected on the Cusp of Power

If you are born on the Cusp of Power (April 19–24), the Cusp of Exposure (August 19–25), or the Cusp of Prophecy (December 19–25) your energies blend well with those of this week. Results should be obtained with little effort on your part.

Cusp of Power people will be listened to as long as they learn to let up on their fierce need to control others. Cusp of Exposure people can succeed now, providing they are more honest and open with their associates. Cusp of Prophecy people use their quiet assurance and high concentration to inspire those around them.

If you are born on the Cusp of Oscillation (July 19–25), the Cusp of Involvement (October 19–25), or the Cusp of Mystery, Violence, and Imagination (January 17–22) you will face problems and challenges during this week. You will have to work harder to achieve your goals.

Cusp of Oscillation people must keep their energies balanced and learn to focus. Cusp of Involvement people should be less occupied with themselves and show others that they really care. Cusp of Mystery, Violence, and Imagination people will have to keep their nerves under control or risk putting those around them under pressure.

The Week of Manifestation

Time to put your plans into practice. During this week the introspection which has taken place during the winter, the reevaluation of the past year's efforts, finally can be put to real use. Perhaps it will even be possible to form an analysis that can lead to improved performance and be implemented in highly practical ways.

Procrastination must be battled, since the forces operating at this time can be easily blunted or sidetracked by sensual desire. Unfortunately, although the time is ripe for action, the increasing warmth and length of days can persuade us to relax into outright indulgence. This conflict between a drive to implement new ways of thinking and the temptation to fall into old patterns is the crux of the difficulties encountered during this week. The key to resolving this conflict could be an emphasis on physical activity, particularly of an outdoor type, such as taking long walks, jogging, tai chi, or aerobics. Working out with others in a social setting is particularly favored.

Another good change to make at this time could be setting up a new living situation either in a house or apartment, alone or with others. This could also extend to family and business opportunities, making it a priority to build close-knit groups around ourselves. Included in such a task will be assigning roles to each member of the group and drawing up lists of specific duties and responsibilities. Should you find yourself at the head of such a group you would do well to encourage others to express themselves through taking initiative and working for the good of all, rather than setting yourself up as a powerful boss.

Avoiding conflict will be difficult during this week, but the key here is social interaction and cooperation. Be particularly attentive to family members, friends, or colleagues who need assistance. A perfect way to implement such endeavors is to work together on a common project, particularly one that benefits the other person. Such activities will ensure that you can expect that favor to be returned later in the year according to your needs. Thus, helping others can be seen as an investment for the future.

As dreaming up ideas and implementing them are favored at this time, we must be able to sense the impracticality of certain projects which may not be viable. Since the danger exists of putting your head down and stubbornly plowing ahead, ignoring danger signals and possibly going off in a completely wrong direction, it is important not to waste your energy on such fruitless endeavors. No doubt others will aid in spotting such mistakes, and it is important at this time to remain open to comments and criticism.

Spring fever can hit hard during this week, favoring all sorts of love relationships. In particular, you will be more prone to falling in love during this time. Falling in love with love can be a real problem here. It is important to at least try to be realistic about the other person and not get caught up in a whirlwind of your own emotions. Remember: Getting into such an unreal state may be easier than getting out of it. The danger exists that relationships formed during this week may refuse to resolve themselves in the coming weeks and months. Issues of control, dependency, and outright addiction in matters of love can create problems for the rest of the year.

The Personology of People Born in the Week of Manifestation

Those born in this week usually have a clear idea of what they want and how to get it. Once they have formulated an idea or concept they will not rest until they bring it into being. Dedicated and trustworthy, they may be relied on as a rock of security by other more needy individuals. However, they are not ones to work alone, and may also rely heavily on those around them to work as a team in getting their projects launched. Generally, although not particularly gifted as leaders, they can be excellent coordinators. They must not allow their stubbornness to gain the upper hand and block progress.

Annual Events That Occur During the Week of Manifestation

April 26: Anzac Day: Landing of Australian and New Zealand forces at
    Gallipoli during the First World War
April 26: National Arbor Day
May 1: May Day
        Law Day
May 2: National Day of Prayer

Major Historical Events That Have Happened During the Week of Manifestation

April 25, 1859: Building of the Suez Canal begins
April 26, 1915: Landing of Allied troops in the Dardanelles
April 27, 1937: Building of Golden Gate Bridge completed
April 28, 1919: League of Nations founded
April 29, 1945: German army in Italy surrenders
April 30, 1789: First U.S. president, George Washington is inaugurated
May 1, 1931: Empire State Building opened
May 2, 1923: First plane flight across the United States

Famous People Born During the Week of Manifestation

Michelle Pfeiffer, Al Pacino, Duke Ellington, Coretta Scott King, Saddam
Hussein, James Baker, Oskar Schindler, Bianca Jagger, Andre Agassi,
Ulysses S. Grant, Uma Thurman, Emperor Hirohito, Ella Fitzgerald, Jerry
Seinfeld, Donna de Varona, Judy Collins, Willie Nelson, Duke of Welling-
ton, Talia Shire, Terry Southern

Birthdays Especially Affected During the Week of Manifestation

If you are born in the Week of Manifestation (April 25–May 2), the
Week of Structure (August 26–September 2), or the Week of Rule
(December 26–January 2) your energies blend well with those of this
week. Results should be obtained with little effort on your part.

Week of Manifestation people will have few problems implementing their visions as long as they keep an open mind. Week of Structure people give much needed structure to the efforts of any group of which they are a part. Week of Rule people lend leadership skills to help get projects on the rails.

If you are born in the Week of Passion (July 26–August 2), the Week of Intensity (October 26–November 2), or the Week of Intelligence (January 23–30) you will face problems and challenges during this week. You will have to work harder to achieve your goals.

Week of Passion people may upset coworkers with their self-centeredness and thus need to keep their egotism under control. Week of Intensity people should keep it light and let up on their criticism. Week of Intelligence people should trust their intuition more and use their logic less.

✳

The Week of Study

MAY 3–10

All forms of education are favored during this week, from attending a formal institution of learning, to reading tech manuals and computer books, to self-study and analysis of your own character.

For those who are in school, final exams are approaching and with them deadlines for papers and reports. People who have encountered real difficulties in a given course should not delay in scheduling an appointment with their teacher. Learning about your personal weaknesses or lack of understanding in a given subject should lead to a resolve to catch up in this area.

Many ideas are attractive now. Indeed, we seem to live in a world of thoughts, concepts, and ideologies, each beckoning to us with its own particular appeal. Holding on to a healthy amount of skepticism during this week will be necessary to avoid being taken in by more misleading or even dangerous philosophies. Also, aesthetic matters, particularly those concerned with sensual and physical beauty, regarding both works of art and living creatures, hold special interest.

Those who find their own seductive powers working in overdrive may have to switch to a lower gear to avoid the flood of attention they seem to be receiving. If such attention proves too much, withdrawing into a more isolated head space should provide safety from emotional onslaughts.

Nothing is more upsetting at this time than seeing disadvantaged or physically challenged individuals being mistreated, either verbally or physically. Even a hint of prejudicial attitudes will be enough to push us into attack mode. Nevertheless, keeping our cool, and perhaps taking the time to deal firmly but kindly with unjust discrimination will enable us to achieve positive results. Allowing tempers to flare out of control will just exacerbate the situation.

The danger exists during this week of becoming too fixed in our attitudes and beliefs. Arguments are likely to arise at home, often due to a refusal to budge. We must learn to listen carefully to what others are saying and at least to consider their viewpoints with an open mind before rejecting them, or we are likely to create a difficult situation for all concerned.

Our involvement with certain ideologies is not in any way contradicted by our hankering after physical exercise or by our sensuality. In fact, the latter will provide a welcome relief and contrast to our mental preoccupations. In some cases it may in fact be possible to bring about a synthesis of the two worlds, giving physical expression to mental activities and using our powers of thought to enhance the more earthy side of our natures. Our need for both is highlighted by the fact that frustration and even depression are likely to result if we are deprived of either for any period of time. If it is possible for you to get involved in a special extracurricular activity at this time, perhaps involving music or dance, coaching sports or fitness, or one involving environmentally related activities, then so much the better.

The Personology of People Born in the Week of Study

Born teachers, Taurus IIs affect their environments heavily, particularly when it comes to setting an example for those around them. Not only good in instructing on a one-on-one basis, those born in this week are able to work well with groups and to become central figures in families and professional groups. They are unlikely to be overly dominant bosses, but allow people to express their own personal initiative and may even make strong demands that their employees or colleagues enjoy themselves. Because they are so opposed to any form of discrimination against individuals, they insist on a fair and open attitude from all they meet, fighting for the underdog and socially oppressed with great fervor.

Annual Events That Occur During the Week of Study

May 5: Cinco de Mayo
May 7: National Teacher Day
May 8: VE Day celebrated in England to mark the end of WWII
   World Press Freedom Day
   World Red Cross Day
May 10: National Receptionist Day
Mother's Day (or following week)

Major Historical Events That Have Happened During the Week of Study

May 3, 1937: *Gone With the Wind* wins the Pulitzer prize
May 4, 1970: Four students shot dead at Kent State University by National Guard
May 5, 1968: Students riot in Paris
May 6, 1954: British medical student Roger Bannister breaks the four-minute mile
May 7, 1945: War in Europe ends as Germany surrenders
May 8, 1921: Sweden abolishes the death penalty

May 9, 1926: Admiral Byrd becomes first to fly over North Pole
May 10, 1940: Winston Churchill becomes British prime minister

Famous People Born During the Week of Study

Karl Marx, Sigmund Freud, Judith Jamison, Audrey Hepburn, Pyotr Tchaikovsky, Johannes Brahms, Golda Meir, Gary Snyder, Keith Jarrett, Glenda Jackson, Candice Bergen, Fred Astaire, Rudolph Valentino, Tammy Wynette, Sugar Ray Robinson, Greg Gumbel, Willie Mays, George Lucas, Katherine Anne Porter, Keith Haring

Birthdays Especially Affected During the Week of Study

If you are born in the Week of Study (May 3–10), the Week of the Puzzle (September 3–10), or the Week of Determination (January 3–9) your energies blend well with those of this week. Results should be obtained with little effort on your part.

Week of Study people may find this the most opportune time of the year to devote themselves to endeavors involving school or learning. Week of the Puzzle people will find their mental challenges here and revel in figuring out all kinds of logical exercises. Week of Determination people can use this week to catch up on written work they have fallen behind in.

If you are born in the Week of Challenge (August 3–10), the Week of Profundity (November 3–11), or the Week of Youth and Ease (January 31–February 7) you will face problems and challenges during this week. You will have to work harder to achieve your goals.

Week of Challenge people must hold themselves back from taking an active role and use this time to examine their mistakes. Week of Profundity people must be aware of slipping into depression or falling prey to procrastination. Week of Youth and Ease people need to stop having so much fun and get more serious about their studies.

The Week of Nature

Seeking inspiration in the lands of woods, mountains, or rivers is characteristic of this week's activities. Getting back to basics and finding our roots in the natural world are both part and parcel of this process.

Moving among natural surroundings means giving up man-made artificial ones, at least for the time being. Spontaneous expressions are a keynote in this week, but unfortunately society may not always prove to be understanding about individualistic displays, which neglect the established mores of the larger group. A rejection of artificiality may be seen as a direct affront to society's values. Conflicts inevitably result from such confrontations, and we must be prepared to fight for our right to express personal values, basically to be ourselves. Showing the more natural sides of our personalities may prove threatening to family groups as well as to professional ones.

Should criticism and disapproval get too heavy to bear, anger at perceived misunderstanding or mistreatment may erupt. If this anger is repressed it may lead to a cycle of alternating depressions and emotional outbursts. However, now is not the time to get bogged down in negativity. Life beckons, in all of its most exciting and colorful aspects, and now is the time to throw ourselves into the stream of daily existence with enthusiasm and fervor. It is not only the straight and narrow which attracts us, but also the detours and byways of more unusual sorts of experience which lure us from the main path. We may find ourselves spending more time with the least likely of new acquaintances while neglecting our dearest friends.

There is, however, a real need for security here. Whatever uncertainties arise, and with them accompanying insecurities, the drive for security will help to surpass these obstacles and may even fuel ambitions to succeed. We attempt to guarantee the stability that we so desperately crave by advancing in our careers, although such ambitions usually do not sustain themselves in the long run.

A thirst for more out of the ordinary experiences and downright rebellious or antisocial behavior can bring drug or sex and love addictions to the fore. During the Week of Nature succumbing to such dangers easily could have a detrimental effect for the rest of the year. Therefore, some real prudence and self-control must be exercised here to avoid disasters.

If a balance can be struck between conventional and extreme forms of behavior, the need for exciting experiences could be satisfied without getting into serious problems. Although self-understanding is difficult to attain at this time, it should be attempted, if only to help us survive. Quite likely the key lies in Nature itself, in its balance, its cycles, and its abilities to correct and readjust. In this last respect, the healing properties of Nature are essential, always granting a second chance to the one who has gone astray. Thus, spending time outdoors and having daily contact with the natural world may prove not only enjoyable but highly instructive.

The Personology of People Born in the Week of Nature

Because of their zany and colorful behavior, people born in this week are often the life of the party. Yet they may fall short of inspiring trust, since their unpredictable behavior and spontaneity are not always valued by people who prefer more stable attitudes. Critical attitudes of family members frequently drive those born in the Week of Nature to go off on their own as soon as possible in late adolescence and early adulthood. Because of anger against such judgmental figures, often driven deep inside, those born in the Week of Nature can suffer puzzling depressions later in life or exhibit sudden explosions of temper. Not infrequently, the insecurities of Taurus IIIs may propel them to excel and to rise to the tops of their professions.

Annual Events That Occur During the Week of Nature

May 12: International Migratory Bird Day
May 15: National Employee Health and Fitness Day

May 15: International Day of Families
May 16: National Bike to Work Day
May 18: Armed Forces Day
        International Museum Day
Mother's Day (or preceding week)

Major Historical Events That Have Happened During the Week of Nature

May 11, 1981: Musical hit *Cats* opens in London
May 12, 1949: Soviet Union lifts Berlin blockade
May 13, 1981: Pope John Paul II shot in St. Peter's Square
May 14, 1948: State of Israel proclaimed
May 15, 1958: First space lab launched by Soviet Union
May 16, 1991: First woman, Edith Cresson, elected prime minister in France
May 17, 1973: Watergate hearings begin
May 18, 1832: George Sand publishes women's rights novel, *Indiana*

Famous People Born During the Week of Nature

Salvador Dali, Martha Graham, David Cronenberg, Margot Fonteyn, Emilio Estevez, L. Frank Baum, Debra Winger, Dennis Hopper, Frank Capra, Jiddu Krishnamurti, Katharine Hepburn, Harvey Keitel, Birgit Nilsson, Daphne du Maurier, Henry Fonda, Joe Louis, Yogi Berra, Natasha Richardson, Liberace, Lindsay Crouse

Birthdays Especially Affected During the Week of Nature

If you are born in the Week of Nature (May 11–18), the Week of the Literal (September 11–18), or the Week of Dominance (January 10–16) your energies blend well with those of this week. Results should be obtained with little effort on your part.

Week of Nature people can be very comfortable with being themselves and not having to adopt any pretenses, yet should be sensitive about offending others. Week of the Literal people will find their common-sense attitude appreciated, as long as it is expressed in an easy manner. Week of Dominance people should use this week to explore their natural surroundings.

If you are born in the Week of Leadership (August 11–18), the Week of Control (November 12–18), or the Week of Acceptance (February 8–15) you will face problems and challenges during this week. You will have to work harder to achieve your goals.

Week of Leadership people should be aware of depression if their natural attitudes are not appreciated by others. Week of Control people need to loosen up, since strict attitudes are not appreciated at this time. Week of Acceptance people need stability now but must be aware of trying too hard to get it.

✳

The Cusp of Energy

MAY 19–24

You may enjoy trying a little bit of everything at this time, like sitting down to a smorgasbord and sampling some of this and some of that. Of course the danger exists here of spreading ourselves too thin over a wide range of activities. In addition, there will be an undeniable tendency to rush things, to push ahead too fast and thereby fail to put in the proper groundwork so necessary for the success of any project. Great patience will have to be exerted during this week in order to avoid such haste, and also to avoid the temptation to address only the more superficial aspects of what may turn out to be quite serious matters.

Feeling an upsurge of energy can work positively, though, fueling our endeavors and guaranteeing success in many areas. Conversely, it also can work to our disadvantage, particularly when we are headed off in the wrong direction, full speed ahead. No energy is limitless. Consequently, to harness the tremendous energies of this week, we must learn to pace ourselves in order to maximize effectiveness and guard against possible burnout.

Sometimes energy directed toward the outer world can be directed inward as well. This can lead to well-needed introspection and ultimately to valuable self-development. Unfortunately, this can also lead to getting bogged down in obsessive behavior, particularly when it comes down to our body and its functions. Rather than worrying about nonexistent maladies, we're better off seeking medical advice during this week, usually of an alternative holistic type. It is also helpful to guard against prospective illnesses by taking the appropriate doses of food supplements. Fortunately, abundant sunshine at this time of the year also can do wonders and work to counteract depression.

In no other area is energy better spent during this week than in exercise, sports, and other physical endeavors. Competitive drives may be viewed as healthy ones now, and desires to excel must be satisfied. Music, dance, and theater may also figure in this equation. Linking our creative drives with the physical side of life will result in increasing pride in our endeavors and an increase in self-esteem. Moreover, it will provide much needed social contact for those who find it difficult to make friends.

This physical involvement may carry over in the realms of sex, love, and friendship. Touching is extremely important at this time, and with close contact will come an increasing intimacy. Nothing can be more pleasurable now than sharing such experiences with that very special person. Breakups are best avoided during this time. It is more advisable to give a relationship a real chance to succeed, even if that means struggling to work out difficult problems with an equally difficult person.

The need to seek constancy in general, to hang in there and refuse to give up, is the most difficult challenge of all. But stick to your guns, and you will ensure that not only will your energies not be split or weakened, but you will be empowered with the ability to move mountains.

The Personology of People Born on the Cusp of Energy

Energy cusp people often are engaged in several different projects at once, giving rise to concerns among family and friends that they are spreading themselves too thin. But a need for versatility and change is so strong in these energetic individuals that they soon grow bored, dissatisfied, and unhappy without them. Unfortunately, those born on this cusp too often neglect the more mundane, everyday aspects of existence in favor of more interesting or challenging activities, for example, leaving the housework to others. Allowing other people to be the center of attention at times and keeping their motor mouth under control are important lessons for energy cusp people to learn.

Annual Events That Occur on the Cusp of Energy

May 22: National Maritime Day
         National Waiter/Waitress Day
May 24: Victoria Day

Major Historical Events That Have Happened on the Cusp of Energy

May 19, 1980: Mount St. Helens erupts violently
May 20, 1910: Earth passes through tail of Halley's comet
May 21, 1927: Lindbergh lands in Paris to end first solo transatlantic flight
May 22, 1972: Richard Nixon becomes first U.S. president to visit USSR
May 23, 1934: Bonnie and Clyde ambushed
May 24, 1833: Brooklyn Bridge is opened

Famous People Born on the Cusp of Energy

Malcolm X, Cher, Bob Dylan, Arthur Conan Doyle, Priscilla Presley, Gary Goldschneider, Peter Townshend, Jimmy Stewart, Mary Cassatt, Queen Victoria, Honoré de Balzac, Nicole Brown Simpson, Richard Wagner, Charles Aznavour, Henri Rousseau, Laurence Olivier, Ho Chi Minh, Lorraine Hansberry, Carolus Linnaeus, Joan Collins

Birthdays Especially Affected on the Cusp of Energy

If you are born on the Cusp of Energy (May 19–24), the Cusp of Beauty (September 19–24), or the Cusp of Mystery, Violence, and Imagination (January 17–22) your energies blend well with those of this week. Results should be obtained with little effort on your part.

Cusp of Energy people can get a lot done now, as long as they realize that there are limits to what they can accomplish. Cusp of Beauty people should widen their horizons but not lose their focus. Cusp of Mystery, Violence, and Imagination people can indulge in outdoor activities that are well suited for their physical type.

If you are born on the Cusp of Exposure (August 19–25), the Cusp of Revolution (November 19–24), or the Cusp of Sensitivity (February 16–22) you will face problems and challenges during this week. You will have to work harder to achieve your goals.

Cusp of Exposure people may put others off with obviously extroverted behavior. Cusp of Revolution people could be tripped up by a belief in their own infallibility. Cusp of Sensitivity people must be aware of falling into obsessive worry patterns.

❂

The Week of Freedom

MAY 25–JUNE 2

Breaking out of all sorts of restrictions is characteristic of this week. You may find it hard to take orders or even keep to a fixed schedule. Although a breakdown of organization is not always the case during this time, attempts to plan and arrange your work may fall flat. Freewheeling energies are better suited for initiating projects than for carrying them through to the end. Also, rules which have applied up to this point in the year can suffer breakdowns, necessitating an entirely new approach.

As the tendency to rebel is so strong here, we must aim for positive goals, rather than wasting energy reacting against restrictions and therefore being controlled by such behavior. When it comes to implementing our visions during this week the possibilities are practically unlimited. Working on our own, rather than in group endeavors, is particularly favored. Since personal initiative is rewarded now, one must develop the capacity to make quick decisions and act on them without taking the time for planning or reflection. Thus, the intuitive side of our nature is favored over the thoughtful or logical side.

With everything moving at such high speed, it is easy to become impatient with those who move at a slower tempo. Such impatience can explode into anger, and great control will have to be exerted to avoid displays of temper, which ultimately have a negative effect on group endeavors and other professional projects. It is essential at this time to minimize stress, and since stress is largely something we inflict on ourselves, self-control must be exerted.

Because the tendency to innovate is so strong here, more mundane domestic tasks may be neglected. In the financial sphere, bills must be paid and money regularly put aside for this purpose. Without constant reminders of the need to save and pay attention to financial matters, all sorts of difficulties could be brewing, many with ramifications for the rest of the year.

Breaking through restrictions may not only be possible on a personal level, but may also serve as an inspirational force for others to follow. Along the way, there is no doubt that an individual's charismatic appeal in such endeavors may attract a whole host of followers—wanted or unwanted. A penchant for preaching from the pulpit is undeniable here, and accompanying it an inability to listen to others. The most successful of endeavors during this week will feature a real effort both to give and take in the sphere of communication.

Grounding energies, such as those found in family or job, will be essential to balance the mercurial and spontaneous tendencies prevalent at this time. Moreover, friends who exert a calming influence will be prized highly. Family members and friends should not feel insulted or neglected when high-flying individuals ignore their wishes, for often the good of the group can be furthered by quick and effective individual endeavors. Also, the opportunity to advance in life is so pronounced during the Week of Freedom that opportunities lost here may well languish in neglect for the rest of the year.

The Personology of People Born in the Week of Freedom

Quick, feisty and, those born in the Week of Freedom must be left alone to pursue their own highly individualistic goals. Although they may leave dozens of unfinished projects in their wake, those born in this week are also capable of following through on those endeavors that really matter most to them (at the time). Those who try to figure out these mercurial individuals will have a difficult time of it, and often Gemini Is themselves may not be sure of what they are about, or even care. However, those born in the Week of Freedom often are convinced that they know what motivates others, and also have strong convictions about what is best for their family, friends, and mates.

Annual Events That Occur During the Week of Freedom

May 25: National Missing Children's Day
Memorial Day

Major Historical Events That Have Happened During the Week of Freedom

May 25, 1935: Jesse Owens sets six world records in one single hour
May 26, 1940: Allied troops evacuated from Dunkirk
May 27, 1949: Mao Tse Tung's communist army captures Shanghai
May 28, 1932: Dutch complete massive dike to isolate Zuider Zee from ocean
May 29, 1953: Edmund Hillary and Tenzing Norgay reach peak of Mt. Everest
May 30, 1989: A million Chinese demand freedom in Tiananmen Square

May 31, 1961: South Africa declares independence
June 1, 1967: Beatles release *Sergeant Pepper's Lonely Hearts Club Band*
June 2, 1989: Chinese soldiers kill over one hundred in Tiananmen Square

Famous People Born During the Week of Freedom

Miles Davis, John F. Kennedy, Marilyn Monroe, Isadora Duncan, Sally K. Ride, Jim Thorpe, La Toya Jackson, Clint Eastwood, Ralph Waldo Emerson, Benny Goodman, Sally Kellerman, Rachel Carson, Brooke Shields, Wild Bill Hickok, Gayle Sayres, Levon Helm, Dashiell Hammett, Peggy Lee, Gene Tunney, Brigham Young

Birthdays Especially Affected During the Week of Freedom

If you are born in the Week of Freedom (May 25–June 2), the Week of Perfection (September 25–October 2), or the Week of Intelligence (January 23–30) your energies blend well with those of this week. Results should be obtained with little effort on your part.

Week of Freedom people find their initiative rewarded and also appreci-ated by friends and family. Week of Perfection people should not lose this opportunity to move forward in their careers. Week of Intelligence people can further the best interests of others through their personal initiative.

If you are born in the Week of Structure (August 26–September 2), the Week of Independence (November 25–December 2), or the Week of Spirit (February 23–March 2) you will face problems and challenges during this week. You will have to work harder to achieve your goals.

Week of Structure people run the risk of inhibiting others through their unyielding attitudes. Week of Independence people should not allow their fantasies to spin out of control. Week of Spirit people should be aware of attracting the wrong kind of admirers.

The Week of Communication

In the communication age few skills are so highly prized as this one. Should verbal communication not be your forte, there is no better time than this one to develop it. You are possibly a good listener, but may not have attempted yet to hold center stage and have others attend to your words. Begin small, perhaps in everyday interactions in stores and at work. Formulate your thoughts well before uttering them, and try to keep things direct and succinct.

It can be quite frustrating to be misunderstood, or perhaps not understood at all. For this reason, we should be prepared to repeat ourselves or patiently explain the idea we are trying to get across. However, in addition to simplifying and clarifying certain concepts, the tendency during this week is also to express ourselves in the most unusual and strikingly different ways. In this case, if others do not understand, then perhaps it is their problem.

Working with the media is also favored here. Whether it's informal PR for your social club or another kind of organization, this week will be a favorable time for you to get across ideas in writing. Putting together a good press release, CV, or grant application is especially favored.

Verbal and written expressions of communication are not the only types to flourish at this time. Many kinds of personal expression involving style—whether clothing, cars, fashion accessories, or hairdo—will bring us to the attention of others. Once we have their attention, we can proceed further using speech.

Be careful not to lose your audience or drive it away by misunderstanding people's needs and capacities. Some listeners may even be downright uninterested, and this disinterest must be respected and not violated.

Because of the beautiful weather during this period, which may not yet have turned too hot, we may find that physical expression will prove equally as important as mental exercise. In fact, through sharing aerobic, competitive sport, or martial arts activities with others, new avenues of communication may open up with established friends or encourage new friendships to blossom through these mutually shared activities.

Should emphasis on the mental aspects of life become too great, the danger exists during this week of hurting others with our words or giving free rein to the critical elements of our nature. We must be extremely careful of repeating old patterns from childhood, particularly those wielded with venom by parents. Old habits die hard, and we may find ourselves becoming the very parent we had so much difficulty with as a child. A sharp tongue or rapierlike wit can leave deep scars.

Due to a fascination with the dark side of life and with black humor during the Week of Communication, we must be careful not to go overboard in this area. Laughter features prominently in this week but should not be of the humiliating type leveled against a more vulnerable person. A cheap shot or flippant remark can wound deeply and not be forgotten for many months, even years.

The Personology of People Born in the Week of Communication

Among the most entertaining of all individuals in the year, Gemini IIs need to communicate their thoughts and feelings to others. Highly expressive, it is not advised that others attempt to put a damper on these exuberant individuals, since this will only result in unhappiness and depression. Learning to handle disappointment is a major task for Gemini IIs, who are generally positive thinkers and prone to expecting the best life has to offer. Because of their need for change and variety, those born in the Week of Communication may be seen as flitting from one project to another like butterflies. Maintaining a realistic attitude and keeping grounded are essential for their mental health.

Annual Events That Occur During the Week of Communication

June 3: Jefferson Davis Day
June 5: Boone Day
 World Environment Day
June 6: D-Day
June 9: Children's Day

Major Historical Events That Have Happened During the Week of Communication

June 3, 1965: Edward White becomes first American to walk in space
June 4, 1944: Rome liberated by Allies in WWII
June 5, 1783: First ascent of hot-air balloon, in France
June 6, 1944: Allies begin Normandy invasion
June 7, 1712: Philadelphia prohibits importation of slaves
June 8, 1930: Romanian Carol II declared king after return from exile
June 9, 1898: Britain granted ninety-nine-year lease on Hong Kong
June 10, 1967: Israel wins six-day war against Arab neighbors

Famous People Born During the Week of Communication

Judy Garland, Allen Ginsberg, Frank Lloyd Wright, Laurie Anderson, Thomas Mann, Aleksandr Pushkin, Josephine Baker, Johnny Depp, Immanuel Velikovsky, Bill Moyers, Madame Chiang Kai-shek, The Artist Formerly Known as Prince (TAFKA), Paul Gauguin, Billie Whitelaw, Federico García Lorca, Barbara Bush, Cole Porter, Francis Crick, E. M. Delafield, Rocky Graziano

Birthdays Especially Affected During the Week of Communication

If you are born in the Week of Communication (June 3–10), the Week of Socialization (October 3–10), or the Week of Youth and Ease (January 31–February 7) your energies blend well with those of this week. Results should be obtained with little effort on your part.

Week of Communication people will revel in the value accorded to the written and spoken word at this time, but must be careful not to wound others with their barbs. Week of Socialization people seek out people who will appreciate their particular brand of humor. Week of Youth and Ease people enjoy nothing better than get-togethers with friends featuring lively conversation.

If you are born in the Week of the Puzzle (September 3–10), the Week of Originality (December 3–10), or the Week of Isolation (March 3–March 10) you will face problems and challenges during this week. You will have to work harder to achieve your goals.

Week of the Puzzle people may feel isolated and unappreciated because of their personal style of communication. Week of Originality people should try to find other unusual types who can understand them and not accept rejection from others. Week of Isolation people will have to make a real effort to explain themselves clearly and patiently so that they can be understood.

❖

The Week of Exploration

JUNE 11–18

Looking for something? You probably are, and chances are good that you will find it—perhaps under some previously unturned stone. Lost something? Now is the time to recover it. Intrigued by an interesting or alluring personality? You stand a good chance in the pursuit of your heart's desire.

Exploring the nooks and crannies of life, not excluding the secret hidden recesses of the human soul, are all characteristic of this week's activities. With many vacations imminent, it is even possible that you will be planning or making trips to faraway exotic places during this time. On the other hand, you may find yourself simply traveling to nearby parks, lakes, rivers, mountains, or beaches to escape from the monotony of daily life. Filled with curiosity, everyday objects and places, even familiar faces, hold a special kind of allure.

However, going beyond the ordinary and pushing back frontiers may prove even more tempting now. We may be drawn to taking risks at this time. Putting everything on the line raises the stakes and promises great rewards, unless of course we happen to fail. Keeping the ultimate goal in mind is important, however, since we may get so caught up in the thrills and dangers of the journey that we get sidetracked into one interesting episode after another and forget about arriving at the destination. Another pitfall may be mistaking the map for the terrain, which in this sense means getting caught up in the idea of exploration and failing to reach the destination. Indeed, an intense need for change and variety characterizes the Week of Exploration.

The energies of this week are seductive, and those seeking to explore may find themselves undermined by indulgence. Feeling too good about ourselves can sabotage our positive energies for advancement, though, and can cause us to wallow in self-indulgent pleasures. Thus, great discipline may be required to underscore one's determination to forge ahead.

The tendency to prevaricate, or at least stretch the truth a bit, can tempt us to embellish reports of our explorations to a captive or gullible audience. The need to share our experiences may prove so strong that we might fool ourselves into believing these tall tales. Thus, illusion is an ever-present danger here, albeit an amusing and innocent one.

The beautiful weather and extra time for play enables us to enjoy many pleasurable outdoor activities during this week. Extra daylight time is abundant, and with the long days come many opportunities for cookouts, hikes, and sports activities. It is difficult to be severe with ourselves or even objective about work when the music of nature is so insistent and ever building to new peaks. With freer dress styles come the allure of sex and the promise of happy marriages.

Exploration of the private world of other individuals beckons. This does not imply being obsessed to dig to great depths, but rather to discover common pleasures and goals. By interacting with another person in such pursuits we are likely to learn more about ourselves.

The Personology of People Born in the Week of Exploration

These active individuals are constantly on the move, rolling back frontiers and testing the limits of experience to the max. In relationships, they may have difficulty establishing constancy in their younger years, but are quite capable later on of making a firm commitment to one partner. Their free-wheeling style gives the impression of chaotic behavior to some, but their ability to impose structural limitations on themselves is also characteristic, often through following a strict daily routine (at least on some days). Teaching or controlling others is not high on their list of priorities. Instead, they allow their family members and friends to go their own ways and develop their own style.

Annual Events That Occur During the Week of Exploration

June 14: Flag Day
June 17: Bunker Hill Day
Father's Day (or following week)

Major Historical Events That Have Happened During the Week of Exploration

June 11, 1847: Arctic explorer John Franklin dies trying to discover North-West Passage
June 12, 1991: Russians go to polls in first democratic election ever
June 13, 1989: Gorbachev and Kohl agree on reuniting Germany
June 14, 1645: Cromwell defeats Royalist forces
June 15, 1215: Signing of the Magna Carta
June 16, 1963: First Russian woman, Valentina Tereshkova, launched into space
June 17, 1775: Battle of Bunker Hill
June 18, 1815: Napoleon meets defeat at Waterloo

Famous People Born During the Week of Exploration

Anne Frank, Paul McCartney, Isabella Rossellini, Adam Smith, Harriet Beecher Stowe, James Brown, Steffi Graf, Jacques-Yves Cousteau, Jeannette Rankin, George H. W. Bush, Waylon Jennings, Che Guevara, Donald Trump, Xaviera Hollander, Jim Belushi, Erroll Garner, W. B. Yeats, Gwendolyn Brooks, Edvard Grieg, Lamont Dozier

Birthdays Especially Affected During the Week of Exploration

If you are born in the Week of Exploration (June 11–18), the Week of Theater (October 11–18), or the Week of Acceptance (February 8–15) your energies blend well with those of this week. Results should be obtained with little effort on your part.

Week of Exploration people may indulge their investigative passion to the limit. Week of Theater people should go on their own private search without broadcasting too much about it. Week of Acceptance people need to get out and enjoy the good weather, perhaps even take a vacation trip.

If you are born in the Week of the Literal (September 11–18), the Week of Expansiveness (December 11–18), or the Week of Dances and Dreams (March 11–18) you will face problems and challenges during this week. You will have to work harder to achieve your goals.

Week of the Literal people will find it hard to accept any far-fetched stories, but could easily get in trouble through the manner in which they reject them. Week of Expansiveness people can exaggerate too much and subsequently be accused of dishonesty. Week of Dances and Dreams people may get into dangerous situations through their curiosity getting the better of them.

Spring Personology Snapshot

MARCH 21 People born on March 21 are forthright, courageous, and persistent. Always practical, they often neglect their social skills, and forget that being no-nonsense is not the same as being overbearing.

MARCH 22 March 22 people are often strongly opinionated, but with a calm confidence. Single-minded and ambitious, they should take care that their desire to reach their goals does not result in arrogant or domineering behavior.

MARCH 23 Those born on March 23 are inquisitive, often searching for answers to the most important existential concerns. Probing and scientific, they often become overly curious and get involved where they shouldn't.

MARCH 24 Spontaneous and direct, people born on March 24 value simplicity and optimism above all. Open to new ideas and experiences, these visionary people are often overly optimistic and have trouble reaching decisions.

MARCH 25 Those born on March 25 are energetic and self-motivated. Vital and active, their energies are not always positive, however, and they run the risk of being overly critical and bitter.

MARCH 26 People born on March 26 are guileless and frank and exhibit innocence in many areas. Excellent at viewing challenges objectively, they must nevertheless be careful not to succumb to passivity and timidity.

MARCH 27 Strongly innovative, those born on March 27 are good at assimilating newly learned ideas. Independent and quick, they may also be impatient and forgetful, and that can make them hard to get along with.

MARCH 28 Helpful and popular, those born on March 28 are very good at concentrating on the task at hand. Often misunderstood, they also need to work at being mindful of the feelings of others.

MARCH 29 People born on March 29 are keen observers and adept at making decisions. Idealistic, devoted, and dedicated, they have to be careful that they do not also become judgmental and distant.

MARCH 30 Honest and persistent, March 30 people have an incredible drive and vision to succeed. Focused and directed, their intensity and perseverance may lead them to stress and isolation.

MARCH 31 The practical and tenacious people of March 31 work hard for their ideas and don't release them easily, unless in times of crisis. Good at working with others, they can also be contentious and confrontational.

APRIL 1 Direct and self-disciplined, those born on April 1 possess an unusual drive and determination. Diligent, and good at pressing on through mundane tasks, they need to take care that they do not become remote and obsessed with work.

APRIL 2 Those born on April 2 are open, genuine, and kind. Extremely idealistic, they can also be naïve, and may have problems reaching their overly optimistic and unrealistic goals.

APRIL 3 Those born on April 3 have a deep understanding of human nature and excel at problem-solving. Candid and direct, they may also be self-centered and, at times, inappropriately blunt.

APRIL 4 Extremely innovative, those born on April 4 can achieve great success in life. Ambitious and energetic, they can also be rash and need to guard against getting involved in too many endeavors.

APRIL 5 Success oriented, April 5 people are magnetic and inspirational. Driven, they sometimes face emotional problems in their private lives.

APRIL 6 The visionary people of April 6 love to experiment and to probe both physical and mental issues. Quick to engage in logical discussions, they must be aware that their inflexible attitudes may alienate those around them.

APRIL 7 Strong and creative ideas are abundant in April 7 people. Directed well, this energy can be of enormous advantage; left unchecked, it can be the source of impatience and anxiety.

APRIL 8 Strong ethics and compassion characterize April 8 people. Selfless and reliable, they may also be shy and self-sacrificing, which can detract from their own happiness.

APRIL 9 Outspoken and uncompromising, April 9 people will find success through their convincing and determined personalities. They have a tendency to be misleading, though, and often forget that they have a strong influence on those around them.

APRIL 10 Independent and daring, April 10 people do not back down from their principles, though they do not enjoy outright confrontation. Risk takers driven by competition, they can also be compulsive and tense.

APRIL 11 Often the center of action, April 11 people are more pragmatic than ambitious. Able to make strong decisions with a diplomatic ease, they may also be inflexible and unwilling to change.

APRIL 12 Community awareness characterizes April 12 people, because they have a keen understanding of society. Kind and compassionate, they would do well to cultivate a stronger knowledge and awareness of themselves.

APRIL 13 Those born on April 13 are often pioneers in thought and seek a place where they can spread their ideas through their outspoken nature. Unconventional and original, they are often cast off by society for their beliefs.

APRIL 14 Thoughtful people who are aware of history and tradition, those born on April 14 spend much time looking for their niche in society. Idealistic, they must learn to be patient so as not to become frustrated or discontented by their search.

APRIL 15 Realistic, intelligent, and confident, April 15 people are acutely interested in the state of human nature. Organized and direct, they often strive to manage the lives of others as well as their own, with the result that they are vulnerable to criticism.

APRIL 16 Thriving on laughter and humor, April 16 people are skillful at using comedy to relieve tension and have fun. Quick-witted, they may also be oblivious to their surroundings and may, without realizing it, choose their own needs over others'.

APRIL 17 Grounded and dependable, those born on April 17 have a real sense of power. Persuasive, they like to use their strengths to influence others and may take great offense when their advice is not heeded.

APRIL 18 Defenders of their ideals, April 18 people are at the head of the progressive movements of their times. Principled and just, their defenses may nevertheless be seen as unrealistic and aggressive.

APRIL 19 Hard workers who believe in a strong career and family, the principal focus of April 19 people is control. Though resilient and often quite successful, they have to watch that they don't become immersed in their own need for power.

APRIL 20 Natural leaders, April 20 people have an internal drive that pushes them, as well as others, to succeed. Ambitious in their public lives, their private lives can be fantasy prone, and they can get into trouble with their illusions.

APRIL 21 Professional success and integrity are extremely important to the intelligent people born on April 21. They have an incredible need to be loved, though, and often find to their disappointment that professional successes may lead to private failures.

APRIL 22 Structured and daunting, April 22 people excel when in charge of some kind of system, such as a family or store. They are often unsociable, though, and can become very materialistic due to their private failures with other people.

APRIL 23 Sociable and talented, April 23 people need to be publicly successful and will search until they find the right place for their skills. Single-minded, they often desire exhilaration and success, and that may leave them rigid and uneasy about change.

APRIL 24 Protective and loving, April 24 people are loyal to their families and friends. Concerned with an acknowledgment and acceptance of their work, they must work hard to avoid an unhealthy reliance on authority.

APRIL 25 Those born on April 25 are concerned with establishing their personality and presence early in life and remain committed once these are found. Steadfast and persistent, they may find that others label them intolerant.

APRIL 26 Talented at creating and maintaining structures, April 26 people fight hard for their relationships and health. Loyal and ambitious, they must learn to be more tolerant of shortcomings—both in themselves and in others.

APRIL 27 Dedicated and strong, April 27 people are usually found in the background, conducting unheralded but essential roles. Unsung heroes, their social skills are often lacking and they may become withdrawn.

APRIL 28 Extremely determined, April 28 people never give up on any project and do not back down from their opinions. Often a positive attribute, this persistence can lead to rigidity and domination if left unchecked.

APRIL 29 Dependable and self-reliant, April 29 people frequently hold positions of responsibility but always take the opportunity to be playful and silly. Nevertheless, they often become frustrated and unhappy with their role in life.

APRIL 30 Those born on April 30 need to be loved and cared for while simultaneously being allowed to live their lives the way they want to. Though loyal and protective of their loved ones in return, they need to understand that their behavior may sometimes be difficult.

MAY 1 Talented and perceptive, May 1 people are skilled observers and good communicators. Serene and sensible, they may also be prone to lethargy and sarcasm.

MAY 2 Insightful and intelligent, May 2 people possess an unusual understanding of human psychology and are therefore difficult to fool. Confident in their abilities—sometimes to a fault—they can also be dictatorial and harsh.

MAY 3 Those born on May 3 have an uncanny ability to understand the way groups work and are eager to assume a leadership role, which is often granted to them. Dynamic, they can also be demanding and stubborn, and must learn how to relinquish control.

MAY 4 Caring and calm, May 4 people are teachers by nature, and they will pass on their knowledge to others whether they teach in a school or not. They may not take enough risks in life, however, and may eventually feel dissatisfied because of it.

MAY 5 Pragmatic and motivating, May 5 people give advice readily and often contribute greatly to the lives of others. Best in the practical world, their intellect is not suited to vague hypotheses or suppositions.

MAY 6 Exceptionally imaginative, May 6 people excel in understanding fantasies and in being compassionate toward others. Empathic and kind when their creativity is used sensitively, they need to take care not to become manipulative.

MAY 7 Incredibly devoted, May 7 people will give all they have to a cause in which they believe. They tend to be troubled and isolated, though, and have difficult social lives.

MAY 8 Extremely outspoken, May 8 people are forceful and opinionated both in speech and in the written word. Convincing, strong, and loyal, they tend also to be critical and demanding when pursuing their cause.

MAY 9 A strong sense of morality and fair play is evident in May 9 people, and they exhibit courage in supporting their beliefs. This moral stance causes problems when they start to set unrealistic goals for themselves, however, and they may have trouble relaxing their beliefs.

MAY 10 Lively and bold, May 10 people work best alone, teaching by example. Many people learn from them, but the impulsive and selfish nature they possess often gets in the way of their success.

MAY 11 Inventive and original, May 11 people usually keep their ideas quiet. Though usually very intelligent, they may find that others regard them as merely eccentric and may not take them seriously.

MAY 12 Mirthful individualists, with a unique style, those born on May 12 also have a serious side. Strong communicators—especially good at refuting the spurious claims of others—they nevertheless tend to find themselves in trouble often.

MAY 13 The relaxed and expressive personalities of May 13 find that popularity comes easy to them. Easy esteem has its price, however, as playing to the crowd makes room for only petty and trivial accomplishments.

MAY 14 An eye for the future is evident in May 14 people, as they are good at blazing their own paths and taking advantage of opportunities. Driven to seek perfection, they may become stressed and uneasy when it eludes them.

MAY 15 Natural and unassuming, May 15 people tend to exemplify what others are unconsciously trying to reach, and thus draw people toward them for reasons that are not immediately evident. Lacking self-confidence, they may find themselves lonely and passive because they do not take risks.

MAY 16 Flashy and unconventional, May 16 people are great communicators who have few ambitions. Passionate, they must work to keep their feet on the ground, lest they become unaware of what is going on around them.

MAY 17 Straightforward and intense, those born on May 17 often make profound statements. Overzealous and abrasive at times, they may risk alienating their loved ones by refusing their help.

MAY 18 Dedicated and practical, May 18 people get their work done in the simplest manner possible, exemplifying constant logic and dependability. They risk getting too caught up in a cause they deem worthy, however, and may be unaccepting of the ideas of others.

MAY 19 Intelligent, energetic, and dynamic, those born on May 19 often attain positions of leadership. Still, they must be careful to properly harness their energies; otherwise they may become controlling or unruly.

MAY 20 Extremely enthusiastic and creative, May 20 people cannot contain their energy, and this enthusiasm inspires others. Restraint can be a problem for them, however, and they may have difficulty being satisfied.

MAY 21 Always ready for a challenge, May 21 people have incredible vision and resolve that allows them to do well in all kinds of situations. They must be careful, though, or their courage may lead to selfishness that may upset family and friends.

MAY 22 Optimistic and productive, May 22 people excel in using their talents in a variety of ways, and can often be found categorizing and organizing. Driven, they need to watch out that they don't give in to egotistical or childish behavior.

MAY 23 Attractive, energetic, and difficult to overlook, May 23 people are naturally alluring in many ways. Always working so that things will work out nicely for others, they risk becoming unnecessarily self-sacrificing.

MAY 24 Opinionated, concerned, and forthright, May 24 people enjoy working to better society. Good at evolving with the times, they nevertheless must learn to guard against narrow-minded behavior.

MAY 25 Exceptionally talented visionaries, those born on May 25 will go to any lengths to achieve the recognition to which they think they are entitled. Both gifted and ruthless, they need to remember that many people have contributed to their success.

MAY 26 Dependable and honorable, May 26 people have strong views and are respected for their methods of communicating them. Violence is a risk for them, though, and they must be careful not to become either perpetrator or victim.

MAY 27 Intelligent and funny, May 27 people usually specialize in one field, are hardworking, and leave no doubt of their opinions. They risk exhibiting arrogance, however, and may be seen as rude and self-righteous.

MAY 28 Original and creative, May 28 people often have difficulty finding the right career but will succeed quickly when it is located. Their unusual style and success are not appreciated by everyone, however, and they need to work hard not to get annoyed by more conventional types.

MAY 29 Defenders of truth and fairness who don't back away from a struggle, May 29 people often seek a group effort to effect change. Stalwart, they need to be cautious that their strong desire for change doesn't lead to narrow-mindedness.

MAY 30 Visionaries driven by freedom and independence, May 30 people succeed through freelance work. Always on the lookout for new endeavors, they often have problems with commitment and accountability.

MAY 31 Outwardly tough, with a demeanor that is capable and direct, May 31 people are actually sentimental and kind. Frequently escapist, they often don't realize that their tough exterior is just a front for some kind of insecurity.

JUNE 1 Interested in seeing and being seen, those born on June 1 are keen and lively. Very friendly people who resist introspection, they should be careful not to gather friends and possessions to veil the loneliness they sometimes feel.

JUNE 2 Those born on June 2 are creative and flexible, always coming up with ways to overcome the small problems with which they are constantly faced. Resourceful, they may become dependent on little dramas, and create problems where none exist.

JUNE 3 Highly original and humorous, June 3 people are strong and convincing communicators. Great at using language, they can become frustrated and even rude if they feel that they are misunderstood.

JUNE 4 Inspirational and intuitive, June 4 people are skilled in stimulating others with their words. Good bosses, they can be undiplomatic and critical with those who do not follow their lead.

JUNE 5 Methodical, intelligent, and direct, those born on June 5 excel when organizing and ordering things. They have trouble understanding when others do not grasp their methods of communication, though, and run the risk of becoming critical and nervous.

JUNE 6 Good at reaching their goals, those born on June 6 possess a unique vision that influences all aspects of their lives. Ambitious, they sometimes set their sights too high. Stubborn, they may refuse to acknowledge their mistakes.

JUNE 7 Engaging and funny, June 7 people know how to please a crowd and are often free of inhibitions. Large in their outlook, they may become preoccupied with the group picture, however, much to the detriment of those who are close to them.

JUNE 8 Highly intelligent and developed, June 8 people are individualistic and unusual. Quick to come up with ideas, they are often too quick to act on them, which is why they may be prone to making mistakes.

JUNE 9 Those born on June 9 are clear-thinking and methodical. Convincing people who don't change their minds easily, they need to understand that others may find them very persuasive and sometimes intractable.

JUNE 10 Brave and capable, those born on June 10 know how to exhibit courage in the face of desperation. They may be overly worried deep down, however, and need to take care that their emotions don't become overly dark.

JUNE 11 Well-directed and persistent, June 11 people are driven to break through barriers, no matter who set them up. Their determination may cause them to be stubborn, however, and they need to work hard not to be abrasive.

JUNE 12 Those born on June 12 are generous people who keep a positive outlook even when things are bad. Always concerned for the welfare of others, they must make sure not to lose their own identities in the process.

JUNE 13 Extremely imaginative, June 13 people love to travel and investigate past mysteries. Daring and adventurous, they are often on the verge of catastrophe and must learn not to overlook the important simple tasks of life.

JUNE 14 Ambitious, convincing, and courageous, June 14 people fight hard when they believe the cause to be worthy. Often successful, they may make enemies through their forceful nature and must be careful not to alienate those they care about.

JUNE 15 Appealing and pleasant, June 15 people rely on their charm to get ahead, using whatever attributes they have to win people over to their point of view. Convincing, they may also be manipulative, and this can cause them to lose true friends.

JUNE 16 Patient and constructive, June 16 people always manage to get something positive from their endeavors. Confident, they risk being too satisfied with themselves, though, and often have trouble making friends.

JUNE 17 Serious and persuasive, June 17 people strive to establish themselves in their careers and to care for their families. Ambitious, they need to work hard to ensure that their drive doesn't get in the way of their relationships.

JUNE 18 Influential and successful, June 18 people are very good with money and understand the best ways to manage their wealth. Prosperous, they may also be impatient, always looking to the next triumph that isn't always attainable.

JUNE 19 Inspirational and challenging, those born on June 19 excel at pushing boundaries. Frequently provocative, they must nevertheless understand that defiant behavior is not always appropriate.

JUNE 20 Expressive and appealing, June 20 people stir the emotions of others as well as themselves. Unusually charismatic, they must work to be balanced, as their lives may become governed by irrationality.

JUNE 21 Vital and attractive, those born on June 21 love life and strive to get the most out of it. Sensual, they need to be careful that their passion for life doesn't lead to undisciplined and addictive habits.

Summer

Summer is ruled by the urge to harvest. The sun is high and the colors are bright. Nature's full-blown ripeness is everywhere. Days are long now, and sunshine is plentiful. This is the time for picnics and barbecues, for swimming, for soaking up the rays of the sun, and for the uninhibited expression of sensual impulses. Body conscious, many of us seek to improve our physical appearance and to strut our stuff with characteristic pride and immodesty. Summer is wanton and abundant. Yet much of this bright extravagance is an illusion, since the amount of natural light available is actually shortening and the ripeness of all things carries with it the promise of imminent decay.

Summer technically begins on the solstice of June 21, but in fact many people begin celebrating summer during the hottest days of spring at the beginning of June. Likewise, a return to school or work in early September seems to herald the beginning of the fall season, when in fact the season of fall does not commence until the equinox of September 23. Some people and cultures shorten the season even further in their orientation and limit it to the hottest months of July and August.

Many people consider summer the most pleasant of seasons; nevertheless, it does have some highly unpleasant aspects about it too. The dangers of hot weather and of abundant direct sunlight are evident to all. The effects of the sun's full powers can have extremely detrimental effects on our health. Likewise, the absence of water in certain geographical areas and the exponential growth of insect and animal populations, regarded by many as pests to be eradicated, pose serious problems. In addition, the possibility of power outages due to increased electricity consumption, and the accompanying rise in energy costs, are ever-present threats. Thus, the combination of pleasant and unpleasant aspects of weather, driven to their extreme through temperature elevation and an overabundance of Mother Nature's gifts, provide a somewhat perplexing set of psychological problems.

We say that those born in the summer, so-called summertime people, are harvesters, in the sense that they need to pick the fruits of their endeavors. Seeds that have been sown in the spring now begin to bear fruit, both in nature and in business. In this way, summertime people need to witness the full flowering fruit of their efforts. Using the faculty of feeling, those born in the summer are best when expressing and monitoring their emotions. Capable of luminous expressions of energy, those born at this time light up those around them with their radiance. Positive in their orientation and intent on producing results, these determined individuals will strive to bring benefits to those in their family, social, or professional groups. Summertime people must bring one project to full fruition before moving on to the next.

In the same way, summertime endeavors mirror the personalities of those born during this season. Whether building additions to our property, working to repair or enlarge already existing spaces, bringing a vacation or travel project to a successful conclusion, or just plain enjoying ourselves in a way not possible during other seasons, we will find it easier to achieve fulfillment now than at any other time of the year. If the summer proves to be a bust due to an unfortunate accident or death of a loved one, huge disappointment and frustration can be felt in the coming fall and winter seasons. For some, summer poses the challenge to complete certain projects with the drive engendered by a now-or-never attitude. However, taking advantage of the seemingly endless hours of hot daylight is not always easy, due to the twin evils of procrastination and enervation caused by the sun itself. Too often, lolling around and wasting time is the result.

Personology shows the coincidence of the yearly cycle of nature with that of the human life and of the zodiac. Summertime thus also symbolizes the second twenty-one-year period of human life, from age twenty-one to forty-two, and of the fourth, fifth, and sixth signs of the zodiac: Cancer, Leo, and Virgo. Human development during these years sees a progression from early adulthood to midlife, in which a human being expects to see the results of their endeavors, whether in terms of career, finances, family, love, marriage, or certain leisure activities. Taking over the role of parent and being truly independent and productive can be the focus of this period. Like the season of summer, when we take joy in watching fruits and vegetables develop in our gardens, taking pride in the growth of our children and the progress of our work, and enjoying these with pride, is highly gratifying.

Likewise, Cancer, Leo, and Virgo events usually unfold slowly and can be watched or guided easily. However, occasional sudden outbursts of hot passion can cause their own sets of problems. People born under these signs benefit from contact with more thoughtful and intuitive individuals who are not as carried away by emotion. The signs of Cancer, Leo, and Virgo state as their mottos "I feel," "I create," and "I serve." The reflective and emotional sign of Cancer prepares us for the hot fecundity and creativity of Leo, which is finally evaluated and structured by the sign of Virgo. Again, the evolution from one sign to the next mirrors that in nature and in human development.

The Summer Personology Periods: June 21 to September 23

The Weeks

The season of summer lasts from the summer solstice of June 21 until the fall equinox of September 23. It is composed of the three astrological signs of Cancer (June 22–July 22), Leo (July 23–August 23), and Virgo (August 24–September 22). This second quarter of the year is further subdivided by personology into the following "weeks," or personology periods:

Gemini-Cancer Cusp: The Cusp of Magic (June 19–24)
Cancer I: The Week of Empathy (June 25–July 2)
Cancer II: The Week of Unconventionality (July 3–10)
Cancer III: The Week of Persuasion (July 11–18)
Cancer-Leo Cusp: The Cusp of Oscillation (July 19–25)
Leo I: The Week of Passion (July 26–August 2)
Leo II: The Week of Challenge (August 3–10)
Leo III: The Week of Leadership (August 11–18)
Leo-Virgo Cusp: The Cusp of Exposure (August 19–25)
Virgo I: The Week of Structure (August 26–September 2)
Virgo II: The Week of the Puzzle (September 3–10)
Virgo III: The Week of the Literal (September 11–18)
Virgo-Libra Cusp: The Cusp of Beauty (September 19–24)

The Cusps

The summer quadrant is given structure by the cusps between the astrological signs, as throughout the rest of the personological year. Demarcating the summer, at its beginning we find the summer solstice, known in personology as the Cusp of Magic, and at its end the fall equinox, the Cusp of Beauty. At monthly intervals between these two power points we find the Cusp of Oscillation (between Cancer and Leo) and the Cusp of Exposure (between the signs of Leo and Virgo). These four cusps—Magic, Oscillation, Exposure, and Beauty—characterize the season of summer as fully as the signs of Cancer, Leo, and Virgo, but in a more human sense.

The Cusp of Magic

JUNE 19–24

The Cusp of Magic corresponds with the advent of the summer solstice in the northern hemisphere. This means that the days are longest at this time of year, and the nights shortest. Traditionally a time of long magical evenings, Shakespeare perhaps best immortalized this season in his enchanting play *A Midsummer Night's Dream*. The wonderful but also dangerous combination of romance, fantasy, and illusion lends a special flavor to this cusp.

The faculty of feeling is perhaps stronger here than at any other time of the year. Emotions run high, and the other faculties of intuition, sensation, and thought may be swept aside. Nature's gentle warmth and light breezes caress the skin and gently fan the flame of love. Rarely violent like the onset of spring, the beginning of summer offers a calm gentleness and comfort rarely found at any other time of year.

Of course, love is an important part of most people's lives, and now is the time to indulge in flirtation, courtship, and outright romance. If you love someone secretly and have never told them how you feel, now is perhaps the moment to reveal your feelings. Of course, you can tell that person in subtle ways, for direct confrontation is not always the best tactic to employ. Platonic love is also favored now, and with it many kinds of affection and friendliness. Giving your heart without reservation can be, of course, fraught with peril. Yet attempting to protect oneself at the same time may be near to impossible, and a choice will have to be faced whether to give all or nothing.

Likewise, within the family unit, we would do well to find that relative who has been missing out on attention or whose gruffness has driven others away. Approaching such a thorny individual during the Cusp of Magic could result in breaking through emotional blocks through empathy and mutual understanding.

Perhaps the greatest danger during this cusp is allowing ourselves to be deceived by illusions. Indeed, as the old song says, "Falling in love with love is falling for make believe." We would do well to remind ourselves that the object of desire is after all a flesh and blood human being who one day will undoubtedly come down off his or her pedestal. The state of being in love can be uplifting and rewarding but also remarkably perilous. If taken to an extreme, it can lead to living in a dream world, totally out of touch with the feelings of the other person.

In the pursuit of love, we would all do well to cultivate the qualities of patience, persistence, and perceptiveness. These three "*p*s" can go a long way toward providing stability and minimizing the chaotic behavior of all parties involved. Rather than a threat of violence, the danger on the Cusp of Magic is that feelings will lead us to become attached to a given love object and exhibit highly dependent, even addictive behavior. Although such love involvements may be easy to foster, they can cause problems for years afterward and be extremely hard to disengage from.

The Personology of People Born on the Cusp of Magic

Romantic to the extreme, those born on the Cusp of Magic combine the airy, colorful qualities of Gemini with the deeper and watery emotionality of Cancer. They are able to cast a spell of enchantment over others and to use their powers of attraction and seduction to get their own way. Drawing heavily on the energies of magical summer nights, those born on the Cusp of Magic have a special relationship with their unconscious mind and secret self, being in touch with themselves at a very deep level. They also are able to be objective about personal matters and also to give structure to their relationships by setting down sensible guidelines.

Annual Events That Occur on the Cusp of Magic

June 21: Summer solstice (longest day and shortest night in the northern hemisphere)

Father's Day (or preceding week)

Major Historical Events That Have Happened on the Cusp of Magic

June 19, 1846: First official baseball game in Hoboken, New Jersey
June 20, 1837: Victoria becomes queen of England
June 21, 1990: Iran earthquake kills twenty-five thousand people
June 22, 1938: Joe Louis knocks out Schmeling to regain heavyweight title
June 23, 1956: Nasser is elected president of Egypt
June 24, 1876: Custer and men massacred at Little Bighorn

Famous People Born on the Cusp of Magic

Nicole Kidman, Jean-Paul Sartre, Billy Wilder, Terry Riley, Cyndi Lauper, Meryl Streep, Phylicia Rashad, Kris Kristofferson, Errol Flynn, Martin Landau, Lou Gehrig, Bob Fosse, Niels Bohr, Aung San Suu Kyi, Salman Rushdie, Benazir Bhutto, Joséphine de Beauharnais, Klaus Maria Brandauer, Prince William, John Dillinger

Birthdays Especially Affected on the Cusp of Magic

If you are born on the Cusp of Magic (June 19–24), the Cusp of Involvement (October 19–25), or the Cusp of Sensitivity (February 16–22) your energies blend well with those of this week. Results should be obtained with little effort on your part.

Cusp of Magic people may indulge preoccupation with romance to the fullest extent. Cusp of Involvement people will be at their most attractive and no doubt have to fight off a swarm of admirers. Cusp of Sensitivity people can be appreciated for their deep emotional orientation.

If you are born on the Cusp of Beauty (September 19–24), the Cusp of Prophecy (December 19–25), or the Cusp of Rebirth (March 19–24) you will face problems and challenges during this week. You will have to work harder to achieve your goals.

Cusp of Beauty people must not fall prey to illusion; otherwise they risk heartbreak. Cusp of Prophecy people are likely to give all for love, but may become dangerously addicted to their passion. Cusp of Rebirth people can be hurt emotionally by their own blind intensity.

The Week of Empathy

Our primary concern during the Week of Empathy should be the feelings of those around us. This is the time to touch base with our loved ones and to tune in to their needs and wants. Not only subjective matters but also practical ones should be attended to. The financial status of our family or club should be carefully monitored and proper adjustments to its investments, savings, tax status, and expense accounts made. New sources of income should be investigated in order to guarantee an advantageous cash flow.

Understanding the needs of others is important, as is taking an active role to protect those incapable of protecting themselves. In this respect, a defensive stance will be more effective than an overly aggressive mode. Children and young adults may need special protection at this time, whether they are in our own family or not. In addition, nurturing those close to us, particularly by trying to bring out their best qualities and encouraging their talents to emerge, will be particularly appropriate to the energy of this period in time.

Should aggressive drives surface now, it will prove important to channel such forces constructively. Martial arts and competitive sports are both ways in which excess energy may be put to constructive use. Again, defensive rather than offensive play is particularly recommended. We may also be more likely to face injury during this week, so we have to exercise good sense and keen judgment to avoid getting hurt or hurting others. Those interested in coaching or teaching sports will find this a good time to launch a career. If we begin such endeavors during this week and continue them for the rest of the year, we are likely to face a favorable outcome.

Although dealing with the feelings of others is germane to this week, certain precautions must be taken. There is an undeniable tendency in the

Week of Empathy to confuse the feelings of the other person for our own. It can be problematic, for example, if we find ourselves feeling anger or resentment and do not realize these feelings are coming from someone else. Moreover, the nature of relationships in general can become extremely complex during this week. Skewed emotions may often result, with the concomitant feeling of being out of tune with a partner, friend, or family member. Great care should be taken during this week to avoid misunderstandings, which can dominate our emotional life for weeks or months to come.

One positive way to view emotional problems is to see them as opportunities to learn about relationships, about others, and about ourselves. For example, those who find themselves feeling depressed may consider this a good time to use their inactivity to really get to the heart of a problem. Too often we do not do enough work on ourselves or on our relationships when things are going well, and choose instead to sweep any difficulties under the carpet. As a result we must take advantage of the hard times in our relationships to examine and understand our more distressing feelings. In this way future depressions can be avoided and better mental health fostered.

The Personology of People Born in the Week of Empathy

Able to put their dreams to work for them, these sensitive individuals can be surprisingly successful in the professional realm. Part of their success with money in their adult years is recognizing it as a fluid medium and not getting unduly uptight over having or not having it. Yet people born in the Week of Empathy may well carry a reputation when young of not being good at handling finances, and unfortunately come to believe it themselves. Because of their empathic abilities, those born in this week are able to see into the minds and hearts of others. Comforting and sympathetic, these individuals are often sought out for advice and psychological evaluations.

Annual Events That Occur During the Week of Empathy

June 28: World War I Day
July 1: Anniversary of first zoo in America

Major Historical Events That Have Happened During the Week of Empathy

June 25, 1903: Marie Curie announces her discovery of radium
June 26, 1963: Kennedy appears before cheering crowds in Berlin
June 27, 1939: First transatlantic air service established
June 28, 1919: First World War peace treaty signed at Versailles
June 29, 1970: First outdoor rock festival held in London
June 30, 1859: Charles Blondin crosses Niagara Falls on a tightrope
July 1, 1858: Darwin presents evolutionary theory in London
July 2, 1881: U.S. President Garfield shot, later dies

Famous People Born During the Week of Empathy

Princess Diana, Carl Lewis, George Sand, Ross Perot, Jean-Jacques Rousseau, Hermann Hesse, Richard Rodgers, Mike Tyson, Dan Aykroyd, Emma Goldman, Mel Brooks, Lena Horne, Babe Zaharias, Greg Lemond, Sidney Lumet, Helen Keller, Pamela Anderson, Kathy Bates, Oriana Fallaci, Pearl Buck

Birthdays Especially Affected During the Week of Empathy

If you are born in the Week of Empathy (June 25–July 2), the Week of Intensity (October 26–November 2), or the Week of Spirit (February 23–March 2) your energies blend well with those of this week. Results should be obtained with little effort on your part.

Week of Empathy people should put their financial abilities in the service of those they love. Week of Intensity people will be appreciated for their emotional intelligence when family or professional disputes arise. Week of Spirit people can form empathic bonds with those who need them.

If you are born in the Week of Perfection (September 25–October 2), the Week of Rule (December 26–January 2), or the Week of Curiosity (March 25–April 2) you will face problems and challenges during this week. You will have to work harder to achieve your goals.

Week of Perfection people will be rejected if they fail to acknowledge the emotional side of life. Week of Rule people should stop paying so much attention to money and try to be happier with the simple joys of life. Week of Curiosity people must be aware of depression when their expectations are not met.

❋

The Week of Unconventionality

JULY 3–10

The energies of this week are a curious blend of introverted and extroverted. On the one hand, flamboyant activities are likely to take center stage, with lots of motion, color, and pizzazz in our daily lives. On the other hand, lots of downtime will be needed to digest all of these experiences, and there will be an accompanying need for peace and quiet. Funnily enough, the extroverted experiences in life are not necessarily contradicted by personal introversion, but can be complemented by it. In this context experiences can be varied and colorful but emotions kept extremely private.

Because vacations are now in full swing, much time is likely to be spent in travel and in outdoor pursuits. At the same time, due to national holidays and celebrations, being at home with our loved ones also has top priority. A pride in both family and country is characteristic now, and along with this will come a desire to make our country a better place in which to live.

Enjoying ourselves is definitely in the cards this week, but obsessive behavior can become a problem. Food ranks high on the list of addictions, but sex and drugs such as alcohol and nicotine also follow in close order. Breaking bad habits at this time will prove extremely difficult, but those who can manage to accomplish this are likely to make it stick. Since the five worst offenders are often alcohol, fat, nicotine, caffeine, and sugar, we should all zero in on at least one of these and try to make some positive changes, however modest they may be.

Going overboard on wacky behavior is certainly a possibility during the Week of Unconventionality. For those who are shy, escaping into a world of fantasy is not at all unusual. The danger here, of course, is that if the fantasies are too gratifying they may continue to dominate our psyche for the rest of the year. Thus, some caution is urged before giving in to the tendency to exercise your imagination unduly.

Sympathy for the plight of the downtrodden or of neglected family members is often felt during this period. Spending time with such unfortunate individuals is highly recommended, both to bring light into other people's lives and also to ground ourselves in the practical matters of everyday life. Strangely enough, the Week of Unconventionality also carries the need for normalcy, and helping others or participating in social activities may be quite reassuring. It can also be a way of atoning for overly flamboyant behavior.

Despite the good weather, watching videos and going to the movies hold their own particular attraction at this time. Subjects relating to the more far-out aspects of life will be especially riveting, particularly science fiction, fantasy writing, and the occult. Films dealing with illegal or illicit activities are hard to resist, as they typify the kind of clandestine behavior that is of particular interest during the Week of Unconventionality.

In general, then, a healthy mix of conventional and unconventional activities will keep us on an even keel while at the same time satisfying our hankering after the bizarre. Once this week passes, however, we may regret having brought downright weird characters into our lives.

The Personology of People Born in the Week of Unconventionality

These unusual individuals understand the twists and turns that life can take. Because of their often eccentric natures they are able to understand and accept the bizarre aspects of life better than most. Having an insight into areas hidden to most, those born in this week can often strike a common chord in their listeners and associates, which allows others to trust them. Characteristically, those born in the Week of Unconventionality make quite a normal impression on first meeting; it is only later, when we get to know them better, that their foibles and idiosyncrasies come to the fore.

Annual Events That Occur During the Week of Unconventionality

July 4: Independence Day

Major Historical Events That Have Happened During the Week of Unconventionality

July 3, 1863: Union defeats Confederacy at battle of Gettysburg

July 4, 1776: Declaration of Independence adopted by Continental Congress

July 5, 1965: Opera star Maria Callas sings farewell concert

July 6, 1535: Defiant Sir Thomas More beheaded for treason

July 7, 1853: Admiral Perry opens Japan to trade

July 8, 1822: British poet Shelley drowns in storm

July 9, 1951: Writer Dashiell Hammett jailed for contempt

July 10, 1985: Greenpeace ship *Rainbow Warrior* blown up

Famous People Born During the Week of Unconventionality

Franz Kafka, Dalai Lama, Tom Hanks, Tom Cruise, Gustav Mahler, Anjelica Huston, Nancy Reagan, Shirley Knight, Sylvester Stallone, Nikola Tesla, Tom Stoppard, Della Reese, Shelley Duvall, Marcel Proust, Elizabeth Kübler-Ross, Wanda Landowska, Pierre Cardin, John D. Rockefeller, Frida Kahlo

Birthdays Especially Affected During the Week of Unconventionality

If you are born in the Week of Unconventionality (July 3–10), the Week of Profundity (November 3–11), or the Week of Isolation (March 3–10) your energies blend well with those of this week. Results should be obtained with little effort on your part.

Week of Unconventionality people should try to find the right balance between introvert and extrovert behavior. Week of Profundity people can indulge their fantasy but must be aware of the attractions of the dark side. Week of Isolation people can seek out their private space without fear of intrusion.

If you are born in the Week of Socialization (October 3–10), the Week of Determination (January 3–9), or the Week of Success (April 3–10) you will face problems and challenges during this week. You will have to work harder to achieve your goals.

Week of Socialization people will arouse resistance to their extroverted behavior. Week of Determination people should not push professionally but instead indulge their more imaginative side. Week of Success people may be overlooking needy friends or family members who are silently asking for help.

❋

The Week of Persuasion

JULY 11–18

Convincing others of the feasibility of our proposals and the efficacy of our plans should be the central focus of this week. Those in tune with the energies of the Week of Persuasion will use subtle means to accomplish these ends, rather than riding roughshod over those perceived as opponents. This last reference is crucial, since the term "opponent" can be turned around with convincing argument to become "ally" or even "colleague." The crucial point here of course is convincing the other person that his or her interests are close to our own, so much so that what benefits one automatically benefits the other.

Giving advice and counsel to others may also be considered part and parcel of this process. This is perhaps most effectively accomplished when the opinions offered are not unsolicited but rather requested. However, this does not imply that the person being sought out for their opinion must behave in an entirely passive manner. Advertising yourself as someone who can help, and who in fact has an excellent track record in doing so, is entirely acceptable and frequently appreciated by the person in need. Whether a fee or favor is requested in exchange for this advice or not, the adviser stands to gain a great deal in stature through a successful outcome.

There is the tendency in this week, however, to go beyond giving counsel and attempting to control the situation excessively. Such behavior surely will arouse resentment in strong-minded individuals or induce crippling dependencies in those lacking the willpower to resist. Thus, someone who is asked for help would do well to judge the character of the individual seeking advice before proceeding thoughtlessly. The trick lies in matching what we say to whom we say it, in a diplomatic and wise manner.

Since persuasion figures so prominently this week, we may be forced to armor ourselves to an extent against unwanted junk mail, door-to-door salesmen, scam artists, and other undesirable intrusions or intruders.

Emotions rule the quadrant of summer, and are especially strong under the sign of Cancer. As a result, the qualities of logic, common sense, and intuition must be brought into play to maintain objectivity. The pleasures of seduction may be enjoyed by those on both sides, primarily as a flirtation, without giving ourselves completely to the experience or buying the product or service offered. Keeping it light in most areas is generally advised during the Week of Persuasion.

Likewise, in our interpersonal relationships a certain amount of good sense will be vital to avoid disasters, or at the very least unpleasant situations. The warm weather during this week is especially conducive to summer romances, usually best confined to a limited time period with few if any expectations of commitment or permanence. It should not be assumed that promiscuity is being recommended here, for refusal or outright abstinence is not always the worst decision to make with regard to a particular person or situation. Learning to say no may frequently prove to be the best course of action when approached by a particularly tempting offer.

The Personology of People Born in the Week of Persuasion

These powerful individuals are capable of convincing others of the correctness of their point of view. Whether using a seductive or a confrontational approach, they are unstoppable once they make up their minds about something. In addition, they do not just rely on their arguments, since their physical presence also can be formidable. They are particularly effective in convincing and influencing larger groups since they have the true interest of such groups at heart rather than only their own personal advancement. Perhaps their most subtle technique is planting their own idea in the mind of the other guy and allowing that person to act on it as if it were his own.

Annual Events That Occur During the Week of Persuasion

July 11: World Population Day
July 14: Bastille Day

Major Historical Events That Have Happened During the Week of Persuasion

July 11, 1804: Aaron Burr kills Alexander Hamilton in duel
July 12, 1920: Panama Canal opened
July 13, 1977: Massive electrical blackout in New York City
July 14, 1789: Bastille stormed by Parisians beginning revolution
July 15, 1954: First flight of Boeing 707

July 16, 1918: Czar and family murdered by Bolsheviks
July 17, 1453: End of Hundred Years War
July 18, 1955: Disneyland opens in California

Famous People Born During the Week of Persuasion

Nelson Mandela, Mother Cabrini, Bill Cosby, Rembrandt van Rijn, Ruben Blades, Mary Baker Eddy, Julius Caesar, Harrison Ford, Richard Branson, Hunter Thompson, Linda Ronstadt, Yul Brynner, Andrew Wyeth, Peace Pilgrim, Kristi Yamaguchi, Kirsten Flagstad, Woodie Guthrie, John Quincy Adams, Emmeline Pankhurst, Bella Davidovich

Birthdays Especially Affected During the Week of Persuasion

If you are born in the Week of Persuasion (July 11–18), the Week of Control (November 12–18), or the Week of Dances and Dreams (March 11–18) your energies blend well with those of this week. Results should be obtained with little effort on your part.

Week of Persuasion people will achieve success if they can persuade others of their views subtly, without being overpowering. Week of Control people may find themselves indulging their desires and achieving great satisfaction in doing so. Week of Dances and Dreams people will enjoy flirting as never before.

If you are born in the Week of Theater (October 11–18), the Week of Dominance (January 10–16), or the Week of Social Betterment (April 11–18) you will face problems and challenges during this week. You will have to work harder to achieve your goals.

Week of Theater people are sure to arouse resistance to their plans if they come on too strong. Week of Dominance people must lower their voices and cultivate the art of listening if they are to be truly persuasive. Week of Social Betterment people will suffer less if they refuse now rather than later.

The Cusp of Oscillation

Great skill will be required to navigate the perils of the Cusp of Oscillation. Because fluctuation and change are so characteristic of this time period, it may be difficult or even impossible to maintain our stability and composure. Riding the waves of emotion and avoiding the danger of extremes of feeling are crucial to our mental health.

Because the sign of Cancer is related to the moon, often associated with feminine qualities, and Leo to the sun, thought of as masculine, this cusp between the two signs shares qualities of both. This implies not only doing your best to deal with women and men in egalitarian fashion, but also to balance the female and male qualities within ourselves.

Not infrequently during this time, swings to extremes in emotion, thought, and action can make us feel like we're on a roller-coaster ride that is difficult or impossible to control. Seismic tremors can be produced in the environment of out-of-control individuals, causing events in their vicinity that may be extremely chaotic. By acknowledging, understanding, and even anticipating such events we may successfully negotiate these dangerous rapids and even put their prodigious energies to good use, like a power plant utilizing the power of a dammed river.

All team endeavors, particularly those involving professional groups, are favored at this time. Such endeavors also will confer the added bonus of providing stability. The most successful groups at this time will be those which combine equal responsibilities and rewards with a maximum of individual initiative within the organization. It is essential that we touch base frequently with our coworkers and not lose sight of the common goal.

Likewise, the importance of stable relationships in our life cannot be emphasized enough during this period. Rather than looking for overly exciting or romantic partners, we would all do well to find those reliable and trustworthy people whom we can count on. This may be especially difficult because of the strong pull we will feel toward exciting experiences at this time. The lure of challenging and perilous adventure is indeed so powerful that our impulses can gain the upper hand and result in self-destructive tendencies. Having the judgment to distinguish between positive and negative influences could even mean the difference between life and death or grave injury in certain extreme situations.

On the other hand this cusp could prove to be the time for more conservative and careful individuals to loosen up and express themselves more fully. For these folks the opportunities inherent in this week to bring some well-needed excitement into their lives could prove highly beneficial. Particularly in the area of love, this could be the time to open our hearts and begin to experience true emotion. Those whose lifestyle is more radical to begin with will need to keep their anarchical tendencies under control to avoid being swept away by the conflicting energies of this time. The great challenge to everyone during this week is to maintain balance and equilibrium without missing out on excitement and challenge.

The Personology of People Born on the Cusp of Oscillation

Change comes naturally to these volatile individuals, who can swing from one mood to another in a short period of time. Because of the reflective influence of the moon (ruler of Cancer) and the dynamic influence of the sun (Leo), Cancer-Leo cusp people can appear extroverted to some and introverted to others. Whether exhibiting their active or passive side, however, most people born on this cusp tend to be exciting and vibrant people who show off their most attractive qualities to full advantage. Physical expression is vital to these exciting people, whether in more intimate spheres, at the fitness center, or on the playing field.

Annual Events That Occur on the Cusp of Oscillation

July 20: Moon Day
July 21: National Holiday of Belgium

July 22: National Hot Dog Day
　　　　National Holiday of Poland

Major Historical Events That Have Happened on the Cusp of Oscillation

July 19, 1545: Flagship of Henry VIII sinks with all hands onboard
July 20, 1944: Hitler survives assassination attempt
July 21, 1969: First man walks on the moon
July 22, 1934: Gangster John Dillinger shot dead
July 23, 1803: Failure of Irish Rebellion
July 24, 1567: Mary Queen of Scots abdicates
July 25, 1909: Blériot first to fly across the English Channel

Famous People Born on the Cusp of Oscillation

Amelia Earhart, Ernest Hemingway, Carlos Santana, Herbert Marcuse, Simon Bolívar, Alexandre the Great, Karl Malone, Monica Lewinsky, Alexandre Dumas, Diana Rigg, Zelda Fitzgerald, Natalia Bessmertnova, Edmund Hillary, Hart Crane, Marshall McLuhan, Danny Glover, Tom Robbins, Woody Harrelson, Robin Williams, Rose Fitzgerald Kennedy

Birthdays Most Affected on the Cusp of Oscillation

If you are born on the Cusp of Oscillation (July 19–25), the Cusp of Revolution (November 19–24), or the Cusp of Rebirth (March 19–24) your energies blend well with those of this week. Results should be obtained with little effort on your part.

Cusp of Oscillation people will find all the excitement they require now, but must maintain some stability too. Cusp of Revolution people can book financial gains this week through taking conservative gambles. Cusp of Rebirth people feed off the inspirational energies of this period, but must be careful not to overeat.

If you are born on the Cusp of Involvement (October 19–25), the Cusp of Mystery, Violence, and Imagination (January 17–22), or the Cusp of Power (April 19–24) you will face problems and challenges during this week. You will have to work harder to achieve your goals.

Cusp of Involvement people are likely to fall prey to self-destructive tendencies unless they exercise good old common sense. Cusp of Mystery, Violence, and Imagination people may be easily caught up in a maelstrom of whirling emotions. Cusp of Power people will have to learn to loosen up if they hope to enjoy themselves.

※

The Week of Passion

JULY 26–AUGUST 2

Trying to avoid burnout can become an important preoccupation during this highly energetic week. Driving ourselves too hard, whether in pursuit of success in our professional life or a desired love object in our personal life, is all too common now. Generally, the tendency is to ignore our limitations in going for it, with subsequent disappointment and frustration threatening to overwhelm us. Finding certain rules to live by or recognizing the authority of a given doctrine or personal teacher may prove to be a way to keep our house in order.

During this week it may be advisable to work on our own as much as possible, since frictions with a boss may prove unsupportable. Rebellious tendencies are bound to emerge, accompanied by displays of temperament. It may also be possible to realize financial success at this time, as long as spending does not get out of control. Planning a strict budget during this week and sticking to it is not at all a bad idea, and the positive effects of bringing such structure into our lives may be felt for the rest of the year.

Because the tendencies of the Week of Passion are so outgoing, we would do well to establish a small space where we may retreat in times of acute stress. This space may be either a psychological or physical one. Sharing intimacy with another person in a relaxed fashion may not be possible at this time, for frenetic energies tend to push us to the limits of exhaustion, particularly in the sexual sphere. However, going for long walks, overnight camping trips, and adventurous explorations in the mountains or by the sea with this person can prove to be positive influences on an already flowering relationship.

Learning to find stillness in the eye of the storm and reaping the rewards of experience through reflection after a passionate experience are true learning experiences that can take us far in life. Often swept away by a maelstrom of emotion during this period, we need time for contemplation and spiritual discovery. Throwing ourselves into life headfirst may lead us ultimately to find out more about our own character. As long as some damage control is operative, there is no need to hold back from the searing experiences that are offered to us now.

Chance encounters with strangers may prove rewarding, particularly in the sexual realm. Somehow, giving ourselves to an unknown person can be remarkably fulfilling. In the sphere of friendship also, this could be the time to make new contacts and to share our experiences and even secrets with a stranger. Generally speaking, it is better not to attempt to transform such chance encounters into permanent liaisons.

This week favors open attitudes rather than hidden ones. The qualities of cheerfulness and optimism are much appreciated. Yet, the danger exists here of refusing to recognize the truth, particularly when it is unpleasant. Thus, it is important to be on guard against being too unrealistic and of falling into dishonest habits out of fear of hurting others or causing difficulty for ourselves.

The Personology of People Born in the Week of Passion

The ambitious individuals born in this week have a passionate desire to rise to the top of their professions. In fact, a passionate approach to life suffuses all of their activities, but at the same time they play by the rules and particularly admire the authorities in their fields whose word is law to them. Ultimately, of course, they secretly wish to become such recognized authorities themselves, and thus are good students of the rules and demeanor of those they admire. Dominant in their attitudes, those born in the Week of Passion will not get out of your way easily but demand to be recognized. Even the shyest of such individuals will eventually emerge to claim their rightful place in the world.

Annual Events That Occur During the Week of Passion

July 26: Liberia's Independence Day
July 27: Cross Atlantic Communication Day
July 29: Founding of NASA anniversary
August 1: Swiss Confederation Day

Major Historical Events That Have Happened During the Week of Passion

July 26, 1956: Nasser nationalizes Suez Canal
July 27, 1685: Spinoza banned by Amsterdam Jewish community
July 28, 1794: Robespierre sent to guillotine
July 29, 1981: Prince Charles marries Lady Diana Spencer
July 30, 1990: British MP Ian Gow murdered by IRA
July 31, 1964: Ranger sends back pictures of the moon
August 1, 1914: Germany declares war on Russia
August 2, 1990: Iraq invades Kuwait

Famous People Born During the Week of Passion

Carl Gustav Jung, Jacqueline Kennedy Onassis, Arnold Schwarzenegger, Pat Schroeder, Primo Levi, Geraldine Chaplin, Herman Melville, Henry Ford, Mick Jagger, Patti Scialfa, George Bernard Shaw, Beatrix Potter, Bobbie Gentry, Peggy Fleming, Mikis Theodorakis, Elizabeth Hanford Dole, Jerry Garcia, Pina Bausch, Alexandre Dumas, Jr., Benito Mussolini

Birthdays Especially Affected During the Week of Passion

If you are born in the Week of Passion (July 26–August 2), the Week of Independence (November 25–December 2), or the Week of Curiosity (March 25–April 2) your energies blend well with those of this week. Results should be obtained with little effort on your part.

Week of Passion people need an outlet for their feelings, whether it is a relationship, a vacation hobby, or their career, and once they find it they will be happy. Week of Independence people should develop their own projects and consider plans to become self-employed. Week of Curiosity people should force themselves to take a vacation, stressing rest and relaxation mixed with milder sorts of adventure.

If you are born in the Week of Intensity (October 26–November 2), the Week of Intelligence (January 23–30), or the Week of Manifestation (April 25–May 2) you will face problems and challenges during this week. You will have to work harder to achieve your goals.

Week of Intensity people are aroused at this time, but can easily get into trouble by indulging their passion, particularly sexual. Week of Intelligence people would do well to follow their intuitions and feelings, since planning and calculating don't work now. Week of Manifestation people risk breakdown if they continue to work during the summer, and thus a workless vacation is mandatory.

✳

The Week of Challenge

AUGUST 3–10

Rising to meet the challenges offered during this week may prove one of the highest points of intensity in the entire year. It is extremely important during this time not to back down from these challenges, but to accept them and fight to achieve our goals. This will demand our perseverance and balanced strength, as well as a stalwart refusal to give up when the going gets tough. The Week of Challenge gives us the power to achieve almost whatever we set our mind to, providing we believe enough in ourselves.

Although we may go far in our pursuits this week, it is also vitally important to be aware of our limitations. Stretching our capabilities to the limit, and even surpassing them, is possible, but an unlimited reserve of energy is not. Furthermore, we can use this week to find out which activities are better suited to our character and ideals. Crucial to this process is recognizing when things have not worked out, for there is an undeniable tendency to refuse to recognize either defeat or failure now. Being able to change course when further progress is impossible will be an important ingredient in our success.

Because depression may sink in when things are not going well, we must learn to handle this debilitating state. Talking ourselves back into an active frame of mind is important, but so is recognizing our problems and doing something about them. As the introspective energies of this week are not high, it may be necessary to talk to a close friend, a spiritual or religious guide, or a professional counselor.

The wilds of nature, the corporate and business world, or the intimate sphere of the bedroom may be arenas in which we strive to achieve our deepest longings for success. In these and other areas, this week is marked by a strong physicality, in which competitive urges come to the fore. Making the connection between true love on the one hand and passionate sexual expressions on the other may not be in the cards now. So great is the urge to dominate and control in every area of endeavor that we must beware that like impulses on the other side do not result in highly aggressive confrontations.

In this latter respect, we would do well to make our goals objective ones, and not to expend all of our energy in personal confrontations. For example, in sports, seeking to surpass our own personal best would be preferable to overcoming a challenging opponent. Yet, the one-on-one struggles both on and off the playing field exert an undeniable hold on us and may prove to be the most gratifying efforts of all.

Since keeping balanced is essential to success now, the fascination of drugs and other stimulants should be monitored and kept under control.

Letting these urges get out of hand, or even indulging in downright addictions, can sabotage all of our endeavors to move ahead. Without stability we may feel that our powers are slipping away and wasted in fruitless bursts of energy. With stability will come the ability to concentrate on the task at hand and realize the very best that we have to give.

The Personology of People Born in the Week of Challenge

Those born in this week are tough, determined individuals who will stick with a company, family, or social group year in and year out with little complaint. Reliable to the extreme, they can be a rock of support to others, although curiously they may not prove to be so dedicated to their own best interests. Because their ambition is not always of the highest sort, they can be quite satisfied with a lower position in a company hierarchy, content to do their job and be rewarded and recognized for the quality of their work. These determined individuals are no strangers to disappointment and learn early in life to pick themselves up, dust themselves off, and proceed on their way with unflappable courage.

Annual Events That Occur During the Week of Challenge

August 4: Coast Guard Day
August 5: Atomic Bomb Day
August 6: Independence Day in Bolivia

Major Historical Events That Have Happened During the Week of Challenge

August 3, 1492: Columbus sets sail for India
August 4, 1914: Britain declares war on Germany
August 5, 1958: U.S. sub *Nautilus* ends two-thousand-mile journey underwater
August 6, 1945: First atomic bomb dropped by United States on Hiroshima

August 7, 1987: Central American leaders sign peace agreement
August 8, 1974: U.S. President Richard Nixon resigns
August 9, 1942: Gandhi arrested in England
August 10, 1966: First U.S. moon satellite launched

Famous People Born During the Week of Challenge

Raoul Wallenberg, Whitney Houston, Neil Armstrong, Dustin Hoffman, Isabel Allende, John Huston, Melanie Griffith, Patti Austin, Percy Bysshe Shelley, Lucille Ball, Louis Leakey, Roland Kirk, Emil Nolde, Rosanna Arquette, Martin Sheen, Mata Hari, David Robinson, Patrick Ewing, Martha Stewart, Courtney Love

Birthdays Especially Affected During the Week of Challenge

If you are born in the Week of Challenge (August 3–10), the Week of Originality (December 3–10), or the Week of Success (April 3–10) your energies blend well with those of this week. Results should be obtained with little effort on your part.

Week of Challenge people will respond well to the intense energies of this week and rise to new heights in their endeavors. Week of Originality people can figure out new ways to get the job done in a highly effective fashion. Week of Success people must keep their fire under control if they are to reach a higher plateau.

If you are born in the Week of Profundity (November 3–11), the Week of Youth and Ease (January 31–February 7), or the Week of Study (May 3–10) you will face problems and challenges during this week. You will have to work harder to achieve your goals.

Week of Profundity people can encounter struggles with others who also choose to control or dominate. Week of Youth and Ease people may find themselves too relaxed to answer the challenges posed during this period. Week of Study people may get too wrapped up in their own private world and fail to actively engage in life's struggles.

The Week of Leadership

AUGUST 11–18

Assuming a leadership role may well prove to be the absorbing passion of this week. Of course, not all of us are cut out to be leaders, but on the other hand not all of us may realize the particular advantages that this week offers in this respect. Those who do recognize the potential for leadership will have a jump on their competitors and also a unique opportunity to assume a role which they may have found difficult in the past. Taking the initiative is the essence of leadership, along with the ability to command, counsel, and guide the destiny of others. Thus, psychology plays an important role in the makeup of any leader.

We would do well to resist battling with others seeking the leadership role within an existing organization, and instead seek to establish our own unique sphere of influence. Leadership may be exerted in almost any direction, and its expression may well prove more important than achieving concrete goals; hence, the means may prove more important than the ends. It is in the act of leadership itself that the most gratifying rewards are to be found.

Through taking the initiative, we can discover the more forceful and spontaneous elements of our own character, raise our self-esteem, and prove that we really can make a difference. Because suffering family groups or businesses may be in dire need of new direction, those from the ranks who jump right in, whether or not they have previous experience, can gain the valued appreciation of the group. Yet we must be sensitive at every step of the way not to trample the feelings and strivings of others, and to remain sympathetic to their innermost needs. We must never forget to listen, or allow ourselves to be carried away by the zeal and challenge of command.

During the hot days of mid-August, learning to pace ourselves and conserve energy is vitally important. Even when in the throes of taking the lead in any endeavor, simple rules of health can well spell the difference between sickness and being well. It is especially important to consume enough pure water, include enough greens and roughage, and limit intake of sugar during this time. Moreover, learning to look after our health will be essential when so much energy is being spent in the service of others.

Nor should personal creative urges be ignored. Art, music, literature, and film may all be areas in which we realize success at this time. Such activities complement the time spent leading others, both as a well-needed diversion and a deep opportunity to express ourselves. In some cases, leadership and creativity may be combined, with spectacular results.

We must beware that passionate feelings do not get out of control during the Week of Leadership. Since the urge to dominate is so strong now, resentments and aggression may be aroused in our partners, resulting in unmanageable conflicts. Also, the breakup of an established relationship may be so debilitating that our urges to take the lead in various endeavors may be subverted and seriously undermined.

The Personology of People Born in the Week of Leadership

These born leaders do not necessarily need to be at the head of a group, but they are quite satisfied when their ideas exert an influence on the groups to which they belong. It is of great importance to these highly complex and emotional individuals that they be regarded as normal, since they are thrown off balance easily when others reject them or consider them peculiar or strange. For these individuals life is an adventure, frequently a heroic one, in which they play a central role, often as queen or king. Because of their high opinion of themselves, those born in this week would do well to cultivate a more realistic attitude and not push beyond their limitations.

Annual Events That Occur During the Week of Leadership

August 11: Family Day
August 15: Feast of the Assumption

Major Historical Events That Have Happened During the Week of Leadership

August 11, 1965: Watts riots begin in Los Angeles
August 12, 1959: Arkansas riots over racial integration
August 13, 1876: Bayreuth theater opens with Wagner's *Ring* premiere
August 14, 1980: Polish workers seize shipyard at Gdansk
August 15, 1965: Beatles concert at Shea Stadium sets outdoor record
August 16, 1960: Cyprus becomes a republic
August 17, 1896: Major gold find in Yukon announced
August 18, 1984: South Africa banned from Olympics for apartheid

Famous People Born During the Week of Leadership

Madonna, Napoleon, T. E. Lawrence, Magic Johnson, Alex Haley, Annie Oakley, Roman Polanski, Lina Wertmüller, Wim Wenders, Alfred Hitchcock, Robert De Niro, Gary Larson, Helena Blavatsky, Pete Sampras, Fidel Castro, Rosalynn Carter, Cecil B. De Mille, Robert Redford, Shelley Winters, Malcolm-Jamal Warner

Birthdays Especially Affected During the Week of Leadership

If you are born in the Week of Leadership (August 11–18), the Week of Expansiveness (December 11–18), or the Week of Social Betterment (April 11–18) your energies blend well with those of this week. Results should be obtained with little effort on your part.

Week of Leadership people take the initiative easily and will be respected by those who follow them. Week of Expansiveness people have the vision to command others and strive for the good of the group. Week of Social Betterment people tend to lead through example, and never expect more of others than they are willing to give of themselves.

If you are born in the Week of Control (November 12–18), the Week of Acceptance (February 8–15), or the Week of Nature (May 11–18) you will face problems and challenges during this week. You will have to work harder to achieve your goals.

Week of Control people may seek to lead but fail through lacking the spark or being able to harness the proper energies. Week of Acceptance people could lack the drive to assume an effective leadership position, suffering frustration. Week of Nature people are likely to be uninterested in commanding others, and thus lose the opportunities granted here.

✳

The Cusp of Exposure

AUGUST 19–25

Keeping secrets is practically inevitable during this week. As shade is sought on these hot summer days, so the tendency here is to escape the earnest scrutiny of the world by concealing our emotions in the shadows. Likewise, all sorts of hidden events may spring out, causing some consternation, unless we are prepared for them. Expect the unexpected to happen with great regularity now, since what was invisible may now materialize suddenly and without warning. Such materialization is emphasized symbolically on this Leo-Virgo cusp by the fire of Leo and the earthy presence of Virgo.

The other side of the coin is that this cusp can also be an ideal time to reveal our plans, particularly those which have been kept hidden for a long while. The element of surprise is potent during this week, and pleasant surprises may be very much appreciated at this time. On the other hand, we must exercise great tact in revealing secrets of a disturbing nature, for they can have a devastating impact on those involved.

Revelations of all sorts may come to us during the Cusp of Exposure, and it will be important for us to assess first whether they are accurate or not, for the danger of being misled is great. Once evaluated, the more profound of these epiphanies can serve to light our way for the rest of the year. Another issue is whether to go public with them or to keep them to ourselves. This question should be carefully considered, and perhaps only shared with one or two close friends.

Observation is usually more important than action during this period. Watching, waiting, and listening are synonymous with the energy of this cusp. All forms of astute examination are favored now, including the study of books or magazines coupled with personal observation. Documentation also may be explored, with special emphasis on home video and recording techniques. Such documents may well be referred to later in the year, particularly during the dark days of winter.

We may well shrink from public displays of emotion during this period, or be associated with an individual who does. Great tact may have to be exercised in the latter case, so as not to embarrass or cause stress for someone in need of special privacy. Any intrusion on another's personal space may elicit a rather extreme reaction, so we would do well to treat others with the greatest respect. Quietude and meditation are most valuable on the Leo-Virgo cusp, and can be sought and practiced fearlessly with good result.

Extrovert tendencies also can surface now, both as an occasional break from an introverted state and to balance the palette of personal expression. But the main emphasis here is a tendency to draw into ourselves, to hide our feelings rather than express them, and to be confronted again and again by interesting puzzles which invite us to solve them. The universe is capable of dishing up some pretty astonishing disclosures, and those making their appearance in this week can be among the most exciting and upsetting of the entire year.

The Personology of People Born on the Cusp of Exposure

Those born on this cusp seize the opportune moment to initiate activity. Because of this sensitivity to *kairos*, the right moment, they are able to be patient and to wait before acting. Often they choose to keep their motives, even their personalities, hidden from others, and only reveal themselves when they feel it is opportune to do so. Others may see them as quiet, even secretive individuals. Their strongest suits are intuition (characteristic of the fire sign Leo) and sensation (the earthy side of Virgo). Consequently, they are at their best when their hunches guide their actions, particularly in the areas of work and sensuous interactions.

Annual Events That Occur on the Cusp of Exposure

August 19: National Aviation Day
August 20: National Homeless Animals Day
August 24: St. Bartholomew's Day
August 25: Independence Day in Uruguay

Major Historical Events That Have Happened on the Cusp of Exposure

August 19, 1960: USSR sentences U-2 spy plane pilot
August 20, 1940: Trotsky assassinated in Mexico
August 21, 1991: Gorbachev back in Moscow after coup attempt
August 22, 1911: "Mona Lisa" stolen from the Louvre
August 23, 1944: Pro-German dictator Antonescu ousted in Romania
August 24, A.D. 79: Mount Vesuvius erupts, buries Pompeii
August 25, 1989: *Voyager* sends back photos of Neptune

Famous People Born on the Cusp of Exposure

Bill Clinton, Sean Connery, Coco Chanel, Jacqueline Susann, Wilt Chamberlain, Princess Margaret of England, Leonard Bernstein, Lola Montez, Shelley Long, Madame du Barry, Connie Chung, Eero Saarinen, H. P. Lovecraft, River Phoenix, Deng Xiao-Ping, A. S. Byatt, Althea Gibson, Cal Ripken, Jr., Orville Wright, Gene Roddenberry

Birthdays Especially Affected on the Cusp of Exposure

If you are born on the Cusp of Exposure (August 19–25), the Cusp of Prophecy (December 19–25), or the Cusp of Power (April 19–24) your energies blend well with those of this week. Results should be obtained with little effort on your part.

Cusp of Exposure people may find it opportune to come out with some very surprising revelations. Cusp of Prophecy people are likely to draw into themselves and make some valuable discoveries. Cusp of Power people put their keen observations to good use.

If you are born on the Cusp of Revolution (November 19–24), the Cusp of Sensitivity (February 16–22), or the Cusp of Energy (May 19–24) you will face problems and challenges during this week. You will have to work harder to achieve your goals.

Cusp of Revolution people may get in trouble through exercising their extrovert tendencies too much. Cusp of Sensitivity people could choose to isolate themselves behind their protective shield and lose opportunities to advance. Cusp of Energy people could get caught up in observing minute details, thereby missing the big picture.

❋

The Week of Structure

AUGUST 26–SEPTEMBER 2

As we prepare to return from summer vacation and get ready for school and fall activities, we feel an intense need to get our affairs in order. Because putting things in order is intrinsic to this week's activities, we would do well to prepare a checklist of preparatory work that needs to be done.

If the preceding weeks of Leo represent results, as symbolized by the harvest of nature's abundance, then this week of Virgo I stresses planning, symbolized by preparing containers to hold the ripened fruit and making plans to ready them for sale and consumption.

Nothing is more effective in establishing order than setting up a routine that can be followed week in and week out. In this way good habits may counteract chaotic tendencies. Readying a personal calendar, making important appointments, establishing priorities, shopping for office or school supplies, and even beginning to think about fall clothes all can be considered germane to this process. Putting our desks or wardrobes in order and considering which staples to stock up on in our kitchens, while being careful to replenish cleaning supplies, are also essential. In order to guarantee that expenses do not run out of hand, a strict budget may have to be implemented.

Now is not the time to thirst after great deeds, but rather to get down to the business of everyday life. In this respect, no detail is too small to be attended to, no task too menial to be performed. Likewise, we have the responsibility to look after not only ourselves but also to serve others. The ideal of service can be very strong in this week, as we become aware of how much our help is needed and appreciated by those around us. Too often, refusing to help with household chores, bookkeeping, and preparing for the visits of guests or family members can be taken by the offended party as an insult or even aggression, rather than simply a lapse of energy or memory.

Of course, the danger exists in this week of becoming compulsive in our quest for order and of imposing a rigidity which will be hard to shake in the weeks to come. It is important to maintain flexibility and to accept alternate ways of doing things. In addition, we would do well to question the wisdom of instituting a plethora of rules, or of sticking by them at any cost. In many ways, establishing excessive guidelines will keep others from exercising their free will and cripple their powers of discrimination and judgment.

We may have to force ourselves to relax and have fun during this week. Hard work should be followed by hard play, enjoyment, and relaxation. Dropping a serious and focused persona in favor of a more light-hearted stance will be essential to good mental health during this highly constructive period. Laughter, in particular, should be highly prized at this time, and sharing the joys of hilarious conversations may be just what the doctor ordered to loosen up.

The Personology of People Born in the Week of Structure

Practical to the extreme, the straightforward individuals born in this week know how to organize their thoughts and achieve tangible results. Although they can function well in the spotlight, they do not demand to be in it and consequently do well as members of a team. Whether they are stars or not, those born in the Week of Structure are capable of working behind the scenes for a period of years with only modest remuneration for their services. They must be careful of letting their need for structure control their daily activities to the point of obsession. Likewise they should avoid becoming fixated on one particular idea or friend.

Annual Events That Occur During the Week of Structure

August 26: Women's Equality Day
Labor Day

Major Historical Events That Have Happened During the Week of Structure

August 26, 1920: U.S. Congress ratifies Nineteenth Amendment to the Constitution, giving women the vote
August 27, 1883: Krakatoa eruption peaks in Indonesia
August 28, 1963: Martin Luther King, Jr., gives his "I Have a Dream" speech
August 29, 1931: Faraday demonstrates first electric transformer
August 30, 1862: Confederates win Second Battle of Bull Run
August 31, 1857: Malaysia wins independence from Britain
September 1, 1939:Germany invades Poland to begin WWII
September 2, 1945: WWII ends with Japanese surrender

Famous People Born During the Week of Structure

Charlie Parker, Mother Teresa, Ingrid Bergman, Johann Wolfgang von Goethe, Dinah Washington, Edwin Moses, Albert Sabin, Frank Robinson,

Maria Montessori, Rocky Marciano, Yasser Arafat, Lyndon B. Johnson, Alan Dershowitz, Jimmy Connors, Geraldine Ferraro, Richard Gere, Gloria Estefan, Peggy Guggenheim, Lou Piniella, James Coburn, Slobodan Milosevic

Birthdays Especially Affected During the Week of Structure

If you are born in the Week of Structure (August 26–September 2), the Week of Rule (December 26–January 2), or the Week of Manifestation (April 25–May 2) your energies blend well with those of this week. Results should be obtained with little effort on your part.

Week of Structure people will have few problems getting their affairs in order. Week of Rule people must remember to relax and have fun once they have worked hard to organize things. Week of Manifestation people can plan ahead and build a solid base for their future activities.

If you are born in the Week of Independence (November 25–December 2), the Week of Spirit (February 23–March 2), or the Week of Freedom (May 25–June 2) you will face problems and challenges during this week. You will have to work harder to achieve your goals.

Week of Independence people are likely to flounder if they are unable to exert control over their wild side. Week of Spirit people should try to ground themselves, otherwise they could produce a chaotic situation. Week of Freedom people should not arouse antagonisms through an overly controlling attitude.

※

The Week of the Puzzle

SEPTEMBER 3–10

Puzzles of all types and how to solve them are the focus of this week. Figuring out how things work, playing mental or actual board and video games, solving mysteries and in general exploring the unknown are all characteristic of the energies and activities found here. We will find it difficult to abstain from tinkering with the technical as well as the emotional spheres in our lives, and therefore the adage "If it ain't broke, don't fix it" may be entirely ignored.

Drawn like a magnet to any problem that requires solving, most of us must use great self-control to avoid being overwhelmed by our preoccupation with detail. Losing the big picture is indeed a danger here. Dealing with financial matters, particularly investments and savings, may well be hampered by a preoccupation with the picayune. Likewise, fiddling around with the feelings of those close to us, probing and peeking into hidden areas perhaps best left alone, may well open a Pandora's box which will be difficult or impossible to close for many months to come.

Maintaining a hands-off attitude and learning to back off are both essential to the well-being of all concerned. During the Week of the Puzzle we are likely to battle with our most obsessive tendencies, helping to develop a deep self-control which will come in handy in the future. In this sense it is possible that our overinvolvement can yield positive results. However, in order for this process to take place, we will need to monitor our behavior and recognize when we are hovering or being overly picky or critical. If this occurs we must immediately use our self-control to change our attitude and cease being so compulsive.

Above all, we must learn to honor the privacy of others at this time. Concurrently we must be aware of our own tendency to withdraw into a private world of hurt or self-pity. Dragging ourselves out of such a state and confronting our problems squarely, particularly marshaling the courage to confront our detractors and address their concerns or even outright slander, will represent an important step forward in our personal developments.

Keeping busy during this week is not usually a problem. However, taking on too many responsibilities can be, and sufficient downtime must be planned into our schedules. If the pace becomes too frenetic and our stress levels prove unmanageable, we will be helped by participating in activities such as swimming, leisurely exercise, long walks in the open air, and more calming forms of recreation, which can allow for enjoyment and stilling the busy mind. Practicing meditation is also recommended to help bring us into a more relaxed and centered state of mind.

As a counterweight to tinkering with the unknown and investigating problem areas around us, we would all do well to investigate our own personal secrets in a concentrated effort at self-discovery. Solving our personal mysteries could produce highly positive results now and help satisfy our desires to explore the unknown.

The Personology of People Born in the Week of the Puzzle

These attractive, even appealing, individuals imbue their own personalities and much of what they do with an air of mystery. Highly secretive, those born in this week know how to keep important matters to themselves and to work out their own problems in silence. Because they do not necessarily draw attention to themselves through speech or outrageous actions, they exert a seductive influence on those who want to peer behind their mask of normalcy. Those who attempt to take advantage of what they see as an easy touch will not try to do so a second time. Because of their demanding and often unforgiving attitudes, they are capable of keeping even the wildest of personalities in check.

Annual Events That Occur During the Week of the Puzzle

September 4: Newspaper Carrier Day
September 8: National Grandparents Day
              Federal Lands Cleanup Day
Jewish High Holy Days: Rosh Hashanah (New Year) and Yom Kippur
   (or following week)

Major Historical Events That Have Happened During the Week of the Puzzle

September 3, 1976: *Viking II* lands on Mars and sends back photos
September 4, 1870: Napoleon III deposed; Third Republic declared

September 5, 1666: Great London Fire finally ended
September 6, 1966: Apartheid architect Vorwoerd assassinated
September 7, 1986: Desmond Tutu made archbishop of Cape Town
September 8, 1944: V2 rockets launched against England
September 9, 1087: Death of William the Conqueror
September 10, 1855: Russian base in Sebastopol falls to Allies

Famous People Born During the Week of the Puzzle

Louis XIV, Leo Tolstoy, Peter Sellers, Stephen Jay Gould, Kenzo Tanget, Joseph P. Kennedy, Louis Sullivan, Buddy Holly, Richard I, Elvin Jones, Queen Elizabeth I of England, Otis Redding, Daniel Burnham, Karl Lagerfeld, Jane Curtin, Amy Irving, Raquel Welch, Sonny Rollins, Liz Greene, Grandma Moses

Birthdays Especially Affected During the Week of the Puzzle

If you are born in the Week of the Puzzle (September 3–10), the Week of Determination (January 3–9), or the Week of Study (May 3–10) your energies blend well with those of this week. Results should be obtained with little effort on your part.

Week of the Puzzle people will do well to keep themselves busy with much needed domestic chores. Week of Determination people will get constructive work done but could learn to relax through meditation. Week of Study people should make lists of what needs to be done.

If you are born in the Week of Originality (December 3–10), the Week of Isolation (March 3–10), or the Week of Communication (June 3–10) you will face problems and challenges during this week. You will have to work harder to achieve your goals.

Week of Originality people should participate in group activities and fight a tendency to be cryptic and difficult. Week of Isolation people need to share their unique visions rather than becoming obsessive with them. Week of Communication people should concentrate on explaining themselves fully and avoid using highly technical language.

The Week of the Literal

We must remember to keep our promises. No one will easily cut us a break this week if we don't come through with the offers we make. As a result, the energies of this week tend to be rather hard and uncompromising. We will be most successful at endeavors which take a huge amount of effort and require persistence in the face of overwhelming odds. Prior meticulous planning and an ability to wait spell a positive outcome for events that occur at this time.

Now is not the time for abstract theory or idle dreams. The intense practicality of this week demands pragmatic thinking and a mastery of technical detail. Keeping our emotions under control is part of this process; therefore, being able to delay gratification, a sign of so-called emotional intelligence, will be a powerful weapon in our personal arsenals. Those who demand immediate emotional gratification, on the contrary, may find themselves falling far short of their goals.

By being truthful with ourselves during the Week of the Literal and refusing to cut ourselves a break out of egotism or solace, we will avoid all forms of pretense at any cost. Of course, the truth hurts, and at some points we will have to smooth ruffled feathers a bit to avoid breakdowns in the rhythm of family or professional life. Likewise, since resentments are aroused easily in those who never really asked to be told the truth in the first place, (particularly unpleasant truths), we should not be surprised if we become the object of their negativity.

Similarly, the tendency to engage in crusades of all types, particularly those directed against the "establishment," is high during this week, and we must not succumb easily to their destructive tendencies. In the Week of the Literal it is best to indulge in activities which can be carried out at the highest professional level and which stand to benefit all concerned. If this implies a sacrifice of individual or special interests for the good of the group, so be it.

To give up on a relationship or back down from a confrontation are not favored at this time. Going that extra yard or mile is the tenor of this week's energies. Perseverance in emotional matters and interpersonal relationships will succeed in keeping a marital, romantic, or family union alive and vital.

Since this week marks the end of the summertime period, when realizing the fruits of our endeavors is required, we may have the feeling now of finally having finished things up and beginning to expect substantial results at last. Should things not work out and the reward is not forthcoming, this week would be the time to implement changes in our organization or orientation, no matter how ruthless. Such pruning, or cutting away of deadwood, will be essential to the further growth of a healthy organic entity, whether a business, family, or individual project. The Dutch saying "Soft remedies make for stinking wounds" is applicable here, despite its extreme tone.

The Personology of People Born in the Week of the Literal

Those born in this week have a way of getting what they want. No matter how much they engage in acts of service to others, their own needs are uppermost in their minds. Because of their forceful mental orientation, they are capable of bringing their logical and rational faculties to bear fully on the situation at hand. However, since their willpower is so strong, they must be careful not to completely dominate those they live with. When they observe others overindulging their emotions or showing a lack of awareness they can be quite merciless in their cold criticism. Yet, for the most part, their nature is warm and friendly and demands satisfaction and attention.

Annual Events That Occur During the Week of the Literal

September 15: National POW/MIA Recognition Day
September 16: Mayflower Day

September 16: International Day of Peace
September 17: Citizenship Day
Jewish High Holy Days (or in preceding or following week)

Major Historical Events That Have Happened During the Week of the Literal

September 11, 2001: World Trade Center and Pentagon attacked
September 12, 1970: Palestinian hijackers blow up three jets
September 14, 1752: Gregorian calendar adopted in England
September 15, 1917: Russian republic claimed by Karensky
September 16, 1620: *Mayflower* sets sail for America
September 17, 1787: New U.S. Constitution is presented
September 18, 1970: Jimi Hendrix dies of drug overdose

Famous People Born During the Week of the Literal

Greta Garbo, Jesse Owens, Jessica Mitford, D. H. Lawrence, Hank Williams, Henry V of England, Agatha Christie, Lauren Bacall, Bruno Walter, Lola Falana, Clara Schumann, Jacqueline Bisset, Jessye Norman, Roald Dahl, Kate Millett, B. B. King, Zoe Caldwell, Oliver Stone, Margaret Sanger

Birthdays Especially Affected During the Week of the Literal

If you are born in the Week of the Literal (September 11–18), the Week of Dominance (January 10–16), or the Week of Nature (May 11–18) your energies blend well with those of this week. Results should be obtained with little effort on your part.

Week of the Literal people will be happy to express their views honestly and forthrightly without rejection. Week of Dominance people should use their strength to support others who need help. Week of Nature people will find themselves lighting up the lives of others with their honest approach.

If you are born in the Week of Expansiveness (December 11–18), the Week of Dances and Dreams (March 11–18), or the Week of Exploration (June 11–18) you will face problems and challenges during this week. You will have to work harder to achieve your goals.

Week of Expansiveness people must be aware of tripping over the details with their eye on a distant star. Week of Dances and Dreams people should realize that not everyone will believe their tall tales. Week of Exploration people may encounter resistance if they probe too deeply into the private lives of others.

Summer Personology Snapshot

JUNE 22 Dramatic and romantic, June 22 people enjoy all of life's adventures. Keen to take any journey, they can be naïve about the workings of the world and may suffer hurt as a result.

JUNE 23 Those born on June 23 are magnetic and intense, valuing nothing above their close relationships. Committed and loyal, they must be careful not to interfere where they do not belong.

JUNE 24 Totally devoted to their work, June 24 people are imaginative and successful. They must be careful to use their talents wisely, though; otherwise they may become overwhelmed and disturbed.

JUNE 25 The perceptive and sensitive people of June 25 are exceptional at reaching their goals. Compassionate toward others, they should take care not to become overly sentimental and temperamental.

JUNE 26 Those born on June 26 are courageous, trustworthy, and reliable. These strong and steadfast people make great friends, but they tend to stifle their own feelings, often to their detriment.

JUNE 27 Determined to protect what is theirs, June 27 people are incredibly persistent in reaching their goals. This drive to succeed can be dangerous, though, and they must be careful not to become inflexible toward others.

JUNE 28 Skilled in the use of humor, June 28 people make good impressions and are exceptional at reaching their coworkers. A strong work ethic will lead them to success; however, they should take care to maintain a sense of humor in times of stress.

JUNE 29 Those born on June 29 are skilled at helping others realize their ambitions and at finding practical ways for dreams to be employed. Well liked by others, they may be passive in their own affairs and must be sure to consider their own interests when necessary.

JUNE 30 Highly motivated to reach their personal goals, June 30 people are commonly very successful, though private and quiet. Mysterious, sometimes even to themselves, they would do well to investigate their own true natures.

JULY 1 Insightful and charitable, July 1 people often endure suffering, which they can usually overcome through their determined demeanor. Valiant in their struggles, they must be careful not to alienate those they care about while they are fighting through their distress.

JULY 2 Those born on July 2 are emotional and exciting, with an active imagination that usually manifests itself only in dreams. Often insecure, they must find a way to balance their inner feelings with the outer workings of the world.

JULY 3 Those born on July 3 are attentive and honest and enjoy defending the common person. Traditional and philosophical, they must be careful not to give unnecessary advice, as they may be seen as know-it-alls.

JULY 4 Not satisfied by private success, the committed and generous people of July 4 like to spend their time representing a group in which they may have roots. They tend to suppress emotions in order to help the group, though, and can become troubled if their emotions are not expressed.

JULY 5 Enthusiastic and unique, July 5 people are always moving from one project to the next, wanting to get all they can out of life. Often moving too quickly to be dependable, they must learn to sometimes slow down in order to keep their friends.

JULY 6 Passion is paramount for July 6 people, and they are often involved in serious relationships with attractive people. Devastated if the relationship ends, they must learn to bolster themselves against hurt.

JULY 7 Confident and honest, July 7 people often let other people know a great deal about themselves. While revelation is important to them, others can sometimes be disturbed by this openness, which can be difficult for them to tolerate.

JULY 8 Those born on July 8 are practical and hardworking and excel at building organizations—whether it be a family or a business. Successful in their outcome, they should be careful not to cultivate a sharp exterior that others will find off-putting.

JULY 9 Inquisitive and creative, those born on July 9 are influential people with the power to put ideas into practice. Easily disillusioned, they must keep their energies focused and avoid getting carried away with impractical plans.

JULY 10 Tolerant and attentive, July 10 people are driven toward personal success while also enjoying a private social life. There is a certain detachment about them, though, and they must work not to become isolated or too introverted.

JULY 11 Highly social and knowledgeable, July 11 people are often up-to-date on all public events, though extremely private about their own business. Socially astute, they need to guard against relying on appearances.

JULY 12 Compelling and influential, July 12 people use sound reason to win over their audience and are skilled in using humor. Intensely loyal, they often run the risk of becoming overprotective, especially of their children.

JULY 13 Those born on July 13 possess an uncanny sense of timing and know when to take a chance and head in a new direction. Though their daring may lead to success, they must be careful early in life, for until they find their own sense of timing, they will make many mistakes.

JULY 14 Some of the most convincing people alive, July 14 people can win over others with their confident honesty and charm. Seductively powerful, they sometimes run the risk of being thought manipulative or deceptive.

JULY 15 Persuasive and energetic, July 15 people are successful because of their dynamic personalities and the ability to enlist the help of others. Highly motivated, their need for control may go too far, resulting in behavior that is controlling and domineering.

JULY 16 Dependable and passionate, July 16 people are incredibly romantic and enjoy nurturing others in all ways possible. They often do not follow their own advice, however, and may be labeled hypocritical and unrealistic in their goals.

JULY 17 Ambitious and self-assured, July 17 people rise quickly to the top once they find the right career, as their sense of humor and calm confidence is very appealing. They need to be careful, though, as others may confuse their confidence with arrogance.

JULY 18 Those born on July 18 have a well-defined set of beliefs and often find themselves in the position of group spokesperson. Courageous and committed, they should be cautious about their dedication getting in the way of their own ambition.

JULY 19 Refined and self-aware, July 19 people excel in presenting themselves to others and are quick to acknowledge a mistake. Successful in what they undertake, they do not take it well when they make repeated errors, and they often need to learn patience.

JULY 20 July 20 people exemplify the extremes in life, as they are often sky high and then hit rock bottom. Adventuresome and active, they like to keep moving and become impatient and frustrated with their current place.

JULY 21 Brave and fun-loving, July 21 people enjoy playful antagonism and are quite capable in stressful situations. They excel in times of conflict but must be careful not to become too argumentative, as this may deter others from interacting with them.

JULY 22 Those born on July 22 are success-driven and courageous and will change careers many times before finding the right place for them to thrive. They need to learn to recognize their faults, however, as not every failure is due to bad luck.

JULY 23 Compassionate and traditional, July 23 people may have some radical views, although they are rooted in conventional values. Though they work through small problems well, they tend to see themselves as more defenseless than they really are and become prone to crises.

JULY 24 Stimulating and adventurous, July 24 people are always looking for a thrill and are thus very appealing to others, especially those reluctant to take risks. They need to work to be able to take the routine of daily life, though, as they can easily become unstable.

JULY 25 Creative and idealistic, the romantic people of July 25 focus on the intentions of others, not just their actions. They need to be careful not to set their sights too high, though, as unrealistic goals can lead to frustration and annoyance.

JULY 26 Influential and dominant, July 26 people find their power in their ability to understand themselves and their surroundings. Very direct about facts, they must be careful not to be too straightforward.

JULY 27 Those born on July 27 often make decisions for the group, due to their ability to organize and plan. They may become too opposed to change, however, and must be careful to choose a career that will bring them success and contentment for a long time.

JULY 28 Never satisfied with being second best, the practical and vibrant people of July 28 strive to be the best at all they do. Sometimes intolerant, they must learn diplomatic communication skills or risk being seen as insensitive and inaccessible.

JULY 29 Dependable and aware, July 29 people excel when predicting the future actions of others and also do well when mediating arguments. They may become prejudiced, however, and must be careful with their opinions.

JULY 30 Decisive and solid, July 30 people focus on physical action and enjoy learning about the workings of things on earth. They must be careful not to ignore their spiritual side too much, however, as they will do themselves good by conducting some introspection.

JULY 31 Tremendously expressive, July 31 people are taken with all aspects of humanity, reveling in philosophical questions and discussing them with others. Caution is necessary when working too hard, though, as family and friends may be ignored in favor of work.

AUGUST 1 Influential and reasonable, regarding knowledge as power, August 1 people are determined to convince others of the rightness of their point of view. They will suffer failures, however, and should be careful not to be rude or judgmental of others when they are not immediately persuaded.

AUGUST 2 Versatile and self-assured, August 2 people are good at taking on a variety of tasks and undergoing changes, while managing to stay confident and grounded. They need to be careful not to put too much stock in the opinions of others, however, as they do not want to become disconnected from themselves.

AUGUST 3 Brave and fearless, August 3 people enjoy danger, whether it be saving others from it, or risking themselves in some way. At times unable to tolerate their daily routine, they journey far from home for excitement and must avoid recklessness in their endeavors.

AUGUST 4 Often cast in the role of guide, people born on August 4 use their quick and clever intelligence to lead a group from behind the scenes. They must learn to be tactful, though, as they may be seen as irresponsible and ignorant of the feelings of others.

AUGUST 5 Though very emotional, August 5 people usually have great control over their feelings, allowing them to lead a well directed and distinguished life. They need to work on being more comfortable in a leading role, since they make good leaders as long as they can control their combative tendencies.

AUGUST 6 Those born on August 6 are drawn toward unusual situations and enjoy being eccentric and unique themselves. Prone to recklessness, they can benefit from learning how to tolerate some form of routine.

AUGUST 7 Curious and secretive, August 7 people are constantly drawn to the covert and enjoy investigating mysteries and unearthing facts. They need to use caution, though, as prying into the lives of others can cause problems with family and friends.

AUGUST 8 Resourceful and talented, those born on August 8 enjoy playing a number of different roles in life, and they go to great lengths to play those roles well. Single-minded and driven, they must learn to strive for a diverse life or risk unhappiness.

AUGUST 9 Those born on August 9 are extremely reliable and loyal and are astute observers of psychology. They must be careful to listen as much as possible and not give advice hastily, though, as they can be of great help to family and friends only if they are patient.

AUGUST 10 Vocal and appealing, August 10 people will give all they have to others as long as they feel they are respected. Extremely reliable, their desire to help others may result in ignoring their own needs, and they must learn to let others help them in turn.

AUGUST 11 Intelligent and difficult to fool, those born on August 11 love nothing better than to search for the truth and grapple with challenging ideas. Quick to reveal their findings, they need to be aware of the pain that truth can cause.

AUGUST 12 Knowledgeable about institutions, August 12 people seek to maintain traditions and uphold the power of long-standing rules. Always keen on order, they should learn to relax and realize that others do not always see things the same way.

AUGUST 13 Persevering through countless challenges, August 13 people seem to have endless patience as they fight to achieve success. Constant hardship may lead to insecurity and frustration, which they must work to keep under control.

AUGUST 14 Reflection and revelation are evident in August 14 people, and they can frequently be found as guides or teachers. They need to work to not show their emotion so readily, however, as this can lead to a need to escape ridicule from others.

AUGUST 15 Leaders by nature, August 15 people are concerned with the big picture and enjoy ruling their family or company through a generally sensitive authority. They may be unaware of their methods of persuasion, however, and must be willing to accept criticism of their ways.

AUGUST 16 Seductive and credible, August 16 people have a magnetic personality that allows them to be very successful. They must work to avoid hypersensitivity, however, since that can lead to an inability to be happy and a rebellious streak.

AUGUST 17 Forceful and grounded, August 17 people strive to be in control of all things, and their outgoing nature is conducive to gaining the trust and respect of others. Sometimes antagonistic to others, they must be careful not to let their authoritarian tendencies get out of control.

AUGUST 18 Resilient and patient, August 18 people enjoy fighting through challenges and value experience over pleasure. They must be careful not to become too caught up in their struggles, though, as they can become an obsession.

AUGUST 19 Those born on August 19 enjoy being mysterious and take pleasure in suddenly revealing their secrets. Influential through their confidence, their concealing nature may lead others to leave them alone rather than try to understand them.

AUGUST 20 Thoughtful and lively, those born on August 20 have private secrets to work through but are commonly determined to help themselves.

Sometimes troubled, they must take care not to slip away from friends—loneliness will be sure to follow.

AUGUST 21 Reliable and sturdy, with a composure that helps them handle all types of situations, August 21 people are great providers. They need to remember that protection should go only so far, however, and that shielding loved ones too much can lead to frustration and withdrawal.

AUGUST 22 Incredibly creative, possessing imaginations that flow from a deep understanding of the natural world, August 22 people are good at keeping their feet on the ground. They need to work on admitting their errors, though, as they might alienate family and friends with their inflexible attitudes.

AUGUST 23 Determined and focused, August 23 people strive to fulfill their goals and will often amass many possessions in life. They must keep their minds open, however, as being too focused and goal oriented can cause them to lose touch with loved ones.

AUGUST 24 Investigative and curious, those born on August 24 enjoy delving into mysteries, specifically those that may be only partially understood. They need to work on their social skills, though, as they tend to become preoccupied with trivial matters.

AUGUST 25 Flashy and outspoken, August 25 people take pleasure in revealing all aspects of themselves to others, though they can be very secretive when necessary. Exuberant and outwardly strong, they must often work to overcome a deep lack of confidence in themselves.

AUGUST 26 Cooperative and unassuming, those born on August 26 prefer to work within a group and not to take the leading role. Although it is often a struggle for them to make the world see their abilities, they will usually find their own place through perseverance.

AUGUST 27 Those born on August 27 identify with the common man and work to better society through their idealistic character. They can easily become depressed if they become too involved, however, and must work to let others help out as well.

AUGUST 28 Those born on August 28 use their expertise with language to teach others and to convince them of their own worth. Devoted and intellectual, they must try to avoid being too rigid and learn to accept different kinds of people.

AUGUST 29 August 29 people like to have all aspects of their life ordered, though they are sensitive to others and can adapt to different kinds of situations. Extremely emotional, they must learn to control their feelings in order to avoid constantly needing escape.

AUGUST 30 Stable and financially sound, August 30 people are generally organized and capable of handling many kinds of situations. They can be overconfident in their abilities at times, however, and must be wary not to negatively influence their loved ones.

AUGUST 31 Often in public view, August 31 people are drawn to important events and frequently stand out in the crowd due to their dynamic personalities. Tending to be critical, they must be careful to admit their own failings and avoid being hypocritical.

SEPTEMBER 1 Practical and thoughtful, September 1 people have very active imaginations, while also possessing the ability to realize their dreams. Financially successful, they can become so focused on their work that they may be inflexible toward other ideas.

SEPTEMBER 2 Straightforward and just, September 2 people are very direct, even about themselves and their own mistakes, and will be quick to defend someone who they believe has been wronged. Their no-nonsense demeanor may lead to explosions of anger, however, and they must guard against being moody.

SEPTEMBER 3 Great vision and complexity characterize those born on September 3, and their beliefs and ideas are often misunderstood. Tending to keep their feelings inside, they need to understand that this stoic facade will often repel people.

SEPTEMBER 4 People born on September 4 take pleasure in constructing things, whether it be a company or a physical structure, and revel in planning and arranging such a project. Concerned with efficiency, they must learn to accept the failures of others as well as their own in order to ensure the respect of others.

SEPTEMBER 5 Idealistic and romantic, September 5 people set very optimistic goals and intend to reach them, as they surround themselves with pieces of their fantasies. Unfortunately, they are inclined to set unrealistic goals and become self-destructive when those goals can't be reached.

SEPTEMBER 6 Compassionate and patient, September 6 people tend to believe that their lives are ruled by fate and to accept what comes. Admirably tolerant, they run the risk of becoming fatalistic, and have to be careful not to succumb to the notion that they have no control over their own future.

SEPTEMBER 7 Resilient and committed, those born on September 7 use their creative energy to find success and to surmount the many obstacles that may come their way. They need to learn to keep an open mind, though, as in their quest for success they tend to become aggressive and intolerant.

SEPTEMBER 8 Those born on September 8 are complex people who like to clean and organize as well as take care of their families. They are inclined to be authoritarian, however, and must take care not to see the world in extremes of good and evil.

SEPTEMBER 9 September 9 people enjoy a good challenge and may even go so far as to make their own trials if there are none ahead. This may bolster their self-confidence, but it may also lead them to be fearful and needy, as they can end up constantly guarding against their fears.

SEPTEMBER 10 Concerned with origins, September 10 people spend a lot of energy looking to define themselves in some sort of pragmatic way. Though wanting to appear balanced and stable, they may be insecure and notably unstable inside and must take care to nurture their private lives.

SEPTEMBER 11 Strongly spirited from an early age, those born on September 11 find that dramatic decisions control their lives. Inclined to strong beliefs, they must learn tolerance and take care not to be critical and overly judgmental.

SEPTEMBER 12 Those born on September 12 are very interested in forms of communication and are bold and humorous, while also understanding the value of restraint. They can be quite dry, though, and should try not to be so sarcastic.

SEPTEMBER 13 Dedicated and unusually intense, September 13 people concentrate very well and may even come to believe that they have some sort of special ability to overcome adversity. They can often be unaware of the problems of others, however, and must learn to commit to another.

SEPTEMBER 14 Effective and active, those born on September 14 are passionate about the society in which they live and work to impart their beliefs to others. Admirable in its intention, this activism can lead to an overly critical quality if left unchecked.

SEPTEMBER 15 September 15 people are unusually gifted specialists, with an expansive outlook that allows them to fully understand their surroundings. Highly successful, they can sometimes become too determined and may risk compromising their principles for financial gain.

SEPTEMBER 16 Those born on September 16 are caring and sincere people who are able to reach their goals through patience and determination. Courageous and direct, they often overstep boundaries with others before fully earning their trust.

SEPTEMBER 17 Serious and committed, September 17 people persevere until they reach their goals and make a name for themselves. Tenacious, they must learn that there is a time to put aside work and make room for fun.

SEPTEMBER 18 Public careers do not stop September 18 people from keeping a secret private life, and their thoughtful approach makes them very appealing. Their private side can get in the way of success, however, and they run the risk of becoming reclusive.

SEPTEMBER 19 Orderly and knowledgeable, September 19 people are very concerned with appearance in all aspects of their lives, but often possess an important deep inner self as well. They must learn to draw a line between being organized and being compulsive, however, and must avoid being too satisfied with material things.

SEPTEMBER 20 Confident in their own ability to handle crises, September 20 people are especially good money managers. Financial problems may be few, but self-assurance can be dangerous, as it can lead to an inflated ego.

SEPTEMBER 21 Progressive and knowledgeable, September 21 people are always up on the current trends and take great pride in their creations. Tasteful and discerning, they must still remember that life is not composed solely of material things.

SEPTEMBER 22 Driven and strong, September 22 people are always looking for new projects to stave off boredom. Individual and self-sufficient, they must learn to open up, as the wall around them will only deter others.

SEPTEMBER 23 Inventive and resolute, September 23 people often struggle through hardship before finding themselves but then become incredibly successful and respected. However, they must remember that success is often uncertain, and so try to guard against dejection.

Fall

WEIGH. CONTROL. PHILOSOPHIZE.

With the arrival of the fall, people inevitably begin to think more conservatively. This is the time to consider making the best of, in a lot of rudimentary societies, steadily decreasing daylight, increasing lack of warmth, and fewer opportunities to find food. The urge to stockpile resources comes upon us now, as slowly we realize that the theme of this season is not initiating new projects as in the spring, or demanding their fruition as in the summer, but rather working steadily to maintain such endeavors and carry them through to completion. Practical and earthy, rather than intuitive or emotional like the preceding seasons, fall is the time in which sensuous impulses come to the fore and in which indoor comforts and pleasures should be guaranteed.

Fall begins with the autumnal equinox, usually encountered on September 23, when day and night are once again equal. A balanced time of the year, quite different in its energy from the frequent violence and unpredictability of the equinox found in the spring, this Cusp of Beauty brings about the first signs of change in the fecundity of nature, in which ripeness begins its metamorphosis into decay. Close ahead lie the magnificent colors of autumn, as deciduous trees prepare to shed their leaves and indulge in spectacular displays. With the onset of fall we inevitably experience a certain sadness at the loss of summer; even the onset of a protracted summer leads us to the inevitability of the cold and dark weather to follow. For the first time in the year we may experience thoughts of death and dying, symbolically related to the changing state of nature around us. We may even sense the onset of SAD, seasonal affective disorder. As the fall progresses these symptoms can become more acute, and in the dark days of November and December result in the so-called "winter blues."

Because maintenance is the key word here, all sorts of preparations for the coming of winter may now be implemented. In the country, canning and preserving of nature's bountiful harvest is under way, guaranteeing good eating and pleasurable family get-togethers in the coming months. Fields must be plowed under, gardens cleaned up and put to bed, porch and patio furniture brought inside, and everything battened down and made shipshape against the coming storms and freezing cold. Likewise, furnaces must be prepared and heating oil stocked up on, even by city dwellers. Gas and wood reserves will also be checked, when relevant.

Maintenance is truly the key word here, not only in the practical sphere. In relationships as well, now is not the time to initiate new beginnings or expect lavish results, but rather to learn to hold on to what we already have. Renewing old friendships or breathing new life into old romantic liaisons are in order now. Perhaps family has never played as important a role as it does at this time of year, and with the settling in for the winter the holidays of Halloween, Thanksgiving, and Christmas are anticipated and planned for.

Such maintenance also applies in the financial sphere. A review of our investments may be in order, and a corresponding pruning of deadwood advisable. New methods may be implemented to aid a suffering or failing business, or perhaps to add to the prospects of a successful one. Conservative thinking is best at this time, and overly ambitious projects with a high risk factor are better avoided. Personology teaches a coincidence of the yearly cycle of nature with that of the human life and of the zodiac. In this way fall also symbolizes the third twenty-one-year period of human life, from age forty-two to sixty-three and of the seventh, eighth, and ninth signs of the zodiac: Libra, Scorpio, and Sagittarius. Moreover, the age of forty-two in psychological terms represents the midlife crisis, which can be seen as a pivotal point in the human life. Looking back to evaluate the first half of our lives and making a realistic assessment of our capabilities is essential now. Because the sensuous aspects of life are favored during the upcoming twenty-one-year period, the pleasures of table and bed are particularly valued and indulged in. Likewise, objectivity and wisdom increase with the approach of middle age, along with the growing authority and (hopefully) respect which advancing age can bestow; these can combine to make life a bit easier and more pleasant. Financial success or accrued benefits from a steady job also can lend their hand in increasing security. In the season of fall and during this time of life, the quality of sleep can become increasingly important, a mirror of the instinct for hibernation found in many mammals. Likewise, the instinct for migration is mirrored by our making our bedrooms, living rooms, or kitchens cozier to protect against the harsh winter weather which increasingly threatens and by mature adults giving energy to refurbishing or rebuilding these parts of their homes.

The events likely to occur in Libra, Scorpio, and Sagittarius and the proper conduct during these signs stress the same kinds of maintenance, care, and conservation found in the fall season to which they correspond. These sensuous people benefit from contact with intuitive and feeling individuals who can lend color and emotion to their lives. The signs of Libra, Scorpio, and Sagittarius state as their mottos "I weigh," "I control," and "I philosophize." The socially oriented and evaluative sign of Libra prepares us for the strong control of Scorpio, which is in turn transformed into the high idealism of Sagittarius. The evolution from one sign to the next mirrors that in nature and in human development.

The Fall Personology Periods:
September 23 to December 21

The Weeks

The season of fall lasts from the fall equinox of September 23 until the winter solstice of December 21. It is composed of the three astrological signs of

Libra (September 23–October 22), Scorpio (October 23–November 21), and Sagittarius (November 22–December 21). This third quarter of the year is further subdivided by personology into the following "weeks" or personology periods:

Virgo-Libra Cusp: The Cusp of Beauty (September 19–24)
Libra I: The Week of Perfection (September 25–October 2)
Libra II: The Week of Socialization (October 3–10)
Libra III: The Week of Theater (October 11–18)
Libra-Scorpio Cusp: The Cusp of Involvement (October 19–25)
Scorpio I: The Week of Intensity (October 26–November 2)
Scorpio II: The Week of Profundity (November 3–11)
Scorpio III: The Week of Control (November 12–18)
Scorpio-Sagittarius Cusp: The Cusp of Revolution (November 19–24)
Sagittarius I: The Week of Independence (November 25–December 2)
Sagittarius II: The Week of Originality (December 3–10)
Sagittarius III: The Week of Expansiveness (December 11–18)
Sagittarius-Capricorn Cusp: The Cusp of Prophecy (December 19–25)

The Cusps

As throughout the rest of the personological year, the fall quadrant is given structure by the cusps between the astrological signs. Demarcating the fall, at its beginning we find the fall equinox, known in personology as the Cusp of Beauty, and at its end the winter solstice, the Cusp of Prophecy. At monthly intervals between these two power points we find the Cusp of Involvement (between Libra and Scorpio) and the Cusp of Revolution (between the signs of Scorpio and Sagittarius). These four cusps, Beauty, Involvement, Revolution, and Prophecy, characterize the season of fall as fully as the signs of Libra, Scorpio, and Sagittarius, but in a more human sense.

The Cusp of Beauty

The Cusp of Beauty corresponds with the advent of the fall equinox in the northern hemisphere. This means that at this time, the days and nights are equal in length. The fecundity and abundance of this period are to be seen everywhere, along with heightened aesthetic qualities. Yet many disturbing elements of this season exist as well, particularly the inevitable decay of overripe fruits and vegetables and their symbolic connection with death and decay.

The faculty of sensation is perhaps stronger during the Cusp of Beauty here than at any other time of the year. We may find all of our senses enhanced and our sensuality is aroused by the flavors of food, the smells of crisp, cold mornings, and the gentle touch of a loved one. Riotous natural displays of color are everywhere.

It was Keats who said "Beauty is truth, truth beauty," but not everyone would agree with this. The Cusp of Beauty also can be a time of illusion and deceit, no matter how pleasant a time it may seem. By dealing only with the surface aspects of our lives we may not go deeply enough into understanding them.

There is an undeniable tendency to avoid confrontations at this time, to enjoy the pleasant sensations around us and to find enjoyment in mellow states of being. The other side of the coin is that we may be easily aroused or irritated by our environments and therefore may seek to make our immediate surroundings more pleasurable. Changing the colors of a favorite room, playing music of a more personal nature, working with recipes which feature aromatic tastes and smells are all typical activities now.

Improving our personal appearance also can be part of the activities undertaken during the Cusp of Beauty. Whether paying special attention to hair, skin, nails, or clothing, we can all raise our self-esteem and pride by working on making ourselves look better. Likewise, interests in new styles in fashion and design are to be expected, and we would all do well to develop them.

Romantically speaking, idealized friendships and platonic love relationships are favored at this time. Deeper emotional involvements may arouse disturbing elements, which are not appreciated now, and passionate love relationships may have to be put on hold or at least cooled down for the time being. A definite disinterest in digging deeply into our own personality or that of others is found here, and if we are to do well during this period and enjoy it, we may have to avoid such explorations.

One real danger that exists at this time is the tendency toward egotistical or snobbish behavior and the impulse to cut ourselves off from our fellow human beings. By judging the behavior or dress of others as being in bad taste, we all run the risk of adopting an elitist attitude that isolates us socially. Sharing our newfound discoveries in taste is highly recommended and can be immensely rewarding to all concerned.

The Personology of People Born on the Cusp of Beauty

Those born on this cusp are very appreciative of the many forms of sensuous beauty. Whether that beauty is found in paintings or people, they are here to admire and enjoy the aesthetic elements of life. People born on the Cusp of Beauty may also be very aware of their own personal appearance and never want to appear in anything but the best light. Wanting to make a good impression, they can be quite fastidious about their hairstyle, skin, dress, and physical health. Because the signs of Virgo and Libra are both concerned with good taste, the legacy of this cusp is one of refinement of the senses.

Annual Events That Occur on the Cusp of Beauty

September 21: World Gratitude Day
     National Hunting and Fishing Day
September 22: American Business Women's Day

September 23: Fall equinox; day and night are equal in length

Jewish High Holy Days (or in preceding week)

Major Historial Events That Have Happened on the Cusp of Beauty

September 19, 1513: Balboa first views the Pacific Ocean

September 20, 1580: Francis Drake lands in England with Spanish
treasure

September 21, 1989: Hurricane Hugo hits east coast of United States

September 22, 1980: Union Solidarity formed in Poland

September 23, 1846: Discovery of planet Neptune

September 24, 1975: British team climbs southwest face of Mt. Everest

Famous People Born on the Cusp of Beauty

John Coltrane, Bruce Springsteen, Sophia Loren, Stephen King, Ricki Lake, Bill Murray, Sister Elizabeth Kenny, Shirley Conran, Twiggy, Jim Henson, Cheryl Crawford, Linda McCartney, F. Scott Fitzgerald, Fay Weldon, H. G. Wells, Joseph P. Kennedy II, Julio Iglesias, Ray Charles, Cardinal de Richelieu, Brian Epstein

Birthdays Especially Affected on the Cusp of Beauty

If you are born on the Cusp of Beauty (September 19–24), the Cusp of Mystery, Violence, and Imagination (January 17–22), or the Cusp of Energy (May 19–24) your energies blend well with those of this week. Results should be obtained with little effort on your part.

Cusp of Beauty people enjoy themselves and pay special attention to their personal appearances. Cusp of Mystery, Violence, and Imagination people are likely to watch videos and films which stimulate their active fantasy life. Cusp of Energy people enjoy redecorating their living space and spicing up their lifestyle.

If you are born on the Cusp of Prophecy (December 19–25), the Cusp of Rebirth (March 19–24), or the Cusp of Magic (June 19–24) you will face problems and challenges during this week. You will have to work harder to achieve your goals.

Cusp of Prophecy people will put others off with their highly serious attitudes. Cusp of Rebirth people should avoid drawing attention to themselves, but instead enjoy the multifaceted world around them. Cusp of Magic people need to pay more attention to their personal appearances.

✴

The Week of Perfection

SEPTEMBER 25–OCTOBER 2

Although we would all do well to clean up our act now, we must be careful of going too far and demanding too much of ourselves and others. Judging the behavior of those around us in a very severe manner can cause hurt and also arouse anger and resentment. Our urge to perfect things can better be spent in dealing with technical matters and fixing material objects which are in need of repair. Also, time can be spent shopping for new items to take their place, after doing careful research on their specifications.

Computer work of all types is recommended now, and especially using the Internet as the valuable research tool it is. Hobbies attract us magnetically during the Week of Perfection, as do other leisure time activities. The only danger here is going overboard with our own interests and forgetting that loved ones may be in need of attention. An important lesson to be learned in this week will be to leave things which don't need fixing alone, not only in the technical but also the psychological sphere.

Many people will feel acute resentment when given unsolicited advice, and such feelings can surface easily, especially if that advice is accompanied by a cavalier or know-it-all attitude. If you feel deep concern about someone's behavior during this period, try to watch, listen, and wait for the right moment to make your observations known. An opportune time will come when your comments will be welcomed or requested.

By applying high standards to ourselves in a quest for perfection, we may achieve higher quality in our work, but in return we may well suffer from tension and stress. We must all be aware of the dangers of becoming a workaholic. Learning to balance a desire to work and a need for rest is crucial to everyone's success and mental health. Also, we must be aware of getting bogged down in endlessly detailed work that keeps us from moving ahead profitably. Neurotic or obsessive behavior particularly must be guarded against.

Humor is important now to guard against becoming overly serious. Laughter is indeed the best medicine, particularly if it occasionally can be directed against ourselves. Playing board or card games, doing crossword and jigsaw puzzles, and indulging in lively repartee with others will give ample exercise to our logical faculties.

This is a good week to put our energies into improving our living situation. All kinds of renovation and painting activities are favored now, particularly those projects which will help protect our homes against the bitter weather ahead. Taking advantage of good weather to work outside can prove both utilitarian and enjoyable. Major projects that require a few weeks of work are best started at this time, rather than being left to the dark days of November.

Occasionally, neglecting emotional matters while attending to technical ones can lead to outbursts of impatience or anger. Students who hit the books with a vengeance may suffer intense reactions from their psyches, left to feel abandoned or ignored. Forget about a philosophy which advocates working hard, then playing hard. Balance is the answer. And remember: Self-understanding and being understanding of others is something which should not be put on the back burner for too long.

The Personology of People Born in the Week of Perfection

Because of their insistence on technical perfection, those born in this week can be extremely demanding, both of themselves and others. Although people born in the Week of Perfection frequently may present a cool exterior, this facade belies the seething emotions that frequently lurk beneath the surface. Among the most witty and charming people of the entire year, these individuals are frequently drawn to deep, complex individuals very different from themselves. One outlet for their passionate nature is their work, which they do not hesitate to throw themselves into, body and soul. Getting stressed out is all too common a problem though, and people born in the Week of Perfection must learn to protect themselves by taking extra time off to relax.

Annual Events That Occur During the Week of Perfection

October 1: International Day for the Elderly
    World Vegetarian Day
October 2: World Farm Animals Day

Major Historical Events That Have Occurred During the Week of Perfection

September 25, 1957: Little Rock school integration begins
September 26, 1934: The *Queen Mary* is launched
September 27, 1938: The *Queen Elizabeth* is launched
September 28, 1964: Warren Commission report denies plot to kill President Kennedy
September 29, 1941: Babi Yar massacre of thirty thousand Jews
September 30, 1938: Munich pact signed ("Peace with honor")
October 1, 1938: Hitler invades Czechoslovakia
October 2, 1835: Texas uprising against Mexican government

Famous People Born During the Week of Perfection

Michael Douglas, Catherine Zeta-Jones, Dmitry Shostakovich, George Gershwin, Barbara Walters, Olivia Newton-John, Brigitte Bardot, Madeleine Kahn, Mohandas Gandhi, William Faulkner, Bryant Gumbel, Annie Besant,

Glenn Gould, Groucho Marx, Jimmy Carter, Marcello Mastroianni, Angie Dickinson, Samuel Adams, Truman Capote, Annie Leibovitz

Birthdays Especially Affected During the Week of Perfection

If you are born in the Week of Perfection (September 25–October 2), the Week of Intelligence (January 23–30), or the Week of Freedom (May 25–June 2) your energies blend well with those of this week. Results should be obtained with little effort on your part.

Week of Perfection people will enjoy tinkering with gadgets and fixing up their living space. Week of Intelligence people mix good humor with a light but caring attitude. Week of Freedom people move easily from one project to the next and are able to get a lot accomplished.

If you are born in the Week of Rule (December 26–January 2), the Week of Curiosity (March 25–April 2), or the Week of Empathy (June 25–July 2) you will face problems and challenges during this week. You will have to work harder to achieve your goals.

Week of Rule people must learn that "if it works don't fix it." Week of Curiosity people should keep their opinions to themselves and not poke their noses into other people's business. Week of Empathy people tend to get bogged down in emotional matters and need to let go of their heavy feelings.

✷

The Week of Socialization

OCTOBER 3–10

It's essential to get out and meet people during this time. All activities that involve interactions with others are favored during the Week of Socialization, and most attempts to go off on our own or adopt an isolated stance will be thwarted. Renewing social contacts may also have a very favorable effect on career and professional matters. Too often, it is not what you know but *who* you know. So many opportunities come our way via acquaintances and colleagues that even the most mundane dinner party or get-together should not be avoided.

It will not always be easy to force yourself to seek out the company of others, since we often prefer to isolate ourselves in a comfortable cocoonlike existence. But such comfort does not seem to be in the cards during this week, for no sooner do we find ourselves alone than the doorbell or telephone rings, or we find an e-mail message popping up on our computer screen. Friends need us, our children need us, parents and associates need us, and finally we accept that at least for this one week out of the entire year we have no choice but to give our lives over to interactions with others.

Of course, during this period we must have a clear idea about what our own values and wishes are. To give up our individuality and simply become a member of the group is not the idea here at all. What we need to do is bring our individual skills and talents to bear on group problems and projects. In a way, the most ideal social organization would be a dedicated group of individualists, each valued for his or her opinions and abilities but dedicated to the highest good of the group and of society in general.

Too often we may be anxious to please and therefore not be strong enough to say no and risk rejection. Such a lack of ego boundaries can leave us at the mercy of unscrupulous individuals or crushed by the dominant nature of the group ethic. This is a good week to remember what John Stuart Mill called "the tyranny of the majority." We must never allow it to stifle our initiatives and opinions.

Probably the highest ideal possible during this week is that of universal brotherhood, a kind of friendship that is more inclusive by nature. Parties that include a fairly large group of friends and perhaps a couple of newcomers can radiate that conviviality which many of us value so highly. Moreover, professional efforts that employ a well-ordered team working together harmoniously are particularly favored at this time.

Socialization also can include family get-togethers. This week is conducive to reestablishing relations with family members with whom we have had little contact for the past months or years and can be a time for bringing disparate and even contentious factions together. No one should feel shut out or excluded during the Week of Socialization.

The Personology of People Born in the Week of Socialization

The paradoxical nature of those born in this week is underlined by the fact that although they are frequently at their best in social situations, they value their time alone and indeed may prefer to be on their own most of the time. Like it or not, however, their destiny in this lifetime is bound up with that of others more than most. People born in the Week of Socialization have deep and profound skills in dealing with humanity. Others sense this and seek them out for understanding and advice. Outspoken, these scrappy fighters often can be found championing the cause of the underdog.

Annual Events That Occur During the Week of Socialization

October 3: Techies Day
October 4: World Space Week starts
October 6: National German-American Day
October 7: Child Health Day
       World Habitat Day

Major Historical Events That Have Occurred During the Week of Socialization

October 3, 1863: Thanksgiving Day holiday created by Lincoln
October 4, 1957: First Earth satellite *Sputnik* launched from Russia
October 5, 1908: Bulgaria establishes independence from Turkey
October 6, 1973: Yom Kippur attack on Israel by Egypt-Syria forces
October 7, 1959: Dark side of moon photos sent back by *Lunik III*

October 8, 1912: First Balkan War begins
October 9, 1871: Fire destroys Chicago
October 10, 1935: *Porgy and Bess* opens in New York

Famous People Born During the Week of Socialization

Susan Sarandon, John Lennon, Jesse Jackson, Vaclav Havel, Le Corbusier, Buster Keaton, Eleanora Duse, Desmond Tutu, Yo-Yo Ma, Bob Geldof, Britt Ekland, Miguel de Cervantes, Jenny Lind, Helen Hayes, Aimee Semple McPherson, Sigourney Weaver, Thelonious Monk, Juan Perón, Imamu Amiri Baraka, Elisabeth Shue

Birthdays Especially Affected During the Week of Socialization

If you are born in the Week of Socialization (October 3–10), the Week of Youth and Ease (January 31–February 7), or the Week of Communication (June 3–10) your energies blend well with those of this week. Results should be obtained with little effort on your part.

Week of Socialization people will make important contributions to the professional and community groups to which they belong. Week of Youth and Ease people can take the initiative in reestablishing ties with neglected family members. Week of Communication people should articulate group needs and concerns.

If you are born in the Week of Determination (January 3–9), the Week of Success (April 3–10), or the Week of Unconventionality (July 3–10) you will face problems and challenges during this week. You will have to work harder to achieve your goals.

Week of Determination people should be aware of feeling sorry for themselves or cutting themselves off from social interactions. Week of Success people must not put their self-interests before the good of the group. Week of Unconventionality people must pay more attention to the wants and needs of their partners and friends.

The Week of Theater

Everything that happens during this week is likely to be imbued with a theatrical flair. Even the simplest of everyday tasks may be done with a flourish, as if to dramatize our individual styles. Most of us have the tendency to put ourselves center stage and request a waiting and appreciative audience. Nor are we averse to being part of the audience at someone else's show, since "the play's the thing" and not necessarily our own egotistical gratification.

Even the most shy and solitary of characters will feel urged by the extroverted tendencies of the Week of Theater to join the show. More introverted types would do well now to try their hand at expressive public displays. Sporting colorful new clothes, indulging in poetic and vivid language, spending time at music, theater, or dance performances are all appropriate to the energies of this week. Likewise, going dancing at clubs, taking part in sport competitions (particularly those of a team nature), and experiencing light entertainment or stand-up comedy will be particularly enjoyable at this time.

People are more likely now to speak their minds, and we should admire that honesty rather than take offense or feel insulted. Events that happen at this time may also be imbued with a sense of the dramatic, whether due to actual content or the tendency of the media to play things up. Likewise, most people will be more conscious of the role they are playing at work, in social gatherings, and even at home with their families. During this week we may begin to question which role we should be playing in the drama of our own lives. Perhaps, feeling dissatisfaction with our assigned role, we might choose to change the role and step out in quite another direction, much to the surprise and, maybe even perhaps the dismay, of our family and friends.

In this latter respect, relationships can experience seismic tremors as one partner decides to take either a more active or passive role and begins acting in a more dominant or subservient manner. Such moves can lead the other partner to examine his or her own role in the relationship more carefully and perhaps respond in kind. In the best-case scenario, both partners may achieve a degree of enlightenment because of their realizations about these shifting roles, although society's view of their relationship may shift significantly as well, causing additional problems.

Liberating influences are felt strongly during the Week of Theater, and in no area is this influence felt as strongly as in sexual mores and practices. All forms of condescension and sexism are despised, and even the shyest of people now demand to be accepted for who they are. For the most part, more vivid sexual expression will have a positive effect on your life, as long as it does not lead you to jealousy or violent and vindictive behavior. Those not engaging in sex may come to realize that sexuality is simply a metaphor for many interpersonal activities, and that friendship may also be imbued with a highly sensual flavor. During this period it is truly fun to flirt, to play, and to indulge in light forms of verbal as well as physical seduction.

The Personology of People Born in the Week of Theater

Those born in the Week of Theater are dominant individuals who exert a powerful influence on their immediate environment. People born in this week are not only interested in getting results, but in getting them in the right way. Thus, they tend to evaluate people for their methods and style as well as their goals. Moral principles are important to them. Right and wrong are not ethical abstractions but ideals intimately connected to maintaining high quality and preserving one's good name. Adept in financial matters, it is important for people born during this week to retain their independence and not allow themselves to rely on others for support.

Annual Events That Occur During the Week of Theater

October 11: National Coming Out Day
October 12: Columbus Day

October 16: World Food Day
October 17: Day for the Eradication of Poverty

Major Historical Events That Have Occurred During the Week of Theater

October 11, 1980: Devastating earthquake hits Algeria

October 12, 1492: Christopher Columbus discovers America

October 13, 1792: Foundation stone laid for White House by Washington

October 14, 1066: William the Conqueror wins the Battle of Hastings

October 15, 1969: Millions demonstrate in antiwar protests in United States

October 16, 1793: Marie Antoinette guillotined in Paris

October 17, 1777: Colonists beat British at battle of Saratoga

October 18, 1989: San Francisco hit by earthquake

Famous People Born During the Week of Theater

Art Tatum, Lenny Bruce, Margaret Thatcher, William Penn, Eleanor Roosevelt, Paul Simon, Oscar Wilde, Edith Galt Wilson, Eugene O'Neill, Luciano Pavarotti, Rita Hayworth, Pierre Trudeau, Martina Navratilova, George C. Scott, Roger Moore, Nancy Kerrigan, Arthur Miller, Mario Puzo, Hannah Arendt, Violetta Chamorro

Birthdays Especially Affected During the Week of Theater

If you are born in the Week of Theater (October 11–18), the Week of Acceptance (February 8–15), or the Week of Exploration (June 11–18) your energies blend well with those of this week. Results should be obtained with little effort on your part.

Week of Theater people can show their more flamboyant sides with confidence. Week of Acceptance people should insist on being accepted as they are and having others trust their judgments. Week of Exploration people are attracted to physical adventure, particularly uninhibited displays of passion.

If you are born in the Week of Dominance (January 10–16), the Week of Social Betterment (April 11–18), or the Week of Persuasion (July 11–18) you will face problems and challenges during this week. You will have to work harder to achieve your goals.

Week of Dominance people need to consider major role changes in relationships which are not working out. Week of Social Betterment people may be losing out in their love relationships because of their inability to face the truth. Week of Persuasion people must learn to keep it light and not take rejection so seriously.

❋

The Cusp of Involvement

OCTOBER 19–25

The energies of this cusp can be wild, unpredictable and stormy. Rarely dull, this period offers a broad palette of experience. It will be difficult to keep from getting our feet wet in the mighty river of life, and in fact we may have to struggle to keep afloat. Many deep experiences in the emotional and intellectual realms hold seductive attractions for us during this week, and in no area may there be more pull exerted than in the sensual and sexual spheres.

The dichotomy between these two areas is important to notice. One does not imply the other, as the stark sexual realities of a relationship may have little to do with the softer sensuous aspects and vice versa. Two types of experience are involved here, one passionate, the other sensuous. Passionate experiences involve periodic, sudden outpourings of feeling and expression, overwhelming in intensity, while sensuous experiences favor regular touching in an everyday setting, as well as expressions of affection. Both surface at this time. Likewise, there may be a definite split between love and sex, with the two firmly compartmentalized.

Intellectual areas such as reading, academic study, fierce discussion, research, lectures, and essay writing also are important now. Nor is there necessarily a contradiction between the intellectual realm and sexual expression, since they may both be present in an intense form in the same day. Moving from the mental to the physical and back again is part and parcel of the energies of the Libra-Scorpio cusp.

However, both areas may have their compulsive or addictive aspects, and we must be aware of the tendencies of this week to pull us into traps and pitfalls from which it may be extremely difficult to extricate ourselves in the coming months. Drugs such as alcohol, nicotine, caffeine, and hallucinogens are capable of exerting especially strong pulls during this week, and the effects may be disastrous. Extreme care must be taken now to avoid such problems.

Fortunately, our powers of discrimination are high at this time, and it is possible to exercise good judgment in these problem areas, but usually only before the fact. Once involved, we can expect a rough ride. A fierce mental orientation in this cusp usually is available to many, but this can be overdone as well, resulting in headaches, worry, and sleeplessness. Balancing the sharp extremes of experience will be difficult now, since the tendency to go overboard in any area is so pronounced. Basically, we are dealing with a deep hunger for experience, which usually cannot be satisfied or put off without an ample dose of the real thing.

Of great help at this time will be subscribing to a healthy lifestyle both in the areas of diet and physical exercise. It will be important to keep involvement moderate, however, to again avoid the penchant of this week's energies for excess. In addition, food supplements are important, as are herbal remedies that can contribute to a calm and relaxed state, when needed. Aromatherapy, massage, meditation, and other spiritual practices are recommended in moderation also.

The Personology of People Born on the Cusp of Involvement

People born on the Cusp of Involvement are outspoken individuals, highly critical in their demeanor. Normally, they will give their opinion in a straightforward manner, whether it is asked for or not. Because of the mental orientation of Libra and the emotional nature of Scorpio, there can be acute conflicts between the head and the heart in those born on the Libra-Scorpio cusp.

Those born on the Cusp of Involvement tend to become deeply involved in issues under discussion and in the lives of those around them, so it is almost impossible for them at times to disentangle themselves from such endeavors. Because of their attractive charm, it is not easy to ignore or forget them.

Annual Events That Occur on the Cusp of Involvement

October 21: Trafalgar Day
October 24: United Nations Day
October 25: St. Crispin's Day

Major Historical Events That Have Occurred on the Cusp of Involvement

October 19, 1781: American War of Independence ends
October 20, 1827: Turkish fleet destroyed by Allies
October 21, 1873: Opening of Sydney Opera House
October 22, 1797: First parachute drop (from a balloon) in France
October 23, 1883: Opening of Metropolitan Opera House in New York
October 24, 1956: Hungarian revolt against communist government
October 25, 1415: Battle of Agincourt pits English against French

Famous People Born on the Cusp of Involvement

Pablo Picasso, Catherine Deneuve, Pelé, Samuel Taylor Coleridge, Carrie Fisher, Franz Liszt, Sarah Bernhardt, Ursula Le Guin, Evander Holyfield, Robert Rauschenberg, Dizzy Gillespie, Benjamin Netanyahu, Jelly Roll Morton, Arthur Rimbaud, Bobby Seale, Antonie van Leeuwenhoek, Auguste Lumière, Princess Michiko Shoda, Peter Tosh, Annette Funicello

Birthdays Especially Affected During the Cusp of Involvement

If you are born on the Cusp of Involvement (October 19–25), the Cusp of Sensitivity (February 16–22), or the Cusp of Magic (June 19–24) your energies blend well with those of this week. Results should be obtained with little effort on your part.

Cusp of Involvement people will experience life to the fullest and meet with success. Cusp of Sensitivity people can come to many new understandings of how to proceed in life. Cusp of Magic people find themselves enjoying highly sensuous experiences.

If you are born on the Cusp of Mystery, Violence, and Imagination (January 17–22), the Cusp of Power (April 19–24), or the Cusp of Oscillation (July 19–25) you will face problems and challenges during this week. You will have to work harder to achieve your goals.

Cusp of Mystery, Violence, and Imagination people may stir up trouble and have difficulty putting out emotional wildfires of their own making. Cusp of Power people who make hard sexual demands may come to regret their inflexible attitudes. Cusp of Oscillation people have to learn to keep their promises and not rationalize away their behavior.

※

The Week of Intensity

OCTOBER 26–NOVEMBER 2

As the night air becomes decidedly cold, the lure of outdoor nocturnal activities intensifies in a buildup to the time of Halloween. Fifty years ago it was common to celebrate chalk night, mischief night, and finally All Hallow's Eve, witnessing a steady crescendo of pranks and nonserious aggression. Behind these practices lie ancient legends of witches, werewolves, vampires, and other supernatural creatures who roamed dark forests and occasionally ventured into villages and towns to work their dark magic.

Pluto, the somber god of the underworld, exerts his strongest influences under the sign of Scorpio, and although the energies of this week have a sunny side as well, his powers can be expected to build until the second week of November. Furthermore, the influences of the planet Mars are likewise felt, showing the aggressive side of the sign of Scorpio. We must take care to guard against all forms of destructiveness during this week, including accidents, but we must also take advantage of the raised level of intensity, which can be put to positive use.

Energy levels are high now when it comes to carrying out maintenance projects, so household endeavors and indoor renovations are especially favored. Likewise, a sharp eye for sales and bargains will locate certain special items of interest avidly sought during the rest of the year. Sound judgment will guarantee the success of important decisions made now. Objectivity is high, and with it the ability to withstand the emotions which tend to bias us in making objective choices. On the other hand, jealousy, revenge, and other intense negative feelings may flood over us periodically. We must do what we can to prevent these Plutonic urges from taking control.

On the sunnier side, this week brings humor, and we can be expected to find it to a high degree day to day. The fun-loving aspects of this Halloween time usually are looked forward to throughout the year. Pranks, jokes, deception, and merriment of all sorts are in abundance now, and with them a lift in spirits and the joy of life.

This week combines an interesting blend of light and dark energies. There is a definite tendency now to be judgmental and unforgiving, but at the same time we are more likely to accept the foibles of others and to be fascinated by the unusual and bizarre aspects of existence. Balance is not in the cards here, but rather a sudden shift from one extreme to the other. Thus, sudden mood changes on the part of a partner or family member may leave us gasping for air and wondering what we might have done to provoke such a reaction.

Outright violence certainly can surface now, but we must also take care not to appear overly fearful or protective, since repressing our own aggressions and fears may lead to attracting these same energies. Taking normal safety precautions is sincerely recommended at this time. During the Week of Intensity we will undoubtedly feel especially protective toward our children and pets, as we instinctively guard them against dark forces which could be roaming at night.

The Personology of People Born in the Week of Intensity

People born in the Week of Intensity are the sunny Scorpios, not as emotionally complex or deep as others born in this sign. Although they can be quite serious, particularly about their work, they have an excellent sense of humor. Those born in this week are more concerned with motives than results. Therefore, they find it important to know why someone did something and are not impressed with a good result achieved through impure motives, no matter how substantial. They highly value quality in everything they do and are unlikely to settle for anything but the best. Because of their high standards they are not impressed by quantity or speed alone.

Annual Events That Occurred During the Week of Intensity

October 27: Navy Day
October 29: International Internet Day
October 31: Halloween
November 1: All Saints' Day
November 2: All Souls' Day
Election Day (or following week)

Major Historical Events That Have Happened During the Week of Intensity

October 26, 1905: Norwegian king elected; country becomes independent
October 27, 1971: Republic of Congo becomes Zaire
October 28, 1962: Russia backs off in Cuba, avoids WWIII
October 29, 1929: Wall Street crashes

October 30, 1925: First TV image sent by John Logie Baird

October 31, 1517: Martin Luther nails ninety-five theses to Wittenberg Church door

November 1, 1755: Lisbon destroyed by earthquake

November 2, 1976: Jimmy Carter elected thirty-ninth president

Famous People Born During the Week of Intensity

Hillary Rodham Clinton, Theodore Roosevelt, Julia Roberts, Christopher Columbus, John Keats, Marie Antoinette, Benvenuto Cellini, Paul Joseph Goebbels, Bill Gates, Dylan Thomas, Sylvia Plath, Niccolò Paganini, Erasmus, Maxine Hong Kingston, Francis Bacon, Gary Player, Jan Vermeer, François Mitterand, Ruby Dee, John Cleese

Birthdays Especially Affected During the Week of Intensity

If you are born in the Week of Intensity (October 26–November 2), the Week of Spirit (February 23–March 2), or the Week of Empathy (June 25–July 2) your energies blend well with those of this week. Results should be obtained with little effort on your part.

Week of Intensity people will enjoy all the dress-up and dramatic qualities of Halloween. Week of Spirit people revel in the intense emotions of this week but should be aware of their dark sides getting out of control. Week of Empathy people should go on shopping trips and find unusual bargains.

If you are born in the Week of Intelligence (January 23–30), the Week of Manifestation (April 25–May 2), or the Week of Passion (July 26–August 2) you will face problems and challenges during this week. You will have to work harder to achieve your goals.

Week of Intelligence people will encounter resistance if they allow their critical faculties to dominate their lives. Week of Manifestation people must learn not to take themselves so seriously. Week of Passion people must be aware of manipulative tendencies, particularly in the sexual sphere.

The Week of Profundity

NOVEMBER 3–11

This is one of the deepest and most serious weeks of the entire year. Now is not the time for trivialities or for a superficial treatment of the subject at hand. The dark days of fall are at last upon us, weather that begins to call up the winter blues through increasing lack of sunlight, high winds, rain, and the first snows of the season. Depression is a constant threat during this week, and we must distinguish between the objective nature of matters which need attention and a subjective state that will make us more inclined to worry and frustration.

Now is a wonderful time to concentrate on inner work that needs to be done. Dealing with your personal problems in an effective way may be one of the most positive occupations to be attempted at this time. It will probably not be easy to talk about what is bothering us, but we should try to remember that only one sympathetic ear is necessary. Likewise, the concentration will be there for professional projects, with the possibility of real progress accruing. As long as we keep our eye on the object and move steadily ahead, some success will be assured.

Money matters should be attended to, both the day-to-day running of a business or professional activity and the making of investments. The most effective investments at this time are mutual funds, bonds, and high-yield accounts rather than options, futures, or other speculative ventures. A half yearly financial review with an accountant or other tax expert will assure that come next April 15 the books will be in good shape.

Deep emotions may be seething beneath the surface during this week, so it is important to avoid provocative behavior and the resulting volcanic outbursts whenever possible. If we find that someone is pushing our buttons, we should work on desensitizing ourselves and disengaging from a reactive mode by developing a whole new set of buttons that cannot be pushed so easily.

During this most Scorpionic of weeks it may be necessary for all of us to retreat at times from the noise and vicissitudes of the world into our own private space. Comforting areas such as cinema, music, hobbies of all sorts, drugs, even sex and love addictions may all exert their particular seductive powers and offer solace. The deepening of interpersonal relationships is most likely at this time and many secure bonds of trust are often formed. On the other hand, we must beware possessive behavior and undue dependency. We would all do well to keep our independence and self-esteem at high enough levels that such dependencies do not become debilitating.

As personal as the energies of this week may prove to be, it is still possible to engage in social activities, particularly those involving family or very close friends. Get-togethers of four or five people over dinner, entertainment, or a quiet party at home are particularly gratifying. This is generally not a good time to change partners, end established relationships, or seek out new job positions, as mutable energies do not run high during the Week of Profundity. Better to stick with a known quantity now than to jump ship.

The Personology of People Born in the Week of Profundity

The influences of the dark planet Pluto are strongest now in these individuals than in any other period of the year, and therefore they are more in touch with their deepest emotions than most people. Their active unconscious life demands many hours of deep sleep each night. Because of their passionate nature, they must beware becoming slaves to certain pleasures, notably those of sex and food. Keeping busy is important to their mental health, otherwise they may sink into brooding and depression. They do well to have as partners more lighthearted individuals who can brighten up their daily life.

Annual Events That Occur During the Week of Profundity

November 9: Sadie Hawkins Day
November 10: Marine Corps Birthday

November 11: Veteran's Day
Election Day (or preceding week)

Major Historical Events That Have Happened During the Week of Profundity

November 3, 1957: *Sputnik 2* launched with dog, Laika, on board

November 4, 1922: Howard Carter discovers tomb of Pharaoh Tutankhamen

November 5, 1605: Guy Fawkes arrested in plan to blow up parliament

November 6, 1991: Yeltsin bans Communist party in Russia

November 7, 1917: Communists take power in Russia

November 8, 1923: Hitler's first big meeting in a Munich beer hall

November 9, 1938: Kristallnacht in Germany results in destruction of Jewish property and mass arrests

November 10, 1989: Crowds pour from East to West Berlin as borders are opened

November 11, 1918: World War I ends with Germany's surrender

Famous People Born During the Week of Profundity

Roseanne Barr, Fyodor Dostoevsky, Ennio Morricone, Joni Mitchell, Marie Curie, Hedy Lamarr, Leon Trotsky, Sam Shepard, Robert Mapplethorpe, Sally Field, Rickie Lee Jones, Mike Nichols, Ivan Turgenev, Roy Rogers, Art Carney, Yanni, William of Orange, Ida Minerva Tarbell, John Philip Sousa, Maria Shriver

Birthdays Especially Affected During the Week of Profundity

If you are born in the Week of Profundity (November 3–11), the Week of Isolation (March 3–10), or the Week of Unconventionality (July 3–10) your energies blend well with those of this week. Results should be obtained with little effort on your part.

Week of Profundity people have heightened concentration but must be aware of depression. Week of Isolation people are in touch with their emotions and are fully able to express them. Week of Unconventionality people find comfort in highly personal activities carried on in their own private space.

If you are born in the Week of Youth and Ease (January 31–February 7), the Week of Study (May 3–10), or the Week of Challenge (August 3–10) you will face problems and challenges during this week. You will have to work harder to achieve your goals.

Week of Youth and Ease people may be disappointed when their ideas are brushed off as too superficial. Week of Study people should be aware of developing dependencies. Week of Challenge people may suffer from feelings of low self-esteem.

The Week of Control

NOVEMBER 12–18

We may find ourselves trying to dominate the environment around us this week, whether in our relationships or professional life. In seeking to gain control over the elements around us, we may be demonstrating a lack of basic self-confidence. Where we might benefit by letting things go in the direction in which they are headed naturally, we may now feel a need to guide and ultimately give structure to those same forces. The danger here is a limiting of spontaneity to a point where it ceases to exist. Fixed pragmatic energies may supplant intuitive ones, and we run the risk of getting mired down in conservatism.

This means that we must all work even harder to remain open during this week, and to stay sufficiently flexible to admit wrongdoing and be capable of changing direction. Even though it may be necessary to take a tough stance, we must beware becoming overly rigid in our attitudes. Being a good boss in any organization, or assuming a leadership role, also implies being sensitive to the wishes of others and being ready to listen to their complaints and criticism. Acute psychological awareness depends heavily on this ability, and also to see what is really there, not just what you want to see. In particular it will be important not only to look for those facts that support one's own point of view but to consider other opinions as well.

During this week it may be necessary for you to terminate a long-standing relationship, probably a friendship, and although this process can be painful it will prove necessary. On the other hand, we will seek more and more the positive benefits which friendships have to offer, and even lean on close friends when mates, family members, or colleagues let you down. Now may also be the time to let your partner know which aspects of the relationship have not been working out. In the sexual sphere, honesty does not always abound, and this week can be opportune to gently inform a partner about which aspects of the relationship are less than ideal in this respect. Working to correct such problems is indeed encouraged.

By taking a realistic view of our professional capabilities, subtle shifts in outlays of time, money, and energy will be possible. This is often a period in which things become clear and we stop deluding ourselves on certain professional matters. Increasing our effectiveness as an entrepreneur, an employee of a company, or as a member of a professional team is possible now, with corresponding advancement possible during the months to come.

We will find that our criticisms and observations about life and people will go down much better if presented in a charming manner rather than in a gruff or abrupt one. Such energies are available now, and there is no reason to subject anyone to a rough ride in this respect. By being polite and considerate, and by speaking softly, others will respond much more easily to us and begin to see the wisdom behind our suggestions. In most cases, a teaspoon of honey, indeed, helps the medicine go down.

The Personology of People Born in the Week of Control

Those born in the Week of Control make excellent bosses and administrators. These individuals have an unusual insight into the running of organizations, whether professional or familial. Thus, they are able to oversee projects and to get the job done without arousing the resentment of those who work under them. Very sensual individuals, those born in this week know how to enjoy themselves, and are especially good at planning vacations which can be satisfying to all involved. Although sure of themselves, those born in this week value the opinions of a close friend highly, particularly one who is strong enough to stand up to them.

Annual Events That Occur During the Week of Control

November 12: St. Martin's Day
November 15: Seven-Five-Three Festival in Japan
November 18: Mickey Mouse's Birthday

Major Historical Events That Have Occurred During the Week of Control

November 12, 1987: Gorbachev fires Boris Yeltsin
November 13, 1945: De Gaulle elected president of France
November 14, 1940: Coventry destroyed by Luftwaffe bombing
November 15, 1864: Atlanta burned to ground by Sherman
November 16, 1940: Petain of France asks Hitler for armistice
November 17, 1988: Benazir Bhutto becomes first Islamic woman leader
November 18, 1477: William Caxton prints first book in England

Famous People Born During the Week of Control

Grace Kelly, Claude Monet, Neil Young, Danny DeVito, Whoopi Goldberg, Prince Charles, Demi Moore, Brenda Vaccaro, Nadia Comaneci, Auguste Rodin, Robert Louis Stevenson, Sun Yat-sen, Joseph McCarthy, Georgia O'Keeffe, Erwin Rommel, Bernard Law Montgomery, Dorothy Dix, Barbara Hutton, Aaron Copland, Jawaharlal Nehru

Birthdays Especially Affected During the Week of Control

If you are born in the Week of Control (November 12–18), the Week of Dances and Dreams (March 11–18), or the Week of Persuasion (July 11–18) your energies blend well with those of this week. Results should be obtained with little effort on your part.

Week of Control people can be effective leaders as long as they respect the feelings of their coworkers. Week of Dances and Dreams people will need to readjust their outlays of money to be more successful. Week of Persuasion people will be listened to if they adopt the right tone in their dealings.

If you are born in the Week of Acceptance (February 8–15), the Week of Nature (May 11–18), or the Week of Leadership (August 11–18) you will face problems and challenges during this week. You will have to work harder to achieve your goals.

Week of Acceptance people can suffer financial setbacks because of overly trusting and idealistic attitudes. Week of Nature people had better exert more willpower rather than just going with the flow. Week of Leadership people will suffer from lack of flexibility unless they can discipline themselves to remain more open.

✳

The Cusp of Revolution

NOVEMBER 19–24

During this week many different forms of opposition may be encountered. Feelings of rebelliousness or at the very least a chafing under the unfair rules which society imposes is felt now, and with it a desire to set things right. The danger here is that sheer rebellion will not get us very far unless accompanied by a positive plan as to how to make things better once the offensive prohibitions are removed. Historically speaking, revolutions have too often only succeeded in placing power in the hands of an even worse dictatorship or resulted in an anarchic reign of terror.

Rebellious feelings need not be so extreme, however, as they may manifest in many mundane areas of life. Such feelings can manifest as protest or objections against inefficiency or ignorance. It is important to make such observations in a positive light and not to arouse unnecessary antagonisms. By making it clear that problems can be mutually recognized and solved by common consent, everyone concerned can feel included in the process and not left out or neglected.

Unless our needs to change things can be brought out in a positive manner, the danger of a downward spiral of accusations, destructiveness, and ultimately all-out conflict may be unavoidable. Although such conflict may finally result in change, it also can arouse animosities that could continue during the weeks ahead. The role of laughter is important here: Everyone involved should be able to stand back and laugh occasionally at their own high seriousness.

Because rebelliousness against an authority figure easily could lead the rebel to turn autocrat himself, we must be sure of our motives. Are we looking to just gain increased power for ourselves or are we truly dedicated to our ideals and the larger good of the group? In this latter respect, the approach of the holiday of Thanksgiving, whether it occurs in this week or the next, will increase your need for the company of family and friends, and also for emotional harmony. The traditional conviviality of this seasonal celebration is also likely to mute the extremes of rebelliousness and provide an effective counterweight to it, to say nothing of the grounding influences of a mercilessly huge meal.

Using the energies of this week to bring about positive change is important, since this is one of the most opportune times of the year to bring new ideas, new systems, and new approaches into being. Not only institutional and professional redirection is possible, but also major turnarounds in personal behavior are also possible at this time. Characteristically, we will have a realization or revelation about things and then work to implement our new ideas in daily life. Taking notes, making checklists, in short, giving order and structure to our realizations may be an effective way to begin such a process. Above all, it will be important to proceed slowly and methodically in the weeks ahead and not simply to waste our energies during this week in a sudden restless bout of enthusiasm. Emotional control is of the essence here, and it is important to act in a wise and intelligent manner.

The Personology of People Born on the Cusp of Revolution

Because of the opposing orientations of this cusp (Scorpio is a water sign and Sagittarius, fire) these people can show acute instability at certain points in their lives. This often manifests as rebelliousness, yet paradoxically they can function well in group endeavors and can even be effective leaders in some cases. However, as they are usually at their best when left to proceed on their own, free of excessive rules of behavior, these dynamic individuals can inspire others with their verve and drive. They must be careful to keep their argumentative side under control, however, and to avoid unnecessary confrontations with those who have a more conservative orientation.

Annual Events That Occur on the Cusp of Revolution

November 19: U.S. Marine Corps Day
November 22: Commemoration of John F. Kennedy's Assassination
Thanksgiving Day (or following week)

Major Historical Events That Have Occurred on the Cusp of Revolution

November 19, 1863: Lincoln delivers Gettysburg Address
November 20, 1818: Venezuela's independence declared by Simón Bolívar
November 21, 1964: Verrazano Narrows Bridge opens in New York
November 22, 1963: John F. Kennedy assassinated
November 23, 1956: British withdraw from Suez under U.S. pressure
November 24, 1963: Lee Harvey Oswald shot by Jack Ruby

Famous People Born on the Cusp of Revolution

Martin Luther, Robert F. Kennedy, Indira Gandhi, Goldie Hawn, Jodie Foster, Ahmad Rashad, Jamie Lee Curtis, Billy the Kid, Billie Jean King, Henri Toulouse-Lautrec, Coleman Hawkins, Ted Turner, Mariel Hemingway, Boris Becker, Charles de Gaulle, Meredith Monk, Frances Hodgson Burnett, Voltaire, Veronica Hamel, Harpo Marx

Birthdays Especially Affected on the Cusp of Revolution

If you are born on the Cusp of Revolution (November 19–24), the Cusp of Rebirth (March 19–24), or the Cusp of Oscillation (July 19–25) your energies blend well with those of this week. Results should be obtained with little effort on your part.

Cusp of Revolution people can institute changes as long as they do so in a nonthreatening manner. Cusp of Rebirth people must remember to proceed slowly and not rush if they want others to follow their more radical ideas. Cusp of Oscillation people will succeed in changing things as long as they avoid extremes of behavior.

If you are born on the Cusp of Sensitivity (February 16–22), the Cusp of Energy (May 19–24), or the Cusp of Exposure (August 19–25) you will face problems and challenges during this week. You will have to work harder to achieve your goals.

Cusp of Sensitivity people will isolate themselves unduly if they do not listen to the criticism of others. Cusp of Energy people should be aware of going too far too fast in demanding change. Cusp of Exposure people may put other people off by making demands for change in an overly flamboyant manner.

The Week of Independence

NOVEMBER 25–DECEMBER 2

Liberating influences run strong in this week. However, we may find it hard to concentrate on any one matter for long due to a strongly chaotic element present at this time. Our greatest challenge during the Week of Independence will be to focus our energies on a single subject or endeavor— and keep it there. The success of such efforts can be realized with perseverance and dedication.

Now is not the time so much for team efforts but for individual initiative. This can manifest itself in a group setting, as long as members act on their own intuitions within the organization. Fortunately, the moral sense which should accompany such efforts is also usually present now. In this way individuals are able to act fairly and honestly, without being swayed or unduly influenced by motives of personal gain.

We should make a concerted effort during this week to establish a tangible bond with nature, whether with our surroundings, small creatures, living a more natural lifestyle, or making outright contributions of time or money to environmental causes. Some of the clearest and most invigorating weather of the year can be experienced at this time, and we would do well to take advantage of it for long walks in beautiful natural surroundings, camping or exploring, and taking part in physically challenging outdoor activities. This is a time when we can truly feel ourselves to be more in tune with the natural cycles and rhythms of nature.

Individual initiative will go a long way to increase our self-esteem. Setting tangible and realistic goals for ourselves will be important, as will setting deadlines to avoid procrastination. We should do all we can to ensure that our goals will be reached in a reasonable period of time. Now is the time to begin implementing plans for a new business or commercial endeavor, consider the possibility of leaving a boring job to begin an entrepreneurial venture, or implement much needed change to encourage individual initiative. Leaving our parents' home, or at the very least beginning to disentangle ourselves from a web of claiming family influences, may very well begin during the Week of Independence. If we can accomplish this in a gracious and appreciative manner, such efforts may arouse admiration and pride rather than unhappiness and resentment in older authority figures.

The energies of this week run very high, and in no area is this more true than in the sexual sphere. Although promiscuity is not necessarily rife here, we may find ourselves fixating our desires on a particular individual and pursuing them doggedly. Relationships of long standing, marriages included, are likely to benefit from this injection of energy, and some pairings which have suffered from boredom or neglect may well be revitalized now. For those not involved sexually, the higher energy levels are likely to raise the quality of their friendships or romantic yearnings to new levels. We must be sure, however, that our feelings are reciprocated, for an insensitivity to the wishes of others may also be present at this time.

The Personology of People Born in the Week of Independence

Those born in the Week of Independence will not be held back. Their irrepressible nature can get them into trouble, but it is more likely to arouse the respect of others because of these individuals' lack of guile and honest, straightforward manner. Extremely effective in their professional life, they are usually self-taught in what they do, regardless of their schooling. Self-reliant and pragmatic, those born in this week are also highly dependable. They are very protective toward animals and children and do well with a very natural lifestyle. At times they can be impulsive and are drawn strongly to intense, even ecstatic experiences.

Annual Events That Occur During the Week of Independence

November 29: Yugoslavia National Holiday
November 30: St. Andrew's Day

December 1: World AIDS Day
Thanksgiving Day (or preceding week)
Beginning of Advent

Major Historical Events That Have Occurred During the Week of Independence

November 25, 1970: Yukio Mishima commits ritual suicide
November 26, 1983: Biggest British bank robbery of all time
November 27, 1893: Women vote for first time, in New Zealand
November 28, 1950: Chinese enter Korean War
November 29, 1945: Yugoslav republic proclaimed
November 30, 1936: Crystal Palace in London is destroyed by fire
December 1, 1990: Britain linked to Europe by Channel Tunnel
December 2, 1859: Abolitionist John Brown hanged in Charleston

Famous People Born During the Week of Independence

Tina Turner, Mark Twain, Jonathan Swift, Shirley Chisholm, Charles Schulz, Randy Newman, Rita Mae Brown, Jimi Hendrix, Bette Midler, Woody Allen, Maria Callas, Monica Seles, Mary Martin, Winston Churchill, Joe DiMaggio, Jacques Chirac, Caroline Kennedy Schlossberg, John F. Kennedy, Jr.

Birthdays Especially Affected During the Week of Independence

If you are born in the Week of Independence (November 25–December 2), the Week of Curiosity (March 25–April 2), or the Week of Passion (July 26–August 2) your energies blend well with those of this week. Results should be obtained with little effort on your part.

Week of Independence people can make excellent progress in their professional lives as long as they are careful to follow a structured course of action. Week of Curiosity people will move forward but to the extent that they can concentrate and avoid being sidetracked. Week of Passion people must take the initiative in order to avoid being ignored or left behind.

If you are born in the Week of Spirit (February 23–March 2), the Week of Freedom (May 25–June 2), or the Week of Structure (August 26–September 2) you will face problems and challenges during this week. You will have to work harder to achieve your goals.

Week of Spirit people should ground themselves in sport or recreational activities, or be prone to losing their focus. Week of Freedom people will tend to forget those near and dear to them in their blind enthusiasm. Week of Structure people must give up some of their rigid insistence if they wish to liberate themselves.

The Week of Originality

DECEMBER 3–10

Ever had a wacky or zany idea that was rudely rebuffed? Ever wonder when it would be time to move ahead with an off-the-wall project? Well, this week could very well be the right one for such endeavors. Nothing is too far out to consider at this time. The more original a project, whether untried or not, it will stand a decent degree of success. This of course implies that we have the courage of our convictions and dare to propose some very advanced notions. Remember that many mainstays of contemporary thought were also once thought to be overly speculative or even absurd before they finally were accepted.

Likewise, unusual hairstyles, clothing, piercings, and other forms of personal expression may be a focus of attention during this week. Seeking to modify your own lifestyle and give it new direction with a highly individual flair, can be very satisfying. Although others may not have the courage or inclination to apply the energies of this week to their own appearance, they are likely nonetheless to be more open about such matters now. A previously disapproving or even hostile parent could be more receptive to his or her children's need to make such an individualistic statement.

Those engaged in unusual projects would do well to seek out others who are of like mind at this time, particularly when it comes to initiating new endeavors. This does not mean to imply that the occupation or field they are dealing with need be far out, for many quite traditional areas can be given a new twist or be turned in an unusual direction now. Quite likely, this could breathe new financial life into a struggling business endeavor. A positive outcome is more likely if such projects are focused in one clear direction from the start rather than using hit-or-miss techniques or trying to adjust by trial and error.

Although love affairs may be especially passionate at this time, they also can be highly unrealistic. Both partners will have to use every ounce of common sense if they are to avoid going off the deep end. There is no end to the excitement which can be generated in the Week of Originality, but unfortunately, there is also no limit on the resulting chaos either. Because this week embodies a great need for physical satisfaction, purely sexual or sensual drives often can be sublimated into sports, exercise, and other physical endeavors.

The bizarre nature of ideas or attitudes generated in this week make rejection or misunderstanding inevitable. Learning how to deal with such responses, to be strong in your commitment to unusual ideas, and finally to be able to pick ourselves up, dust ourselves off, and proceed after having been knocked down are important lessons to be learned. If we know in our hearts that we are right, and we are convinced that our individuality is not a serious threat to anyone's well-being, we should feel free to move ahead. Expressing our real selves during this week will contribute to a much needed sense of identity and self-worth, which we can carry proudly right up until the new beginnings of springtime.

The Personology of People Born in the Week of Originality

One of a kind, the unusual individuals born in this week are not apologetic about being different from others. Because they are so different they may encounter opposition in their professional lives. Usually, however, their charm and ability to convince others of the feasibility of their far-out ideas stands them in good stead. It is best if they associate both personally and professionally with those who are sympathetic to or appreciative of their idiosyncrasies. Although recognition is not overly important to them, those born in this week often achieve success through unexpected twists of fate.

Annual Events That Occur During the Week of Originality

December 6: St. Nicholas Day
December 7: Pearl Harbor Day
December 10: Nobel Prize Day
               Human Rights Day

Major Historical Events That Have Occurred During the Week of Originality

December 3, 1967: First successful human heart transplant done by
   Christiaan Barnard
December 4, 1989: East Germany's communist leader forced to resign
December 5, 1933: Prohibition is repealed
December 6, 1877: First sound recording made by Thomas Edison
December 7, 1941: United States enters WWII after attack on Pearl Harbor
December 8, 1980: John Lennon murdered in New York
December 9, 1990: Solidarity leader Lech Walesa elected Polish president
December 10, 1901: Nobel Prizes first awarded

Famous People Born During the Week of Originality

Sinead O'Connor, Walt Disney, John Malkovich, Joan Armatrading, Emily Dickinson, Tom Waits, Larry Bird, George Custer, Ira Gershwin, Sammy Davis, Jr., Jean Luc Godard, Kenneth Branagh, Joan Didion, Kirk Douglas, Redd Foxx, T. V. Soong, Francisco Franco, Marles Martin Hall, Anna Freud, Joseph Conrad

Birthdays Especially Affected During the Week of Originality

If you are born in the Week of Originality (December 3–10), the Week of Success (April 3–10), or the Week of Challenge (August 3–10) your energies blend well with those of this week. Results should be obtained with little effort on your part.

Week of Originality people will enjoy feeling more appreciated for their far-out ideas and lifestyles. Week of Success people should shift the emphasis in their business affairs toward less rather than more conservative approaches. Week of Challege people should be sure to get enough physical exercise, and can expect success if they are in good health.

If you are born in the Week of Isolation (March 3–10), the Week of Communication (June 3–10), or the Week of the Puzzle (September 3–10) you will face problems and challenges during this week. You will have to work harder to achieve your goals.

Week of Isolation people will have to struggle not to become involved in unrealistic love relationships. Week of Communication people may be swept away by chaotic energies and need every ounce of common sense they can muster. Week of the Puzzle people must be careful not to let their curiosity lead them into dangerous situations.

✹

The Week of Expansiveness

DECEMBER 11–18

Seeing the big picture and not being afraid to think in big terms are both characteristic of the energies of this week. Now is not the time to get caught up in small details but to express the largest vision of which we are capable. This does not mean to imply impracticality or loose thinking. We will be more successful, in fact, to the extent that we have mastered the techniques of our craft. Although in tune with the success-oriented energies of the week, we may be out of sync with family members and close friends, who may view us as going off full steam ahead in the wrong direction. And wearing blinders, at that. Taking the time to reassure them of the soundness of our plans may not be in the cards, and at least for these few days they will have to be accepting, albeit in the dark about what is going on.

During these dark days before Christmas we will begin to feel much of the season's magic. Last-minute shopping is under way, and a sense of enchantment can be seen in children's eyes. Indeed, a part of our larger plans may involve Christmas itself, whether we are working on a monumental presentation, getting a family dinner together, or simply dealing with the drama of the holiday season. We will feel a great desire to share with others now, and if they can participate in our planning for the holidays, so much the better.

Problems abound during this week, and solving them can be a major challenge. Not the least of these may be our struggles to find the money to pay for our big plans, and too often going broke is the only answer. Indeed, worrying about things later seems to accompany the energies of this week. Philosophical attitudes and higher thoughts abound now, which will again protect you from having to think of more mundane financial concerns.

The idealism of the Week of Expansiveness is unmistakable. Critical thinking and negative ideas may not get a very enthusiastic reception at this time. And it is important to realize that optimistic thinking can have a positive impact on the outcome of any projects we may be engaged in now. The only thing which is required of us is wholehearted involvement, since projects that we approach halfheartedly do not carry much chance of success. As far as fate and free will are concerned, this is a week in which strong willpower can overcome even the most powerful restrictions which destiny imposes. Indeed, it was Beethoven, born in this week, who said, "I will take Fate by the throat." Although such arrogance is not advised for mere mortals, we can all strive to implement our grand visions and to believe in our modest abilities to affect the outcome positively. Finally, as always, it behooves us to tune in to God or another source of universal inspiration and to ask for guidance, support, and above all the power to see our projects through.

The Personology of People Born in the Week of Expansiveness

It is the big picture and the large gesture which characterize these idealistic individuals. Generous to an extreme, they are not likely to get bogged down in pettiness or hung up on details. Because they are action-oriented, they must be careful not to arouse opposition with their forcefulness. Others may have to take a hard line with them, since people born in the Week of Expansiveness will only show respect for those who can stand up to them. Putting their prodigious energies in the service of a cause can have a positive outcome as long as they remain realistic.

Annual Events That Occur During the Week of Expansiveness

December 12: Independence Day in Kenya
December 13: Feast of Lights in Sweden
December 15: Bill of Rights Day

Major Historical Events That Have Happened During the Week of Expansiveness

December 11, 1936: Edward VIII abdicates to marry Wallace Simpson
December 12, 1901: First transatlantic radio transmission by Marconi
December 13, 1862: Lee defeats Union army at Fredericksburg
December 14, 1911: Roald Amundsen is first to reach South Pole
December 15, 1989: Bulgarians demand end to communist rule
December 16, 1773: Boston Tea Party
December 17, 1903: Wright brothers make first powered flight
December 18, 1865: Thirteenth amendment abolishes slavery

Famous People Born During the Week of Expansiveness

Ludwig van Beethoven, Steven Spielberg, Paracelsus, Frank Sinatra, Dionne Warwick, Liv Ullmann, Alexandr Solzhenitsyn, Teri Garr, Michael Ovitz, Margaret Mead, Helen Frankenthaler, Gustave Flaubert, Carlo Ponti, Emerson Fittipaldi, J. Paul Getty, Muriel Rukeyser, Arantxa Sanchez Vicario, Fiorello La Guardia, Dick Van Dyke, Arthur C. Clarke

Birthdays Especially Affected During the Week of Expansiveness

If you are born in the Week of Expansiveness (December 11–18), the Week of Social Betterment (April 11–18), or the Week of Leadership (August 11–18) your energies blend well with those of this week. Results should be obtained with little effort on your part.

Week of Expansiveness people find that their idealistic and generous attitudes are fully appreciated. Week of Social Betterment people can fully implement their dreams and visions. Week of Leadership people will be appreciated by others for their care and interest.

If you are born in the Week of Dances and Dreams (March 11–18), the Week of Exploration (June 11–18), or the Week of the Literal (September 11–18) you will face problems and challenges during this week. You will have to work harder to achieve your goals.

Week of Dances and Dreams people may be bewildered when things don't work out; they need to listen to others more carefully. Week of exploration people need to back off a bit in their eagerness to help. Week of the Literal people should drop their critical attitudes and think more positively.

Fall Personology Snapshot

SEPTEMBER 24 Spirited, with active imaginations, people born on September 24 love to wander. Natural travelers, they may have problems settling down, and that may leave them vulnerable to loneliness.

SEPTEMBER 25 Skilled communicators, those born on September 25 work to effect positive changes in society. Dedicated to those around them, they are often self-effacing and may have difficulties opening up to others.

SEPTEMBER 26 Patient and persevering, those born on September 26 work very hard to get what they want. Positive people not easily deterred from their goals, they must nevertheless be careful that determination does not lead to neurotic behavior.

SEPTEMBER 27 Innovative and creative, people born on September 27 are interested in puzzles and paradoxes. Confident on the outside, and often successful, they may be insecure and have difficulty dealing with failure.

SEPTEMBER 28 Often the center of attention, September 28 people are enchanting and attractive. Lovers of excitement, they tend to get bored quickly and give up too easily, especially where mundane tasks are involved.

SEPTEMBER 29 September 29 people are skilled in management and organization and are often integral to the success of others. Calm on the outside, they are often surrounded by tumult and may easily become insecure about their own worth.

SEPTEMBER 30 Inquisitive and involved, those born on September 30 excel at finding the truth and the correct way to convey it to others. Always searching, they must be careful to find balance and to accept that there are things in life that cannot be explained.

OCTOBER 1 Dignified and intelligent, those born on October 1 have a positive outlook that often leads to success. Confident in their work, they tend to vacillate in their personal lives and are prone to crises.

OCTOBER 2 Charismatic and expressive, those born on October 2 often surprise others with their unfailing ability to communicate their ideas in a straightforward manner. Enthusiastic, they are sometimes too blunt and have to watch that their tongues don't get them into trouble.

OCTOBER 3 Acutely aware of social trends, those born on October 3 also have an appreciation of tradition and know how to combine the two successfully. Superficiality may be a trap for them, though, and they must work hard to stay on their true course.

OCTOBER 4 People born on October 4 are independent and direct and like to lead their lives according to their own code. Innovative and hardworking, they may be stubbornly self-sufficient and often unable to yield to authority.

OCTOBER 5 Focused on justice, those born on October 5 seek to expose corruption and oppression and to enlist others to join them in their campaigns. Convincing and proud, they should take care that their confidence doesn't turn to arrogance.

OCTOBER 6 Lively and outgoing, those born on October 6 enjoy life and do their best to shorten routine jobs in order to make time for fun activities. Fond of comfort, they have to work hard to maintain good habits and avoid self-indulgence.

OCTOBER 7 Dedicated to their ideals, October 7 people often strive for power in order to work toward their idea of how society should be structured. Often on the lookout for leadership roles, they must take care that their ambition doesn't cause conflict.

OCTOBER 8 Creative and romantic, those born on October 8 are free spirits who love adventure and give all they have in order to find true love. Fond of their fantasies, they have to be careful not to become withdrawn or unrealistic.

OCTOBER 9 Those born on October 9 are insightful and compassionate and possess the ability to understand what is going on around them. Keenly appreciative of the trials and triumphs of others, they nevertheless may lack insight into their own lives.

OCTOBER 10 Dependable and diligent, those born on October 10 are exceptional managers, especially with money. Though honest themselves, they often do not trust others and may find it difficult to open up.

OCTOBER 11 Loyal and dependable, those born on October 11 have a strong sense of social responsibility and can be trusted to help others. They sometimes have difficulty finding the right career, however, and need to push themselves to try new things.

OCTOBER 12 Social and refined, October 12 people like to be noticed and respected. Often in the spotlight, they need to remember not to neglect the feelings and needs of others, especially in their private lives.

OCTOBER 13 Determined and serious, October 13 people are career oriented and often employ a tough demeanor to help them reach their professional goals. Compassionate and kind to their loved ones, they would help themselves by being more forgiving of their colleagues.

OCTOBER 14 Patient and reserved, those born on October 14 recognize the importance of moderation in their lives and work hard to stay balanced. Overly careful, they must learn when to take a chance in order to attain success.

OCTOBER 15 Knowledgeable, appealing, and strong, those born on October 15 have great influence on those around them. Often tempted to show off their talents, they must learn to be contented with quiet respect.

OCTOBER 16 Intelligent and objective, those born on October 16 are judgmental but fair. Good at determining value and assessing character, they should nevertheless keep in mind that objectivity can sometimes lead to detachment.

OCTOBER 17 Daring and brave, people born on October 17 lead balanced lives despite their love of risk-taking. Success may lead them to become reckless, however, and they would do well to understand the lessons of their setbacks.

OCTOBER 18 Natural born leaders, those born on October 18 are great at inspiring confidence and at striking a balance between ambition and humility. Proud and generally self-assured, they need to realize that they do not always have to hide their feelings.

OCTOBER 19 Active and individualistic, October 19 people liven up their surroundings with their outgoing natures. Animated, they can also be opinionated and inflexible and must work not to seek confrontation.

OCTOBER 20 Creative and energetic, those born on October 20 are acutely aware of the trends of their time, though they may not always approve of them. Hardworking in their hobbies, they do best when they apply some of the same diligence and creativity to their careers.

OCTOBER 21 Unique and appealing, those born on October 21 manage to fit in well at work even though they are different from most people. Private affairs are more of a struggle for them, however, and they often have trouble truly connecting.

OCTOBER 22 Attractive and seductive, those born on October 22 nevertheless have great control over their emotions. Charismatic and usually very popular, they still need to remember that not everyone is charmed by them.

OCTOBER 23 Spontaneous, natural, and quick-witted, those born on October 23 are great improvisers. Often taken by impulse, they can have trouble achieving balance in their lives and may become possessive of things they are frightened of losing.

OCTOBER 24 Combining drama and attentiveness, October 24 people have personalities that draw attention to their actions. They often have difficult private lives, however, as they tend to put too much energy into work while ignoring their loved ones.

OCTOBER 25 Imaginative people, those born on October 25 will be incredibly successful if they can find the right method to express their ideas. Though dependable, they are sometimes too easily satisfied and so don't reach their full potential.

OCTOBER 26 Talented in development and restructuring, those born on October 26 are intelligent people who excel when leading a group. Not always altruistic, they need to acknowledge (if only to themselves) that some acts are undertaken for their own gratification.

OCTOBER 27 Dynamic and influential, those born on October 27 are driven to find success for themselves and their loved ones. Extremely determined, they can become destructive when they fail and must learn to rely on friends for support.

OCTOBER 28 Intelligent and systematic, those born on October 28 are thorough and organized in all their endeavors. Efficient in their methods, they must learn to be spontaneous or else risk becoming compulsive.

OCTOBER 29 Innovative and diligent, October 29 people like to research and prepare before they implement new ideas. Often insecure in their personal lives, they may be suspicious, and overly attached to those they trust.

OCTOBER 30 The highly capable individuals born on October 30 bring managerial skills to all areas of their lives, personal and professional. They must beware of getting bogged down in details and losing sight of the big picture.

OCTOBER 31 Meticulous and incisive, those born on October 31 are very good at concentrating on the task at hand. Practical and protective, they must avoid letting trivial concerns throw them off course.

NOVEMBER 1 Dedicated and energetic, those born on November 1 will be very successful once they find a profession that challenges and excites them. Daring, they must be careful of their desire for danger, as it may eventually catch up with them.

NOVEMBER 2 Fated to undergo important personal changes, November 2 people have tremendous power over everything around them. Sometimes unaware of how much influence they have, they must be conscious of directing it in an ethical way.

NOVEMBER 3 Persistent and strong, those born on November 3 are constantly trying to improve their own status both through personal achievement and defeat of others. They tend to make fierce enemies, though, and their tactics can be ruthless.

NOVEMBER 4 Quiet, with a conservative demeanor, November 4 people do not immediately let on how stimulating and charming they can be. Interested in the lives of others, they need to remember that interest can sometimes lead to their being overly controlling.

NOVEMBER 5 Grounded and honest, those born on November 5 tend to exemplify the times in which they live. Candid and sincere, they enjoy exposing lies, even when other people think of them as interfering.

NOVEMBER 6 Invigorating and confident, with an energy that comes from a deep source, November 6 people stimulate all those around them. Tactful in showing others their faults, they must nevertheless remember that the truth can be upsetting.

NOVEMBER 7 Adventurous and inquisitive, with a deeply rooted desire for discovery, those born on November 7 lead exciting lives. They are often impatient with daily routines, however, and must learn that balance is the key to fulfillment.

NOVEMBER 8 The dedicated individuals born on November 8 are interested in exploring the limits of human nature. Appearing to conform on the surface, they are often consumed with their explorations, which may cause them to push away the people they love.

NOVEMBER 9 Sensuous and exciting, November 9 people enjoy discovery and pondering philosophical questions. Often impetuous, they will find life more rewarding if they can resist the temptation to surrender to the moment.

NOVEMBER 10 Knowledgeable and patient, those born on November 10 take time to mature and transform into the people they are meant to be. Sluggish at times, they must work to maintain their motivation to continue their growth.

NOVEMBER 11 Talented organizers, November 11 people do well when in charge of a unit or group, as they are also very protective. Reflective and probing, their inner struggles may lead them to be both troubled and distant.

NOVEMBER 12 Unusual and talented, November 12 people are able to perform what appear to be miracles. Often admired by others, they must take care not to let their ego get in the way of their personal fulfillment.

NOVEMBER 13 Outspoken individuals who attract attention, November 13 people have the ability to stir up controversy with their commentaries. Rebellious and striving only for justice, they would nevertheless benefit from a more even temper.

NOVEMBER 14 Adventurous and committed, those born on November 14 desire to explore their surroundings and to let others know their beliefs on society. Motivated to express their morality, they are sometimes overly direct and blunt.

NOVEMBER 15 Resolute and strong, those born on November 15 do not back down from a challenge. Steadfast, always ready to defend their beliefs, they are sometimes volatile and unyielding.

NOVEMBER 16 Naturally commanding and intelligent, November 16 people do well in leadership positions, as they handle most situations well. Outwardly directed and good at guiding others, they are often not comfortable being by themselves.

NOVEMBER 17 Fair and evenhanded, those born on November 17 are often called upon to mediate the conflicts of others. Helpful and kind, they must nevertheless be careful not to impose their ideals in every situation.

NOVEMBER 18 Energetic and emotional, November 18 people appear extremely self-controlled. Composure is sometimes difficult for them, though, and they don't always do well in stressful situations.

NOVEMBER 19 Convincing and driven by the possibilities of change, those born on November 19 dedicate themselves to identifying problems and coming up with solutions. Independent, they may be resistant to established ideas and overly preoccupied with their projects.

NOVEMBER 20 Extremely loyal and idealistic, November 20 people are dedicated to their beliefs and would fight before compromising. Sometimes overly contentious, they have to work not to become compulsive.

NOVEMBER 21 Sophisticated individuals, November 21 people look to update established traditions without losing the spirit of that ideal. Not given to introspection, they would do well to spend some time studying themselves, as they will never be truly happy until they know themselves.

NOVEMBER 22 Confident and free, those born on November 22 make their own rules and follow their own ideas. Lovers of challenge, they often construct their own, which may lead them into difficulty.

NOVEMBER 23 Intelligent, loyal, and dogmatic, those born on November 23 take any opportunity to voice their opinions. Confrontational, they have problems with authority that may lead them to physical harm.

NOVEMBER 24 Spirited and social, those born on November 24 put a great deal of effort into their work and want to be appreciated. Loyal friends, they make fierce enemies and tend to be argumentative.

NOVEMBER 25 Capable, practical, and strong, November 25 people know how to use their abundant energy so that they will have enough left for that final push. Strongly moral, they must be careful not to impose their ideas on those who disagree with them.

NOVEMBER 26 Philosophical and imaginative, November 26 people are more concerned with the quality of their work than with awards. Independent idealists, their need for freedom can make them reluctant to commit.

NOVEMBER 27 Surrounded by tumult, those born on November 27 are impulsive and fun-loving. Sometimes impatient, they have to be careful not to adopt a "live now, pay later" attitude which will get them into trouble.

NOVEMBER 28 Intellectual and complex, November 28 people often seek arguments in order to fight against generalizations. Prone to contradictions, they would do well to cultivate consistency and balance.

NOVEMBER 29 Feisty and truthful, those born on November 29 are very good at keeping others honest and at bringing troubling issues to the fore. Often unequivocal, they need to learn to be more diplomatic with their methods.

NOVEMBER 30 Dedicated and formidable, November 30 people put an incredible amount of thought into their actions. Often misunderstood and sometimes judgmental, they would benefit from learning to accept criticism themselves.

DECEMBER 1 Outspoken and fearless, December 1 people use humor to convince others of their ideals. Strong-minded, they often ignore the reactions of others and don't realize when they have gone too far.

DECEMBER 2 Tenacious and authoritative, those born on December 2 often surprise people with their influence, even though they may not be physically imposing. Candid, they may sometimes be tactless in their judgment of others.

DECEMBER 3 Determined innovators, not concerned with fame or money, December 3 people can work through any obstacle to realize their private goals. Hardworking, they need to understand that they don't always have to hide their feelings and dreams.

DECEMBER 4 Elegance and strength combine in those born on December 4 to allow them to reach their lofty goals. Their determination can often be ruthless, however, and they need to be more forgiving of those who don't share their resolve.

DECEMBER 5 Those born on December 5 are confident in their abilities and seek to learn through experience. Optimistic and self-assured, their certainty may at times be misplaced, and this may prompt them to set unrealistic goals.

DECEMBER 6 Analytical and directed, the organizational skills of December 6 people lead them to uncover the best in any situation. Practical and expressive, they must be careful not to become overbearing.

DECEMBER 7 Eccentric and independent, December 7 people are tremendously imaginative. Often wildly unique, they may nevertheless not understand that they are unusual, and this may cause them to become with-drawn.

DECEMBER 8 Those born on December 8 are committed and steadfast, giving everything they have to a worthy person or profession. Outwardly sociable and full of life, they can be overly introspective and may become disturbed.

DECEMBER 9 Flashy and fun, December 9 people are creative and love being the center of attention. Imaginative, they may be controlled by their fantasies and have to work hard to direct their energies.

DECEMBER 10 Sensitive and devoted, those born on December 10 are skilled communicators and spirited individualists. Fun-loving practical jokers, they are also given to introspection and risk becoming overly withdrawn.

DECEMBER 11 Those born on December 11 combine strong mental prowess with a strong physical presence. Very influential, they often do not realize the extent of their authority and must work hard not to become controlling.

DECEMBER 12 Perceptive and intelligent, those born on December 12 have an unusual ability to read the hidden signals of others. Insightful witnesses, they must nevertheless learn that there are times when their observations should not be shared.

DECEMBER 13 Progressive yet restrained, those born on December 13 can reach any goal, large or small. Unpredictable, they can often be unyielding and must learn that compromise is often the only way out.

DECEMBER 14 Physically confident and revealing of their bodies, those born on December 14 are daring and unpredictable. Eager to display their animal nature, they tend to keep their emotional secrets locked up, and this can make them moody and lonely.

DECEMBER 15 Those born on December 15 like to craft big dreams and often reach them through their understanding of authority. Optimistic and exceptionally ambitious, they can also be possessive and unrealistic.

DECEMBER 16 Incredible vision and creativity distinguish those born on December 16. Driven to achieve a high state of spiritual awareness, they are sometimes cut off from the more mundane aspects of existence.

DECEMBER 17 Practical and pragmatic, those born on December 17 are very results oriented. Good at taking action, they are not so good at taking risks and need to learn to move away from routine in order to be truly satisfied.

DECEMBER 18 Persevering and ambitious, December 18 people will do anything in order to realize their grand plans. Determined, they often become frustrated with mundane problems and must work to maintain flexibility.

DECEMBER 19 Brave and strong, December 19 people overcome their difficulties through intense personal struggle. Direct, they are sometimes harsh in their reactions and need to remember that at times a softer face is called for.

DECEMBER 20 Preferring initiation to management, those born on December 20 like to generate new ideas. Always on the lookout for the next big thing, they need to understand that constant motion is no substitute for balance.

Winter

If spring is a time for new beginnings, summer an occasion for fruition, fall a period of maintenance, then winter is a time for evaluation, a time to review what we have accomplished during the past seasons and consider what we would like to achieve in the months ahead. We may dread winter for its extreme hardships of freezing temperatures and difficult weather, but we also appreciate its pristine snowfalls, cozy days indoors, and the feeling of invigoration that the colder months bring. Most important, however, we appreciate the way in which winter announces that the time has come to think of making plans for setting the whole cycle in motion again.

Winter begins with the winter solstice, which usually occurs on December 21, when days are shortest and nights longest. The sun seems to lessen its life-giving influence during the winter period, and the pull of the dark powerful forces generated from deep within the unconscious wield their strongest force at this time of year. Life becomes more private and withdrawn during the winter months, and we must come to grips objectively with the cold, hard facts of existence. Traditionally a time of prophecy and metaphysical influence, winter was the time when sightings were taken at Stonehenge to determine the exact occurrence of the solstice.

Although the earth seems dead and barren at this time, strong forces are at work underground. As Rudolph Steiner has pointed out, the powers of the planet Saturn are most active under the soil, preparing and transforming the ground in readiness for spring plantings. Where the magic of the summer solstice is apparent in a rich enchantment of fecundity, the charm of the winter solstice is hidden, and it is only revealed through study and miraculous revelations.

Christmas and New Year's Eve dominate the beginning of the winter season. Holiday spirits abound, and with them the hope for a better year ahead. Children recognize this as their time; Christmas is, after all, the traditional time for Santa's visit and the giving of gifts. And yet, the relationship between the pagan tree and the birth of the Christ child seem contradictory. Are we dealing here with a pagan or a Christian celebration? The answer is both, since this crucial time of year has served many purposes for differing ideologies and world views.

The key concept for the winter season is that of evaluation. The traditional act of making New Year's resolutions is very much part of this process. The faculties of intuition, feeling, and sensation are no longer dominant. Thought takes over in the winter months. And in the evaluation of what has gone before and the planning for what lies ahead, we must push our mental processes and our logical and pragmatic outlooks to the limit in developing a coherent course of action. We are given time for reflection now, because of the holidays and the weather conditions that keep us indoors. However, those who love winter sports will find that a sports vacation (skiing, skating, snowboarding) also offers a wonderful opportunity for reflection and rejuvenation.

Personology teaches a coincidence of the yearly cycle of nature with that of the human life and the zodiac. Winter thus also symbolizes the fourth and last twenty-one-year period of human life, from age sixty-three to eighty-four years of age, and of the tenth, eleventh, and twelfth signs of the zodiac: Capricorn, Aquarius, and Pisces. At the age of sixty-three many of us are preparing for, or already beginning, our retirement, and that can be viewed with much joy and relief. Experiencing the reward of finally having free time to do what we want day-to-day—spend time with grandchildren, take trips, catch up on reading, rest, and relaxation—may at last be possible. The events likely to occur in the signs of Capricorn, Aquarius, and Pisces, and the proper conduct during these signs, stress the character of quietude and inner reflection in the winter season to which they correspond. Thinking individuals benefit from contact with sensuous and intuitive people who can bring pleasure and a vivid subjectivity to their more mental orientation. The signs of Capricorn, Aquarius, and Pisces state as their mottoes, "I master," "I universalize," and "I believe."

Because Capricorn, Aquarius, and Pisces are ruled by the heavy planets Saturn, Uranus, and Neptune, which move very slowly and have far-reaching effects on mankind over long periods of time, their forces represent the most advanced concepts of the whole year or lifetime. The strong and wise pragmatism of Capricorn is transformed into the high idealism of Aquarius, and finally into the religious depths of Pisces, at the end of which we are prepared to merge our individual energies with those of the cosmos, prior to a new rebirth. When the cycle begins again in Aries with the onset of spring, death is revealed as an illusion. The eternal movement into yet another cycle here on Earth is mirrored symbolically both in the cosmos and the lifetime of mankind, creating a perfect correspondence between nature, the zodiac, and human development.

The Winter Personology Periods:
December 21 to March 21

The Weeks

The season of winter lasts from the winter solstice of December 21 to the spring equinox of March 21. It is composed of the three astrological signs of Capricorn (December 22–January 20), Aquarius (January 21–February 19), and Pisces (February 20–March 20). This fourth quarter of the year is further subdivided by personology into the following "weeks" or personology periods:

Sagittarius-Capricorn Cusp: The Cusp of Prophecy (December 19–25)
Capricorn I: The Week of Rule (December 26–January 2)
Capricorn II: The Week of Determination (January 3–9)
Capricorn III: The Week of Dominance (January 10–16)

Capricorn-Aquarius Cusp: The Cusp of Mystery, Violence, and Imagination (January 17–22)

Aquarius I: The Week of Intelligence (January 23–30)

Aquarius II: The Week of Youth and Ease (January 31–February 7)

Aquarius III: The Week of Acceptance (February 8–15)

Aquarius-Pisces Cusp: The Cusp of Sensitivity (February 16–22)

Pisces I: The Week of Spirit (February 23–March 2)

Pisces II: The Week of Isolation (March 3–10)

Pisces III: The Week of Dances and Dreams (March 11–18)

Pisces-Aries Cusp: The Cusp of Rebirth (March 19–24)

The Cusps

As throughout the rest of the personological year, the winter quadrant is given structure by the cusps between the astrological signs. Demarcating the winter, at its beginning we find the winter solstice, known in personology as the Cusp of Prophecy, and at its end the spring equinox, the Cusp of Rebirth. At monthly intervals between these two power points we find the Cusp of Mystery, Violence, and Imagination (between Capricorn and Aquarius) and the Cusp of Sensitivity (between the signs of Aquarius and Pisces). These four cusps: Prophecy; Mystery, Violence, and Imagination; Sensitivity; and Rebirth characterize the season of winter as fully as the signs of Capricorn, Aquarius, and Pisces, but in a more human sense.

The Cusp of Prophecy

DECEMBER 19–25

The deepest and darkest point of the year, the Cusp of Prophecy has always been a highly significant time for the Celts and other early tribes and nations. Supernatural phenomena are so commonplace around this time that their presence is barely remarkable. Children are enchanted by the physical presence of a white-bearded man who can fly around the world in a magic sleigh and deliver presents individually to every child. Adults are caught up in the Christmas rush and desperate that all their plans turn out right. Yet throughout this activity we sense a stillness here, unmatched in the rest of the year. A carol like "Silent Night" underlines this feeling of holiness and awe.

Perhaps the key to the dichotomy found here between activity and stillness is to be found in the two planets that rule this cusp: Jupiter (the ruler of Sagittarius) and Saturn (the ruler of Capricorn). The former symbolizes jollity and enthusiasm, the latter seriousness and practicality. Saturn can be seen as the Capricorn father, seriously giving advice to his Jupiterian, independent, and feisty Sagittarius son. Earth-fire energies are also at work here, with Capricorn (earth sign) merging with Sagittarius (fire sign). A Christmas tree covered with lights can be seen as a truly graphic representation of earth and fire.

The Cusp of Prophecy is of course dominated by the Christmas holiday, but to find its true significance we must dig deeper. Because it also marks the end of the long nights and the beginning of the cycle of longer days, the Cusp of Prophecy can be seen as a beacon of hope, while at the same time representing the ultimate death of things growing in nature. From now on the days will get progressively longer and more sunlight will come into our lives. This is a real turning point in the year, perhaps the most important one. We now look unmistakably toward the future as we begin to prepare our New Year's resolutions, which will be made the following week. The expression of positive prophecy here asserts man's strength to triumph over the powers of darkness and to light up the world with joy over the birth of the son of God. It thus becomes a time of love and of hope. This is just the opposite of the energy of the cusp of the summer solstice, whose energy speaks more of the magic of romance. This love is a religious love of all mankind for each other, and as such anticipates the coming of Aquarius in January, the sign of universal brotherhood.

Mankind celebrates its universal heritage during the Cusp of Prophecy, and prides itself on its achievements during the year. Prayer and celebration are both important here, for we give thanks to God for having made it all possible. Unfortunately, religious aspects of Christmas are sometimes downplayed in the commercial rush. Nevertheless, the birth of a world avatar, a savior, is being celebrated here, and indirectly the birth of all avatars of all religious faiths and spiritual movements. Thus, the energies of this week are truly transcendental, and reach to the farthest confines of the universe.

The Personology of People Born on the Cusp of Prophecy

Powerful in their silence, those born on this cusp can make their feelings known without words. Their innate expressiveness comes from a very deep place, and so they often give the impression of being weighty individuals. Born at the darkest time of the year, those born on this cusp know something about the serious aspects of life. Yet they love to have fun, too, and often choose friends, mates, and lovers of a much lighter disposition. The sensuality of these highly intuitive individuals is marked, and they are capable of binding others to themselves magnetically.

Annual Events That Occur on the Cusp of Prophecy

December 21: Winter solstice (shortest day and longest night in the
    northern hemisphere)
            Forefathers Day
December 24: Christmas Eve
December 25: Christmas Day

Major Historical Events That Have Happened on the Cusp of Prophecy

December 19, 1991: Gorbachev resigns as president of the USSR
December 20, 1802: Louisiana purchase made by United States from France
December 21, 1988: Pan Am jet crashes at Lockerbie, Scotland

December 22, 1989: Romanian dictator Ceausescu overthrown
December 23, 1922: First entertainment radio broadcasts by BBC
December 24, 1943: Eisenhower appointed head of European invasion
December 25, A.D. 800: Charlemagne crowned emperor by the pope

Famous People Born on the Cusp of Prophecy

Joseph Stalin, Jane Fonda, Uri Geller, Rod Serling, Michel de Nostradamus, Florence Griffith Joyner, Joseph Smith, Frank Zappa, Edith Piaf, Richard Leakey, Ava Gardner, Clara Barton, Annie Lennox, Anwar Sadat, Giacomo Puccini, Mitsuko Uchida, Robert Bly, Cicely Tyson, Jean Genet, Lady Bird Johnson

Birthdays Especially Affected on the Cusp of Prophecy

If you are born on the Cusp of Prophecy (December 19–25), the Cusp of Power (April 19–24), or the Cusp of Exposure (August 19–25) your energies blend well with those of this week. Results should be obtained with little effort on your part.

Cusp of Prophecy people can give full rein to their lighter side and have plenty of Christmas fun. Cusp of Power people enjoy giving Christmas presents to one and all in great abundance. Cusp of Exposure people like being able to reveal their true feelings of joy without feeling threatened.

If you are born on the Cusp of Rebirth (March 19–24), the Cusp of Magic (June 19–24), or the Cusp of Beauty (September 19–24) you will face problems and challenges during this week. You will have to work harder to achieve your goals.

Cusp of Rebirth people should try to forget their troubles by joining in the Christmas spirit. Cusp of Magic people must not get emotionally fixated on one person but share affection and happiness with a larger circle. Cusp of Beauty people will have to pay some attention to their outlay for Christmas presents to avoid disaster later.

The Week of Rule

There is definitely a conservative and traditional bent during the Week of Rule. No matter how riotous a New Year's celebration, there exists an undercurrent of seriousness that urges us to correct our past mistakes, clean up our act, and prepare for the new year ahead. Too often, New Year's Eve parties and celebrations have a tendency to spin out of control; but the spectacle of thousands, even millions, celebrating together their common joy and enthusiasm, in a nondiscriminatory and inclusive manner, stressing friendship rather than hostility, is an amazing sight each year.

In order to share in the very best this week has to offer, we would do well to take on additional responsibilities, both personal and social. Making sure that no one is left out or forgotten during the holiday celebrations is extremely important, for a start. And don't hesitate to jump in and lend a hand with the most menial of jobs, including post–New Year's Eve cleanup. Making sure that even the most socially disadvantaged individuals in our immediate environment have what they need to truly celebrate—and even contributing to charities that help distribute food and clothing— can be extremely rewarding at this time of the year.

If friends are lackadaisical in these respects, or downright unwilling to help, it may be necessary to take the lead to galvanize a social group into action. In other words, even people who have never held leadership positions may have to assume them ad hoc, if such interventions are required. Thus, leading by default we may find it necessary to assume command, at least for the time being. Not infrequently, the taste for true leadership acquired during the Week of Rule may reassert itself regularly in the future, creating a new and most useful set of abilities. Be careful not to get carried away with power, or to become an outright dictator. Try to remain effective. Don't elicit opposition, antagonism, or resentment from others.

Acquiring a healthy respect for law is quite possible during the Week of Rule. Even rebellious individuals may do a complete turnaround now and proclaim the values of home and country. They may even show little sympathy for transgressors at this time, except perhaps to extend pardons to those who have been unjustly convicted or imprisoned. Arguing for the rights of man is an activity most appropriate for the Week of Rule, and expresses both a belief in justice and a need to fight for the rights of the underdog.

Some of us will have to fight to become more open and accepting during this week, since despite the holiday spirit the imposition of highly moral or even prejudiced ideas (possibly expressing a religious bias) is an ever-present danger. Too many acts of a violent and unforgiving nature have been committed during this time, and were wrapped in the holy mantle of patriotism or creed in order to justify them. We would do well to examine the dogmatic tendencies in ourselves during this time, and to make sure that they don't gain the upper hand.

The Personology of People Born in the Week of Rule

These dominant individuals rarely leave any doubt as to who is in control. Authoritarian by nature, those born in this week are comfortable with assuming a leadership role in any family or professional organization. Yet their greatest talents emerge when working alone, for they can accomplish far more when they are not distracted by the needs and wishes of others. Pragmatists, they are open to almost any approach that produces results. They are very aware of society's rules, but they also know how to get around them. On the other hand, they set up strict rules for themselves which they rarely or never transgress.

Annual Events That Occur During the Week of Rule

December 31: New Year's Eve
January 1: New Year's Day

Major Historical Events That Have Happened During the Week of Rule

December 26, 1908: Jack Johnson wins heavyweight boxing title

December 27, 1831: HMS *Beagle* sets sail with Charles Darwin aboard

December 28, 1908: Huge earthquake destroys Messina, Sicily

December 29, 1170: Murder of Thomas à Becket in Canterbury Cathedral

December 30, 1916: Rasputin murdered by poison, shooting, and drowning

December 31, 1891: U.S. government opens Ellis Island as an immigration center

January 1, 1959: Cuba's Castro overthrows dictator Batista

January 2, 1492: Muslim stronghold Grenada falls to Spain's Isabella

Famous People Born During the Week of Rule

Denzel Washington, Pablo Casals, Mary Tyler Moore, Tracey Ullman, Henri Matisse, Marlene Dietrich, Henry Miller, Mao Tse Tung, Ted Danson, Maggie Smith, Gerard Depardieu, John Denver, Paul Revere, Louis Pasteur, Elizabeth Arden, E. M. Forster, Isaac Asimov, Rudyard Kipling

Birthdays Especially Affected During the Week of Rule

If you are born in the Week of Rule (December 26–January 2), the Week of Manifestation (April 25–May 2), or the Week of Structure (August 26–September 2) your energies blend well with those of this week. Results should be obtained with little effort on your part.

Week of Rule people inevitably will forget their seriousness in tumultuous New Year's Eve celebrations. Week of Manifestation people can succeed in making realistic and highly responsible new year's resolutions. Week of Structure people enjoy quiet celebrations of the new year with a few family members or friends.

If you are born in the Week of Curiosity (March 25–April 2), the Week of Empathy (June 25–July 2), or the Week of Perfection (September 25–October 2) you will face problems and challenges during this week. You will have to work harder to achieve your goals.

Week of Curiosity people must be aware of accidents around the new year, particularly involving cars. Week of Empathy people will have to protect themselves from becoming the prey of needy individuals. Week of Perfection people will have to pay for past mistakes unless they make resolutions to change in the coming year.

✺

The Week of Determination

JANUARY 3–9

This is the week to forge ahead. Our professional lives need attention now, and the energies of this week favor a push toward commercial success. Single-mindedness and a sense of purpose are vitally important.

Ambition is the crucial question here. We all know how destructive drives can push us to succeed at any cost—driving ourselves over the edge, sacrificing our personal life, stepping on others to get to the top, and finally doing almost anything to stay there. Yet, unless we give it our best shot and go for it without reservation, we may fall short of what we are capable of in the worldly sphere and never fully realize the best we have to offer the world.

Daring to fail is extremely important. Sitting at home and dreaming or planning becomes counterproductive after a while, for only in action can our dreams be realized. Switching over into an active mode involves taking risks, and with risk comes the whole question of giving up what we already have—or losing it. Even further, action risks failure, and we might convince ourselves that by sitting at home we are keeping ourselves from failing. However, it also could be argued that we are already admitting failure by sitting out the big game on the sidelines of life's struggles.

The Week of Determination is the perfect time for getting a résumé together. We should all take this time to let others know what we have done and what we are capable of. The Week of Determination is a good time to consider interviewing for a more advantageous position or to rise in the hierarchy of an existing professional structure. For those of us who find that no further progress is possible in our own fields, now is the time to at least consider a change in career. Don't give up until every avenue has been explored.

Some people are cut out for independent work, others are not. The same goes for entrepreneurial endeavors, including partnerships. People who have worked a steady job for their whole lives and are suffering from stagnation or lack of appreciation could well find this the right week to consider going off on their own, professionally speaking. Consulting books on the subject and speaking to friends and family about it can be useful in directing our energies. Risk-taking is involved here, and we would all do well to remember how important it is to find the courage to give up the known for the unknown.

Now that the New Year's celebration is over, the times favor giving immediate direction to our careers. We should all try to harness the energies of the Week of Determination, and to not let weeks drag by before taking action. Some people will be able to simply implement the New Year's resolutions made a week or two earlier; others may have to push themselves to implement the binding resolutions that demand perseverance in the coming months. At any rate, the energies of this week strongly favor taking a stand and making a commitment. Losing this chance could well result in sinking into the doldrums.

The Personology of People Born in the Week of Determination

Among the most ambitious individuals of the year, those born in this week strive to rise in their professional and social group. Even when their talents are quite modest, those born during the Week of Determination know how to push themselves to the limit, often guaranteeing success. The danger, of course, is that they may push themselves too hard and too fast, causing a stressful situation which ultimately threatens them with burnout. People born during this week face the important personal challenges in learning to recognize their limitations and to relax. They must also touch base with their moral precepts to keep from going off in a wrong direction. Their talents are often employed best in following idealistic pursuits.

Annual Events That Occur During the Week of Determination

January 5: Twelfth Night
January 6: Epiphany
January 8: Jackson Day
January 9: Balloon Ascension Day

Major Historical Events That Have Happened During the Week of Determination

January 3, 1959: Alaska admitted as forty-ninth U.S. state
January 4, 1948: Burma becomes independent of British Commonwealth
January 5, 1968: Alexander Dubcek becomes head of Czechoslovakia
January 6, 1945: German attempt to break through Allied lines fails in Battle of the Bulge
January 7, 1789: George Washington elected first president of the United States
January 8, 1959: General de Gaulle becomes president of France
January 9, 1799: Income tax introduced in Great Britain

Famous People Born During the Week of Determination

Richard Nixon, Alvin Ailey, Simone de Beauvoir, Elvis Presley, Nancy Lopez, Shirley Bassey, J. R. R. Tolkien, Mel Gibson, Zora Neale Hurston, Charles Addams, Earl Scruggs, Stephen Stills, Kahlil Gibran, William Peter Blatty, Isaac Newton, Stephen Hawking, Victoria Principal, Paramahansa Yogananda, Diane Keaton, Crystal Gayle

Birthdays Especially Affected During the Week of Determination

If you are born in the Week of Determination (January 3–9), the Week of Study (May 3–10), or the Week of the Puzzle (September 3–10) your energies blend well with those of this week. Results should be obtained with little effort on your part.

Week of Determination people won't let any grass grow under their feet before beginning their drive to success in the new year. Week of Study people will need a bit more time for planning before shifting into high gear in their new year's projects. Week of the Puzzle people will no doubt withdraw from the rat race and spend time getting their acts together.

If you are born in the Week of Success (April 3–10), the Week of Unconventionality (July 3–10), or the Week of Socialization (October 3–10) you will face problems and challenges during this week. You will have to work harder to achieve your goals.

Week of Success people run the danger of driving themselves too hard and making a mess of their personal lives. Week of Unconventionality people need to listen carefully to what their employers and clients want to avoid going off track. Week of Socialization people must forget about others for a while and spend time finding out what they themselves want to do.

✳

The Week of Dominance

JANUARY 10–16

The drive to dominate comes to the fore in this week, whether in family, career, social group, or in sports and other leisure activities. Although this drive must be satisfied, it should be expressed in a fashion that does not arouse excessive opposition and thus undermine its potential to succeed.

Perhaps the best kind of dominance expressed in this week is that over the materials with which we work. To the extent that this implies organization and mastery, the energies of this week can be put to work in a highly creative and nondestructive manner.

Physical expression can assume importance in this week. Rather than adopting a dictatorial stance toward a team or other unit we are coaching, the dominance here could imply taking control of the game and making it work in our own team's favor. Likewise, we need to stress the importance of physical control over our muscles and the corresponding flexibility in the skeletal system, particularly the back. Keeping our emotions under control and operating with a clear head will allow for stress reduction and increased direction.

Another outlet for our physical energies may be found in serving the needs of others, or simply by giving a helping hand when needed. The danger here, of course, is that we may allow ourselves to be taken advantage of and not get to spend a lot of our time on our own needs and wants. Making our limits clear, that is, giving up to a point but not beyond, can allow for unconditional giving but also, on the other hand, guard us against being taken advantage of.

Service implies taking responsibility for others, and it is here that the responsible nature of Saturn, ruler of Capricorn, comes to the fore. Taking broad responsibilities on our shoulders is part of the message of the Week of Dominance, but this must never be expressed in a condescending way that implies pity. Those in need should be treated as equals in whatever way possible. Moreover, once individuals are helped they must be aided in the slow process of learning to stand on their own two feet. It is not in the nature of these responsible energies to encourage dependency, either. The sooner that we can help someone get on his or her feet, the more the rehabilitation process becomes an exercise in self-realization.

Of course, turning into a workaholic can be a real danger during the Week of Dominance. We may misjudge our abilities and head for a stressed-out state, or, finally, a breakdown. Learning to pace ourselves and expend energy in an easy and flowing fashion will be difficult but essential to learn. Above all, we must remain positive and beware turning to the solace of self-pity or complaining to ease our pain when failures surface. Should we allow negative thoughts to dominate, then self-confidence may become eroded with a corresponding loss in self-esteem. Being proud of our work, but never arrogant, and being able to go on without lavish praise is essential to our success now.

The Personology of People Born in the Week of Dominance

Exerting a stabilizing effect on most groups to which they belong, those born in the Week of Dominance hang in there for the duration, no matter how long. Rather than ambition, they usually manifest a desire to attain a modest goal and hang on to it. No matter how high the odds against them, they usually will succeed in such endeavors through sheer guts and willpower. Of course, they must learn to share power with others and participate as equals in group endeavors. One great challenge for them is to learn to take chances, or else they run the risk of leading fairly dull and uneventful lives.

Annual Events That Occur During the Week of Dominance

January 12: Stephen Foster Memorial Day
January 15: Martin Luther King, Jr.'s, birthday
January 16: Prohibition Remembrance Day

Major Historical Events That Have Happened During the Week of Dominance

January 10, 1920: League of Nations established
January 11, 1970: Nigerian civil war ends
January 12, 1970: First jumbo jet flight from New York to London
January 13, 1898: Zola accuses French army in Dreyfuss affair
January 14, 1986: *Voyager 2* passes Uranus
January 15, 1900: Hippodrome theater opens in London
January 16, 1991: Gulf War begins with bombing of Baghdad

Famous People Born During the Week of Dominance

Martin Luther King, Jr., Joan of Arc, Yukio Mishima, Alexander Hamilton, Aristotle Onassis, Faye Dunaway, Gamal Abdel Nasser, George I. Gurdjieff, Jack London, A. J. Foyt, Dian Fossey, Maharishi Mahesh Yogi, George Foreman, William James, Howard Stern, Mary J. Blige, Kirstie Alley, Pat Benatar, Horatio Alger, Ethel Merman

Birthdays Especially Affected During the Week of Dominance

If you are born in the Week of Dominance (January 10–16), the Week of Nature (May 11–18), or the Week of the Literal (September 11–18) your energies blend well with those of this week. Results should be obtained with little effort on your part.

Week of Dominance people will be effective professionally if they can maintain flexibility, physically and mentally. Week of Nature people must buckle down to one task at a time to be most effective. Week of the Literal people know exactly where they are headed and fully intend to get there.

If you are born in the Week of Social Betterment (April 11–18), the Week of Persuasion (July 11–18), or the Week of Theater (October 11–18) you will face problems and challenges during this week. You will have to work harder to achieve your goals.

Week of Social Betterment people are too likely to let themselves be taken advantage of and wind up doing all the work. Week of Persuasion people must be aware of arousing antagonisms through their overly domi-nant attitudes. Week of Theater people risk loneliness unless they learn to share power with others.

The Cusp of Mystery,
Violence, and Imagination

JANUARY 17–22

If energies spin wildly out of control during this week, as they frequently do, violence may easily result, and with it irreparable damage. In order to maximize damage control during this week, special care should be taken to avoid accidents of all sorts. It will be impossible to repress the colorful energies of this week, and inadvisable as well, but the forces of mystery, violence, and imagination must be given positive direction whenever possible.

This can be a really fun time of the year. Giving ourselves over to party and play is a real temptation here, and usually the effects are not harmful. Films, humor, sports, and other extracurricular activities exert a strong influence now. Anything that takes our fancy or drives our imaginations wild will flourish during this time period. Daydreams may be particularly vivid, and our dreams at night especially exciting. It is not at all uncommon to look forward to bedtime simply to continue the next episode of a particularly enjoyable serial.

Equally, the nightmare world also will exert a strong influence during this cusp. Once Pandora's box is opened, there is no telling what sort of spirit may pop out, and the same is true of our unconscious mind during the Cusp of Mystery, Violence, and Imagination. Trying to repress the dark side is not a good idea, either. The more anger, violent urges, fear, or jealousy are shoved down into the unconscious, the more they will erupt from it in unpredictable outbursts. Another danger is that by repressing violent urges, for example, we will only attract them, like someone who puts extra locks on their doors only to suffer more and more massive break-ins.

How then to avoid being at the mercy of our demons during this time? The answer lies, perhaps, not in descending into the unconscious and doing battle with such devils, but rather in meeting them, recognizing them, accepting them, and ultimately making friends with them. For too often, such dark powers are the basis of creative drives and frequently what is our most powerful source of energy.

Mystery, violence, and imagination also can be thought of as being at the core of sexual expression. Sexual energies run very high this week, and although they should be expressed, they must be well guided to avoid running riot. Furthermore, since out-of-the-way and kinky forms of sex are especially of interest now, we must guard against unhealthy interests gaining the upper hand. Sex and love addictions may begin or peak during this week along with other obsessive forms of behavior.

Because of the instability of this cusp, we may find it necessary to seek grounding influences by doing simple household tasks and other everyday chores. Not only the structuring of such activities in our daily life, but also the mundane nature of the tasks themselves will help keep our feet on the ground. Also, a diet that stresses simple, earthy foods and avoids exotic or spicy flavors will serve a similar purpose.

The Personology of People Born on the Cusp of Mystery, Violence, and Imagination

No matter how normal these people seem the first time we meet them, we may be sure that they have colorful fantasies and dreams. Because of the intense activity of their unconscious minds, they are highly imaginative in their private and professional lives. Those born on the Cusp of Mystery, Violence, and Imagination are liable to attract all kinds of strange people, and if they repress or ignore their deeper feelings they are likely to attract unwanted and somewhat dangerous experiences as well. Many born on this cusp make no secret about their hidden side, however, and impress the world as highly flamboyant and vivid personalities.

Annual Events That Occur on the Cusp of Mystery, Violence, and Imagination

January 17: Benjamin Franklin's Birthday
January 19: Robert E. Lee Day

Major Historical Events That Have Happened on the Cusp of Mystery, Violence, and Imagination

January 17, 1977: Gary Gilmore executed by firing squad in Utah
January 18, 1943: Red Army breaks siege of Leningrad
January 19, 1942: Japanese invade Burma
January 20, 1988: Palestinians begin intifada against Israel
January 21, 1793: Louis XVI beheaded by revolutionary government
January 22, 1949: Mao Tse Tung's victorious army marches into Peking

Famous People Born on the Cusp of Mystery, Violence, and Imagination

Benjamin Franklin, Muhammad Ali, Joe Frazier, Janis Joplin, D. W. Griffith, Sergey Eisenstein, Jim Carrey, Dolly Parton, Rasputin, John Hurt, Moira Shearer, Geena Davis, Placido Domingo, Cynthia Sherman, Jill Eikenberry, Jerome Kern, Edgar Allan Poe, Stonewall Jackson, Al Capone

Birthdays Especially Affected on the Cusp of Mystery, Violence, and Imagination

If you are born on the Cusp of Mystery, Violence, and Imagination (January 17–22), the Cusp of Energy (May 19–24), or the Cusp of Beauty (September 19–24) your energies blend well with those of this week. Results should be obtained with little effort on your part.

Cusp of Mystery, Violence, and Imagination people can let their vivid fantasies roam over a wide range of human experience. Cusp of Energy people may discover new excitement in a special romantic or sexual liaison.

Cusp of Beauty people could find a special painting, musical composition, or poem which provides inspiration.

If you are born on the Cusp of Power (April 19–24), the Cusp of Oscillation (July 19–25), or the Cusp of Involvement (October 19–25) you will face problems and challenges during this week. You will have to work harder to achieve your goals.

Cusp of Power people may have problems with nightmares or disturbed sleep patterns. Cusp of Oscillation people can encounter the instabilities of sex and love addictions. Cusp of Involvement people must walk thin lines between suppressing and expressing violent urges.

❋

The Week of Intelligence

JANUARY 23–30

In no other week of the year is the use of the modality of thought more favorable than this one. This means not only using our logical faculties and intelligence, but also our common sense, rather than relying too heavily on intuition or feeling. To think intelligently, to express ourselves clearly and concisely, to avoid sloppy thinking, and to try to cut through ignorance, prejudice, and superstition are all part of the picture.

Individualistic tendencies are favored over group endeavors during the Week of Intelligence. Not only building character, but also being a character is favorable to the energies of this week, and with them the furthering of unusual, kooky, and even bizarre ideas. This is not to imply that such ideas are impractical either, for they may not only attract attention now, but may even achieve commercial success. However, it's important to toughen up a bit to avoid being knocked off balance by the slings and arrows of resentful or unsympathetic colleagues.

Because the energies of this week can become so frenetic, setting up a quiet retreat may prove necessary. Finding such a hideout and using it off and on for the rest of the year could spell the difference between leading a balanced life and becoming periodically stressed out. For some, this week may bring a decision to work alone in the coming months, since contact with fellow workers only proves to be upsetting. Indeed, not working with people at all but engaging in pursuits of a technical, scientific, or artistic nature (projects which favor isolation) may be preferable to those that bring us into daily contact with people and their emotions.

Marketing our own uniqueness is not always easy. To proceed along this path during the Week of Intelligence will require some tact, diplomacy, and occasionally fancy footwork. Furthermore, when this week is over, since the energies of following weeks are not as conducive to these sorts of activities, we would do well to lay the foundations of this highly indi-vidualistic track that we intend to pursue. Others may choose to only use this week as an outlet for our most personal forms of expression and carry on as a more social entity, but with a fuller knowledge of who we really are and of the unique gifts we have to offer the organizations in which we work.

There is little doubt that during this week it may be difficult to sit in the classroom and absorb ready-made information from textbooks or spend time memorizing reams of theoretical material. Experience plays an impor-tant role in this week, and experience encourages self-teaching and one-on-one tutoring rather than institutionalized learning. Throwing ourselves headfirst into the stream of life and learning from our mistakes, through trial and error, is the kind of learning most suited to the Week of Intelli-gence. Books may be used as backup and reference sources, but not as the primary wellspring of inspiration.

The Personology of People Born in the Week of Intelligence

Those born in this week are not necessarily smarter than anyone else, but usually pick things up very fast. In their childhood years particularly they may stand out for their early development and their ability to assimilate material more quickly than others. These individuals do well in jobs that stimulate and challenge them, and conversely can suffer in less interesting occupations. Those born in this week do well to develop their physical abilities through exercise and sports of all kind, to serve as a counterweight to their intensely mental orientation. In this respect, music, dance, and theater are particularly recommended for their development and health.

Annual Events That Occur During the Week of Intelligence

January 23: National School Nurse Day
January 26: National Day of Australia
January 27: Vietnam Day
January 29: Carnation Day

Major Historical Events That Have Happened During the Week of Intelligence

January 23, 1973: President Nixon announces end of Vietnam War
January 24, 1848: Gold discovered at Sutter's Mill in California
January 25, 1924: First Winter Olympics are held in France
January 26, 1788: First landing of British convicts at Sydney, Australia
January 27, 1926: Baird demonstrates TV to Royal Institute in London
January 28, 1986: Space shuttle *Challenger* explodes
January 29, 1987: Gorbachev calls for free elections in USSR
January 30, 1933: Adolf Hitler becomes chancellor of Germany

Famous People Born During the Week of Intelligence

Humphrey Bogart, Jeanne Moreau, Edith Wharton, Virginia Woolf, Robert Burns, Angela Davis, Oprah Winfrey, Thomas Paine, Franklin D. Roosevelt, Wolfgang Amadeus Mozart, Nastassja Kinski, Hadrian, Vanessa Redgrave, Gene Hackman, Barbara Tuchman, W. C. Fields, Germaine Greer, Bridget Fonda, Mikhail Baryshnikov, Douglas MacArthur, Robert Motherwell, Maria Tallchief

Birthdays Especially Affected During the Week of Intelligence

If you are born in the Week of Intelligence (January 23–30), the Week of Freedom (May 25–June 2), or the Week of Perfection (September 25–October 2) your energies blend well with those of this week. Results should be obtained with little effort on your part.

Week of Intelligence people would do well to make plans to maximize their own individuality careerwise. Week of Freedom people will benefit if they insist on their personal gifts and talents being recognized. Week of Perfection people should be appreciated for their verbal and written language skills.

If you are born in the Week of Manifestation (April 25–May 2), the Week of Passion (July 26–August 2), or the Week of Intensity (October 26–November 2) you will face problems and challenges during this week. You will have to work harder to achieve your goals.

Week of Manifestation people may find the frenetic energies of this week quite upsetting. Week of Passion people easily could be pushed over the edge and get stressed out. Week of Intensity people must toughen up to avoid being wounded by the criticism of their colleagues.

❋

The Week of Youth and Ease

JANUARY 31–FEBRUARY 7

One of the most relaxed weeks of the entire year, the Week of Youth and Ease impresses us with its motto, "No hassles." The easiest way to be rejected by our social or family group during this week (or to be lowered in estimation or station at work) is simply to cause problems. Anyone who rocks the boat during this week can be assured of swift and decidedly negative reactions from those in the immediate vicinity.

This is not a time for being miserable but for feeling happy about life. The weather may still be fairly grim, but the joys of comradeship and conviviality are never stronger. Dinner with friends, family get-togethers, office parties—all of these are favored now. Laughter and mirth are in the air, and lighthearted fun is being had by just about everyone. This doesn't imply an inability to get things accomplished, for since the tendency is to leave others alone, the space and time will be granted to get a lot done, whether on a personal, social, or professional level. Nor should this opportunity be lost, since it could prove unique to this time.

Of special interest is the evaluative work on past performances during the previous spring, summer, and fall. Such evaluations will be very useful when the start-up energies of spring roll around again; indeed, the beginning of spring is only seven weeks away. Writing down our thoughts and then making recommendations in the form of a checklist to be used at that later time is highly recommended.

Because of the high youthful energies of this week, special interest may be taken in children, whether they are our own or the children of others. A fascination with all things childlike is present during the Week of Youth and Ease, and with it an opportunity to learn from what Nietzsche called "the seriousness that one had as a child at play." All forms of childlike invention and imagination, along with the delightful knack of being silly, are most appreciated now. The curiosity of children can be reflected in a renewed interest in technical matters and in seeing how things work. Fix-up projects around the house can be started with renewed energy and carried through to completion in a relaxed yet thorough manner. A perfect coordination of energies could be achieved by working with children on such matters, or by sharing the joys of board and video games.

Although the energies of this week speak of ease and lack of problems, we must not necessarily assume that these energies are superficial. An interest in all things profound, particularly when it comes to emotional matters, and a fascination with complex emotions is the other side of the coin during the Week of Youth and Ease. As if to balance the light and airy energies here, we may feel the need to delve and probe into the deep feelings of a dear friend, family member, or lover. Bringing such a person out of a deep depression or troubled state may grant enormous satisfaction to both parties.

The Personology of People Born in the Week of Youth and Ease

These folks dislike trouble more than most, and are usually content with a life uncomplicated by stress and conflict. Since they prefer it when things go easily, they are unlikely to provoke confrontations or rock the boat of their company or family group. Having a good time is a high priority for them, and therefore they seek out many varied forms of amusement and entertainment. Because they run the risk of avoiding their personal problems through such behavior, they would do well to make a conscious effort to get to know themselves at a deeper level. In addition, they must beware becoming too agreeable simply to gain the approval of others.

Annual Events That Occur During the Week of Youth and Ease

February 1: National Freedom Day
February 2: Groundhog Day
February 4: Kosciusko Day

Major Historical Events That Have Happened During the Week of Youth and Ease

January 31, 1943: Surrender of German army at Stalingrad
February 1, 1990: F. W. de Klerk ends apartheid in South Africa
February 2, 1989: Russia pulls back last troops from Afghanistan
February 3, 1919: League of Nations convenes for first time
February 4, 1945: Stalin, Roosevelt, and Churchill meet at Yalta
February 5, 1922: *Reader's Digest* first published in New York
February 6, 1840: Britain annexes New Zealand
February 7, 1960: Dead Sea Scrolls discovered

Famous People Born During the Week of Youth and Ease

Franz Peter Schubert, Anna Pavlova, Clark Gable, Gertrude Stein, James Joyce, Jascha Heifetz, Fritz Kreisler, Charlotte Rampling, Natalie Cole, Charles Dickens, Princess Stephanie of Monaco, Boris Yeltsin, Ayn Rand,

Babe Ruth, Jackie Robinson, Betty Friedan, Blythe Danner, An Wang, Ronald Reagan, Ida Lupino

Birthdays Especially Affected During the Week of Youth and Ease

If you are born in the Week of Youth and Ease (January 31–February 7), the Week of Communication (June 3–10), or the Week of Socialization (October 3–10) your energies blend well with those of this week. Results should be obtained with little effort on your part.

Week of Youth and Ease people insist that everyone around them keep cool and relaxed. Week of Communication people will succeed in their chosen professions by keeping their language simple and nonthreatening. Week of Socialization people could have as much fun this week as they can handle, if they wish to.

If you are born in the Week of Study (May 3–10), the Week of Challenge (August 3–10), or the Week of Profundity (November 3–11) you will face problems and challenges during this week. You will have to work harder to achieve your goals.

Week of Study people will have to lighten up to avoid the disapproval of those they live with. Week of Challenge people will battle their guilt over enjoying themselves so much. Week of Profundity people could work out their problems with the help of an understanding friend.

※

The Week of Acceptance

FEBRUARY 8–15

The theme of acceptance governs this week and appears as an issue now in many forms. There are two principal challenges that emerge for all of us. In matters where we are not exercising an accepting spirit, we are urged to learn to be more open and forgiving. In matters where we are too accepting, our challenge is to draw firmer ego boundaries and learn to say no. Thus, we must find a balance in all things between being too accepting and not being accepting enough.

During this week we may have to face up to our fear of rejection and our need to be considered normal. As far as the latter is concerned, we will feel many pressures to conform now, and above all, not to stand out from the crowd. Although idiosyncratic and even bizarre behavior can easily manifest itself during this week, such actions should not be flaunted, but rather played down and even made to work toward one's advantage. Developing a vivid style or intriguing manner of speech may well help us gain attention and even improve our chances for success.

Fear of rejection also can be a big obstacle now, and with it a desire to please and, of course, be accepted. Yet this fear must be mastered during the Week of Acceptance. Only by overcoming the fear of rejection will we become stronger and more self-sufficient. We should try to be honest with others and learn how to take a hard line without being afraid of being hurt in return. The need to please others is one that we must keep in check, substituting in its place the normal desire to interact in a friendly but never obsequious or self-degrading manner.

Our attitudes should be more fearless toward ourselves—this is me, take it or leave it. As a result we will become more self-accepting and may even raise our self-esteem to become proud of who and what we are. Such acceptance will counteract the real danger in this week, which is to indulge in self-blame and strongly disapproving attitudes springing from guilt and shame.

Although personal struggles within our own psyches figure prominently now, we should not neglect our outer life, particularly when it comes to exercise. Jogging, gymnastics, and swimming will keep us healthy and happy, particularly if accompanied by a sensibly balanced diet. Putting our energies into helping disadvantaged persons also can be a powerful stimulus to combat prejudice and also widen one's view of the world. Working with an ethnic or immigrant group will expand our sense of tolerance and put the positive energies of this week to good use. The gratification gained from such work should bolster our drive toward the acceptance that is so vital to this week's energies.

Furthermore, we should try also to work as the champion of the underdog within our family, classroom, or work group. We should approach and hold out our hand in friendship to the little guy in need of protection and support. By doing so, we gain in social stature and also in depth of character.

The Personology of People Born in the Week of Acceptance

Highly idealistic, those born in this week seek out endeavors in which they can express their ideas and strong convictions. Whether supporting causes or giving help to the underdog, those born in the Week of Acceptance are usually found on the side of the disadvantaged and downtrodden. They are usually free of snobbism, preferring to treat everyone in an equal manner in their personal lives as well. Their courage in the face of fire is outstanding, and they are not likely to back down from even the sternest of confrontations or judgmental onslaughts. However, they must learn tactfulness to avoid making themselves the target of criticism and rejection.

Annual Events That Occur During the Week of Acceptance

February 8: Boy Scout Day
February 12: Lincoln's birthday
February 14: St. Valentine's Day

Major Historical Events That Have Happened During the Week of Acceptance

February 8, 1904: Russo-Japanese War begins
February 9, 1775: British parliament announces American rebellion
February 10, 1962: Spy-plane pilot Gary Powers released by Russians
February 11, 1975: Margaret Thatcher becomes first woman to lead
    Britain's Conservative party

February 12, 1912: Monarchy ends in China with emperor's abdication

February 13, 1935: Bruno Hauptmann found guilty in Lindbergh child's murder

February 14, 1929: Mobsters gunned down in St. Valentine's Day massacre

February 15, 1942: Singapore surrenders to Japanese

Famous People Born During the Week of Acceptance

Alice Walker, Jules Verne, Boris Pasternak, Thomas A. Edison, Abraham Lincoln, Charles Darwin, Claire Bloom, George Segal, Susan B. Anthony, Bertolt Brecht, Bill Russell, James Dean, Leontyne Price, Georges Simenon, Stella Adler, Brendan Behan, Peter Gabriel, Galileo Galilei, Oliver Reed, Mia Farrow

Birthdays Especially Affected During the Week of Acceptance

If you are born in the Week of Acceptance (February 8–15), the Week of Exploration (June 11–18), or the Week of Theater (October 11–18) your energies blend well with those of this week. Results should be obtained with little effort on your part.

Week of Acceptance people feel free to develop their own unique way of doing things. Week of Exploration people could decide to put their energies in service of the disadvantaged. Week of Theater people should advertise their unusual qualities in a very subtle manner in order to advance professionally.

If you are born in the Week of Nature (May 11–18), the Week of Leadership (August 11–18), or the Week of Control (November 12–18) you will face problems and challenges during this week. You will have to work harder to achieve your goals.

Week of Nature people must learn to say no without feelings of guilt engulfing them. Week of Leadership people should be aware of getting trapped in their own inner life. Week of Control people risk ill health unless they begin a steady regimen of exercise.

The Cusp of Sensitivity

FEBRUARY 16–22

In order to navigate the currents of this week successfully, we may have to grow a thicker skin. Irritating situations of all types really can get to us now. Many stimuli can push our buttons, and perhaps the only effective way of dealing with them may be to grow a whole new set of buttons which are not so easy to push. The principal difficulty with any armoring techniques which protect us against the world, though, is that in building too impenetrable a defense we may cut ourselves off from the outside world. Thus, the most successful defense could be quite damaging, particularly in the area of preventing love from getting through.

Crucial to this week's energies is finding out just who our friends really are. The issue of trust figures prominently here, and it will be important to know who we can trust and who we cannnot. Examining this trust a bit more closely, we find two different kinds are operative. The first is the kind of trust we put in a bridge we walk over. That is, we trust that someone or something will live up to promised capabilities and that they may be relied on not to collapse or fall apart. The other kind of trust is knowing that we can lean on someone emotionally when we are in need, and that they will come through for us in terms of understanding, discretion, and responsible behavior. Usually, both of these kinds of trust are required.

Seeing the big picture is important now, but also dealing sensitively with the intimate side of life. Thus, the universal and the personal both loom large on the Cusp of Sensitivity. We must divide our attentions sensibly between more humanitarian and idealistic pursuits and those areas that deal with love and feelings in particular. These two areas influence each other. Friendship is a good example, since these relationships may assume more universal and less personal significance in this week. We may find ourselves less possessive toward individual friends and more willing to share them with others. Moreover, the kinds of passions that involve jealousy or claiming behavior may give way to less emotional and more objective attitudes.

Exercising good sense is required now, and the quality of our thoughts may well set the tone for the quality of our lives.

In addition, with the end of winter finally in sight, now may be the time to begin making plans for spring cleaning, picking out a spring wardrobe, saving for vacations in earnest, making reservations, and finalizing our evaluations of our actions during the preceding seasons of spring, summer, and fall.

A drive toward success is also undeniable on this cusp, and we must be aware of not being too ruthless in our endeavors. Again, sensitivity is the key, for only by remaining empathic with others will we force ourselves to consider the other person's needs and motives.

The Personology of People Born on the Cusp of Sensitivity

Those born on this cusp tend to have suffered greatly in childhood from the criticism of others. In order to stave off such criticism and protect themselves against it, these individuals often wall themselves off, thus denying access to their feelings. The problem arises in adult life when they find themselves the victim of their own childhood—that is, unable to open up to those close to them and to the world in general. Dismantling this wall, piece by piece, and freeing up their trust and emotions can become the major work of their lives. Although such highly personal themes often dominate their lives, an unmistakable drive toward worldly success also characterizes those born in this week.

Annual Events That Occur on the Cusp of Sensitivity

February 17: National Public Science Day
February 18: Presidents Day

February 22: Washington's birthday
Purim

Major Historical Events That Have Happened on the Cusp of Sensitivity

February 16, 1932: Fianna Fail party wins Irish election
February 17, 1979: Chinese invade Vietnam
February 18, 1930: Planet Pluto discovered
February 19, 1921: First helicopter flight
February 20, 1962: John Glenn orbits Earth
February 21, 1965: Malcolm X assassinated in New York
February 22, 1879: Woolworth's opens in New York

Famous People Born on the Cusp of Sensitivity

Frédéric Chopin, Toni Morrison, Michael Jordan, Yoko Ono, Amy Tan, John Travolta, Marian Anderson, Andrés Segovia, Nicolaus Copernicus, Ansel Adams, Nancy Wilson, Anaïs Nin, Edna St. Vincent Millay, Ivana Trump, Sidney Poitier, Charles Barkley, Julius Erving, Gloria Vanderbilt, Helen Gurley Brown, Edward M. Kennedy

Birthdays Especially Affected on the Cusp of Sensitivity

If you are born on the Cusp of Sensitivity (February 16–22), the Cusp of Magic (June 19–24), or the Cusp of Involvement (October 19–25) your energies blend well with those of this week. Results should be obtained with little effort on your part.

Cusp of Sensitivity people can make real strides in their personal development. Cusp of Magic people are likely to find out who their real friends are. Cusp of Involvement people can work on planning their spring wardrobes or vacation.

If you are born on the Cusp of Energy (May 19–24), the Cusp of

Exposure (August 19–25), or the Cusp of Revolution (November 19–24) you will face problems and challenges during this week. You will have to work harder to achieve your goals.

Cusp of Energy people are too likely to get upset and easily irritated. Cusp of Exposure people may prove too ruthless in their drives toward success. Cusp of Revolution people could be insensitive to the needs and wants of family members.

✳

The Week of Spirit

FEBRUARY 23–MARCH 2

The devotional aspects of life take center stage now. Our religious or spiritual orientation is extremely important at this time, implying that working on our connection with God or another higher spiritual source is necessary and particularly rewarding. Here we may be dealing with established religions and churches or delving deeply into the devotional beliefs we find in our own heart. Whether more doctrinal or personal, our orientation now is toward areas far beyond our own personal interests and more in the direction of service to God and mankind.

Developing our spirit also can apply to the joy of living. Improving our lifestyle definitely figures here. By raising the quality level of our life, a healthier and more enjoyable daily existence may well result. This can be achieved perhaps through relocating to a more desirable living space, changing our job, or getting more of what we want out of an existing professional pursuit, improving our appearance, or developing our interests and talents.

Because of the abundance of new ideas and spiritual disciplines in the Aquarian age, this week will be especially favorable for investigating such doctrines. Whether the writings of Krishnamurti, Gurgieff, Rudolph Steiner, Tich Nat Han, Osho, or Meher Baba, it is appropriate to take an interest in one or more of these thinkers. Perhaps attending lectures or meetings also will give us a better idea of how these ideas may be incorporated into our everyday life and will grant us an opportunity to learn about them firsthand from devoted practitioners. Several of these spiritual disciplines overlap with established religions such as Buddhism and Christianity and may thus serve as a bridge between the two areas.

For those who do not feel comfortable with group practices, it may be advisable to seek spiritual guidance on their own, or through a one-on-one interaction with a spiritual guide or teacher. Still others may choose the direct pipeline to God, preferring to communicate directly with the deity through prayer. All of these activities, which stress the spiritual rather than the materialistic aspects of life, are favored at this time. This is not to say that material matters must be dismissed from our life now, but that money, material objects, and economic studies should be put in their proper perspective and that connections with the spiritual world should be explored with emphasis on the latter. For example, money may be seen as a type of energy and a means of putting our spiritual orientation to its best use. The use of economics to aid disadvantaged people around the world through financial help and investment also could be of interest during the Week of Spirit.

Because of a desire to leave the world a better place, many individuals, particularly those of an advanced age, may choose to put a part of their financial resources at the service of environmental causes now. In this way, any individual over forty-two may assure themselves that a significant contribution toward saving the planet could have been made during their lifetime and a palpable influence felt after their departure.

The Personology of People Born in the Week of Spirit

Those born in this week will feel at home in the nonmaterial areas of life, often preferring spiritual and religious values to worldly ones. This need not imply their lack of success in the world, however, and frequently these sensitive individuals have a talent for making money. But their hearts are usually in artistic and devotional endeavors, which put their talents in the service of a higher power. Espousing causes, or at the very least having sympathy for the more idealistic thoughts of those around them, those born in the Week of Spirit tire easily of a humdrum or uneventful life. They must beware overidealizing their relationships and putting undue expectations on their partners.

Annual Events That Occur During the Week of Spirit

February 23: Iwo Jima Day
March 1: International Association for Women of Color Day
March 1: St. David's Day in Wales
March 1: Chalandra Marz in Switzerland
March 2: National Sales Person Day

Major Historical Events That Have Happened During the Week of Spirit

February 23, 1945: American flag raised on Iwo Jima by U.S. marines
February 24, 1920: Nancy Astor becomes first woman in British Parliament
February 25, 1913: Suffragette Emmeline Pankhurst goes on trial for bombing
February 26, 1990: Vaclav Havel announces departure of Soviet troops from Czechoslovakia
February 27, 1933: Burning of the Reichstag in Berlin
February 28, 1973: Takeover of Wounded Knee by Native Americans
February 29, 1988: Archbishop Tutu arrested at Cape Town demonstration
March 1, 1932: Kidnapping of Lindbergh baby
March 2, 1836: Texan-Americans declare independence from Mexico

Famous People Born During the Week of Spirit

Victor Hugo, Adelle Davis, Mikhail Gorbachev, W. E. B. Du Bois, Meher Baba, Rudolph Steiner, Elizabeth Taylor, Linus Pauling, Gioacchino Rossini, Ann Lee, Alberta Hunter, Sandro Botticelli, George Frideric Handel,

Bernadette Peters, Lawrence Durrell, Enrico Caruso, Tom Wolfe, John Irving, Dexter Gordon, Dinah Shore

Birthdays Especially Affected During the Week of Spirit

If you are born in the Week of Spirit (February 23–March 2), the Week of Empathy (June 25–July 2), or the Week of Intensity (October 26–November 2) your energies blend well with those of this week. Results should be obtained with little effort on your part.

Week of Spirit people will find their spiritual goals furthered through meditation and study. Week of Empathy people develop their deep feelings of compassion for those around them. Week of Intensity people could benefit from following the precepts of a spiritual master.

If you are born in the Week of Freedom (May 25–June 2), the Week of Structure (August 26–September 2), or the Week of Independence (November 25–December 2) you will face problems and challenges during this week. You will have to work harder to achieve your goals.

Week of Freedom people can get bottled up in thoughts and worries. Week of Structure people must struggle with their need to control money matters and finances. Week of Independence people should place less emphases on the material world to avoid unhappiness.

✺

The Week of Isolation

MARCH 3–10

We should try to take advantage of the opportunity to withdraw from the world during this week, for it may be our last chance to take a breather before the intense activities of the new personology year beginning with the advent of spring. The energies of this week also favor work at home, and this is true for working on professional projects as well as making domestic improvements. Preparing for the weeks ahead is important now. Tax matters should be put in order, new endeavors carefully considered and evaluated against past performance, educational opportunities investigated, and budgets drawn up for basic living expenses.

Because the energies of this week so strongly favor pulling back from social involvements, the intimate side of a special relationship can benefit now and consequently should be developed. Sharing deep emotional interactions with a close friend, lover, or life partner are particularly appropriate now. We should leave time for long conversations about our relationships, and attempt to define and refine them more closely to fit our mutual needs and wants. Taking long walks, spending quiet evenings at home together, and developing a wide range of sensual or sexual inter-actions can all be tremendously rewarding during the Week of Isolation.

One danger which can surface during the Week of Isolation is drug dependency. Whether we are speaking about nicotine, caffeine, and alcohol on the one hand, or so-called soft or even hard drugs on the other, we will have to fight not to allow the use of such products to run out of hand. Problems may emerge for parents who see their children indulging and thereby slipping away from them. Great tact, care, and understanding will have to be demonstrated in such matters to avoid outright breaks in the harmony of day-to-day family existence.

The benefits of withdrawing into ourselves to accomplish positive interiorized goals also must be weighed against the hazards of falling into an unreal fantasy world accompanied by idle daydreaming. Because we may no longer feel able to rely on society's standards and the guidance of friends, it will in many cases be necessary for us to develop a somewhat objective personal standard by which to measure our own sense of reality—a diffi-cult task indeed. Although increased subjectivity is inevitable now, the mental processes involving simple common sense, logic, and pragmatic thought should be able to exist side by side with our imagination, to keep it on course and give it direction.

Scheduling one or two group meetings during this week, of either a social or professional nature (even if we do not really feel like it), could work to increase our reality factor. Others will have to be understanding of our needs to be alone, however, and perhaps a kind of mutual respect and trust could allow many individuals to withdraw into their own private world without fear of criticism or censure. Once the positive results of such behavior are recognized by society, it may be possible to set the Week of Isolation aside each year to develop private initiatives and reach deeper private goals.

The Personology of People Born in the Week of Isolation

Those born in this week are often loners who spend many hours each day absorbed in their own thoughts. Conversely, they value friendships highly and find it difficult to be happy without constant interaction with those closest to them. A strange blend of private and social individuals, those born in the Week of Isolation enjoy both spending time on their own and being in the company of their closest friends. Highly selective in their tastes, both in people and in clothing and accessories, these individuals convey the impression of elegance and nuance in their dress as well as their thoughts. Because of their emotionality and a tendency to be wounded easily by sharp words or unkind attitudes, they must learn to defend themselves against the everyday vicissitudes of life.

Annual Events That Occur During the Week of Isolation

March 3: National Anthem Day
March 6: Alamo Day
March 7: Peace Corps Day
March 8: International Women's Day

Major Historical Events That Have Happened During the Week of Isolation

March 3, 1918: Treaty of Brest-Litovsk is signed by Russia and Germany
March 4, 1980: Mugabe becomes head of an independent Zimbabwe
March 5, 1953: Death of Joseph Stalin

March 6, 1836: Last stand of Texans at the Alamo
March 7, 1917: First jazz recording released
March 8, 1989: Martial law declared by Chinese in Tibet
March 9, 1831: French Foreign Legion founded
March 10, 1876: First official telephone call made by Alexander Graham Bell

Famous People Born During the Week of Isolation

Alexander Graham Bell, Anna Magnani, Harriet Tubman, Lynn Redgrave, Michelangelo, Elizabeth Barrett Browning, Rosa Luxemburg, Gabriel Garcia-Marquez, Oliver Wendell Holmes, Raul Julia, Cyrano de Bergerac, Luther Burbank, Bobby Fisher, Ornette Coleman, Piet Mondrian, Jackie Joyner-Kersee, Aidan Quinn, Maurice Ravel, Yuri Gagarin, Irina Ratushinskaya

Birthdays Especially Affected During the Week of Isolation

If you are born in the Week of Isolation (March 3–10), the Week of Unconventionality (July 3–10), or the Week of Profundity (November 3–11) your energies blend well with those of this week. Results should be obtained with little effort on your part.

Week of Isolation people must not forget to discharge daily social obligations. Week of Unconventionality people will benefit from an analysis of their behaviors in the previous months. Week of Profundity people should feel free to express their needs for privacy without fear of censure.

If you are born in the Week of Communication (June 3–10), the Week of the Puzzle (September 3–10), or the Week of Originality (December 3–10) you will face problems and challenges during this week. You will have to work harder to achieve your goals.

Week of Communication people can be accused of superficiality unless they take more serious views. Week of the Puzzle people could get too involved in technical matters at the expense of emotional ones. Week of Originality people should consider opening up a work space at home, no matter what the cost.

The Week of Dances and Dreams

MARCH 11–18

In this last week of winter it is time to wrap up our ruminative activities and prepare for a more active life, including outdoor projects. Since this can be viewed as the most highly evolved week of the personological yearly cycle, highly philosophical thought and activities are most favored at this time. Taking a step back and looking at the larger picture and questioning ourselves about personal and professional goals will inevitably meet with some success.

We will all feel the urge to help others in their endeavors during the Week of Dances and Dreams. A real empathy with the feelings of those around us and a desire to help satisfy their needs is in the air at this time. Some care must be taken, however, not to foster the dependency of overly needy individuals, nor to deprive friends, colleagues, and family members of the opportunity to do things for themselves. On the other hand, the joys of helping others and sharing in the important moments in their lives can be highly rewarding.

The metaphor for this week, that of dances and dreams, applies to a very high cosmic order of meaning. Play in the highest sense is emphasized here, developing our ability to let our minds roam over the largest questions of human existence here on Earth and their relation to more universal questions, like those involving other levels of reality. Dancing and dreaming should be seen as positive and highly productive endeavors, rather than as activities that foster unreal states of mind. Doing the cosmic dance implies coming into closer touch with reality, rather than withdrawing from it.

Colorful forms of expression exert a tremendous pull now, whether involving music, fashion and design, painting and sculpture, theater or other forms of performance art. Flaunting our individuality and fully expressing our convictions and deepest feelings create an extroverted mood in our immediate surroundings, but it is a mood which proceeds from a deep place within ourselves. Although often shocking, such behavior will not have a superficial cast nor appear as merely rebellious or defiant in nature. Thus, we may all empower ourselves in moving forward together as a human, world collective.

This may well be the time in which many miracles occur. Things thought to be impossible are suddenly possible, even likely to happen. Rather than pushing or trying too hard, it is more appropriate now to allow things to happen and permit the universe to bestow gifts by remaining open to new forms of experience. This kind of "nonactivity" will be difficult for many people who are used to working hard for what they get, but we must be assured that God and the universe will provide for us at this time, if only we are open to it.

In this final week of the year, we have our last chance to touch base with mysterious and mystical powers of a very high order, and to channel their energies to fuel our daily lives and enrich them. Likewise, joining hands with our fellow human beings in such positive attitudes is also favored now, so that no one need feel left out or forgotten.

The Personology of People Born in the Week of Dances and Dreams

Grounding their energies in practical activities is essential to those born in this week. Because they are often called dreamers in their early life, they may react by developing a pragmatic side which will accept only that which can be proved. Many born in this week develop intensely practical skills and function well in the world of technology. Yet rarely do they lose their capability to dream and even to manifest paranormal talents. Because of their sensitivity to the feelings of others, they are often sought out for advice and counsel. Sympathetic to the extreme, they are unlikely to deny a hearing to those in need or to open their doors and their heart to those who ask for assistance.

Annual Events That Occur During the Week of Dances and Dreams

March 12: Girl Scout Day
March 15: The Ides of March
March 16: Black Press Day
March 17: St. Patrick's Day

Major Historical Events That Have Happened During the Week of Dances and Dreams

March 11, 1985: Gorbachev takes office in the USSR
March 12, 1938: Germany annexes Austria
March 13, 1930: Gandhi begins mass protest march
March 14, 1492: Jews expelled from Spain
March 15, 44 B.C.: Julius Caesar assassinated
March 16, 1900: Sir Arthur Evans finds Minoan treasure
March 17, 1969: First Israeli woman prime minister, Golda Meir, elected
March 18, 1890: Bismarck is fired by Kaiser Wilhelm II

Famous People Born During the Week of Dances and Dreams

Albert Einstein, F. W. de Klerk, Liza Minnelli, Percival Lowell, Diane Arbus, Sylvia Beach, Charley Pride, Jerry Lewis, Vaslav Nijinsky, Michael Caine, Rudolf Nureyev, Irene Cara, Edgar Cayce, Bobby McFerrin, Diane Nemerov, L. Ron Hubbard, Nat King Cole, Bernardo Bertolucci, Billy Crystal, Ruth Bader Ginsburg

Birthdays Especially Affected During the Week of Dances and Dreams

If you are born in the Week of Dances and Dreams (March 11–18), the Week of Persuasion (July 11–18), or the Week of Control (November 12–18) your energies blend well with those of this week. Results should be obtained with little effort on your part.

Week of Dances and Dreams people will be more appreciated in the long run if they give more responsibility to others. Week of Persuasion people should follow their most universal and philosophical impulses. Week of Control people do well to indulge in the more playful aspects of life.

If you are born in the Week of Exploration (June 11–18), the Week of the Literal (September 11–18), or the Week of Expansiveness (December 11–18) you will face problems and challenges during this week. You will have to work harder to achieve your goals.

Week of Exploration people must maintain some practicality to avoid disasters. Week of the Literal people should lighten up on their insistence that friends and family act more sensibly. Week of Expansiveness people may find it harder work to do nothing and let things happen than to push ahead.

Winter Personology Snapshot

DECEMBER 21 Skilled in communication, December 21 people tend to put less emphasis on speech, relying on nonverbal methods to convince others of their opinions. Not without confidence, they must respect their skills and try not to use them to control others.

DECEMBER 22 Prepared and organized, those born on December 22 are well organized and detail oriented. Successful people who are patient with their goals, they must learn to control their tempers and to guard against frustration.

DECEMBER 23 December 23 people are visionaries who enjoy using their knowledge and intuition to plan for the future and break new ground. Confident and self-assured, they may also be stubborn and authoritarian due to their commitment to ideals.

DECEMBER 24 Those born on December 24 find that their organized and direct approach to life helps them deal with uncertainty. Adept at overcoming obstacles, they must learn to rely on their self-discipline or run the risk of becoming distracted and confused.

DECEMBER 25 An interest in all supernatural things is evident in December 25 people, and the routine concerns of others seem unimportant to them. Always searching for ways to reach a higher state of being, they often become restless due to their unusual interests.

DECEMBER 26 Rebellious from a young age, December 26 people are also methodical and direct. Honest and committed, they must learn to be flexible with their ideas and those who may oppose them.

DECEMBER 27 Generous and caring, December 27 people are very concerned with the welfare of their friends and family. Completely devoted to those they love, they must be aware that giving too much can sometimes result in a lack of self-confidence.

DECEMBER 28 Sophisticated and sure, those born on December 28 are hardworking people who remember their roots. Often triumphant, they need to watch that their hard work doesn't lead to loneliness—success can be empty without others to share it.

DECEMBER 29 The capable people of December 29 often find themselves in influential positions, even though they are not overly ambitious. They can be blunt and careless at times, though, and must remember to think through their actions thoroughly.

DECEMBER 30 Efficient and realistic, December 30 people stick to proven paths and minimize faults well by being quick to admit them. They often have problems with authority, though, and must take care to realize that their way is not the only way.

DECEMBER 31 Those born on December 31 have a keen understanding of the needs of society and know how to make a strong contribution without being reactionary. Adept at helping others, they must take care not to be seen as narrow-minded and domineering.

JANUARY 1 Loyal to ideas, studious, and extremely organized, January 1 people understand the value of education. They run the risk of being authoritarian, though, and should take care not to control the lives of others.

JANUARY 2 Those born on January 2 have very high standards and are always striving to prove their worth. Serious and hardworking, they tend to be very critical of themselves and must learn to take pride in their accomplishments.

JANUARY 3 Dedicated and involved, January 3 people give all they have once they commit to something, especially when serving others. While devotion to work is often positive, they must take care that their commitment doesn't make them stubborn and secretive.

JANUARY 4 Adept at solving problems, January 4 people have the ability to understand and resolve mundane issues as well as crises. Their vast intellectual skills may lead them to become closed-minded, however, and they must learn to respect the ideas of others.

JANUARY 5 Resourceful and determined, the people born on January 5 often have difficult lives, but their self-confidence usually allows them to overcome their hardships. Once things become stable, however, they need to take care not to become smug about the difficulties of others.

JANUARY 6 Investigating truth is very important to those born on January 6, and they often dedicate their lives to proving what they believe to be true. Dedicated and probing, they need to find balance or run the risk of being thought of as eccentric.

JANUARY 7 Unusually observant, those born on January 7 notice what many do not, whether in the physical world or within the human mind. They must hone this ability, though, as it is easy for them to overanalyze trivial things without realizing it.

JANUARY 8 Influencing everything around them, January 8 people are noted for the clarity of their communication. Often having a profound and seemingly effortless influence on their surroundings, their evident confidence may lead them to become conceited if they are not careful.

JANUARY 9 Focused and determined, January 9 people rarely miss an opportunity to better their lives. Resilient and strong, they must learn to relax, to cherish their accomplishments, and to admit their failures.

JANUARY 10 Realistic and honest, January 10 people understand how to approach any situation. Direct and true, they must be aware that some people will find them to be blunt and insensitive.

JANUARY 11 Those born on January 11 are able to evaluate any situation, and to analyze the quality of objects or systems. They can easily become too judgmental, though, and must learn to be more flexible.

JANUARY 12 Devoted and honest, those born on January 12 put everything they have into their work once they find the right career. Generous, they must learn to cap their generosity or run the risk of giving too much of themselves.

JANUARY 13 The strong-willed people of January 13 are concerned with all kinds of security. Always looking to improve their status in life, they must take care that their constant motion doesn't lead to insecurity.

JANUARY 14 A clear vision enables those born on January 14 to see past the details and understand the true meaning of most situations. Determination can be dangerous, though, and they must learn not to adopt a hard-nosed position.

JANUARY 15 Often heroic, January 15 people do not realize their potential until a serious challenge is set before them. Forgiving, they should learn to temper their forbearance, as they have a tendency to let hurtful people back into their trust.

JANUARY 16 Steady and strong, January 16 people spend their lives striving for true fulfillment and satisfaction. They may distract others in their personal quest, though, and must learn that some projects are better completed alone.

JANUARY 17 Understanding the motivations of others, January 17 people often find great success. Self-discipline is paramount to them, so they must try not to dominate the lives of others.

JANUARY 18 Playful and fun, those born on January 18 use their sense of humor to keep life from becoming daunting. Childlike ideas are not always positive, though, and they must learn to mature while maintaining their enjoyable lives.

JANUARY 19 Those born on January 19 use their imagination and influence to reach their lofty goals. Unrealistic at times, they must fight to remain stable and grounded or their imagination could run wild.

JANUARY 20 Those born on January 20 respond well to any challenge, as they are accepting of what life serves up. Tolerant and understanding, they sometimes may upset others with their chaotic emotional state.

JANUARY 21 Ambitious and relaxed at the same time, January 21 people are very successful once they realize the extent of their aspirations. They love to have fun, though, and must be careful not to let their determination to succeed be overcome by the desire for pleasure.

JANUARY 22 Those born on January 22 find success through their combination of attention to detail and creativity. Control over their emotions must be learned, however, as they tend to be explosive and reckless at times.

JANUARY 23 Distinctive and individual, those born on January 23 are ethical people who make strong impressions on others. They may become overly involved in their own thoughts and ideas and must learn to cultivate social skills.

JANUARY 24 Admired and lively, January 24 people have attractive personalities that lead them to be seen as icons. Admiration can lead to arrogance for them, however, and they may have to work to remain humble about their abilities.

JANUARY 25 The success of the talented individuals born on January 25 depends on the prosperity of the times in which they live. They must fight to stay emotionally stable, though, as success and failure often have a great influence on their sense of self-worth.

JANUARY 26 Bold and methodical, those born on January 26 have endless determination to reach their personal goals. They must learn to not ready themselves for failure, though, otherwise they may become destructive.

JANUARY 27 Often finding their talent at an early age, those born on January 27 may find themselves in a profession dealing with the development of children. They may fight too hard to stay young, however, and must learn to mature.

JANUARY 28 Those born on January 28 often find incredible physical success through strong perseverance. They can be impulsive, though, and must learn that many actions need a plan to accompany them.

JANUARY 29 Confident in reason and logic, those born on January 29 enjoy letting problems work themselves out on their own, although they are willing to intervene when necessary. Compliant, they must learn the correct balance, as it is easy for them to become passive.

JANUARY 30 Born leaders, January 30 people use their communication skills and judgment to resolve crises. Persuasive, they must learn to manage this talent; otherwise they run the risk of becoming manipulative.

JANUARY 31 Attractive and respected, January 31 people like to gain the spotlight to express themselves. Depression is a possibility if they are repressed, though, and they must learn to function out of the limelight.

FEBRUARY 1 Clever and thorough, February 1 people combine their work ethic with improvisation, and are able to overcome almost any situation. They often have emotional problems that stand in stark contrast to their great mental prowess.

FEBRUARY 2 Refined but unusual, those born on February 2 tend to cling to their cultural heritage no matter where they go in life. This strong group identity may cause them to neglect personal matters, however, and they may have difficulty maintaining relationships.

FEBRUARY 3 Extremely attentive to detail, those born on February 3 seem to have an ease with materials, and that affords them an unusual perspective on life. Prone to vacillation, they can have problems making decisions and may never settle down in a serious relationship.

FEBRUARY 4 Needing to do things their own way, February 4 people are honest and uninhibited and do well as long as they have a say in the structure of their work environment. Easily bored, they often use their energy in many different places, never finding the one area in which to direct it all.

FEBRUARY 5 With fluency and elegance, February 5 people know how to approach any situation and to communicate without words. The grace they have with action is lacking in speech, however, and they need to work on not being abrupt.

FEBRUARY 6 Likable and outgoing, February 6 people are often admired and commended by those close to them. Rarely satisfied with the respect of others, they tend to be insecure about their own worth.

FEBRUARY 7 Critical of inequalities, those born on February 7 often speak out against the existing order with their own vision for the future. Good judges of character, they must nevertheless learn that candor is not always appreciated.

FEBRUARY 8 Those born on February 8 are often thought to be able to read the future, though usually they are just perceptive enough to see the importance of ordinary things. Despite possessing this sixth sense, they struggle to find the right partner and may suffer emotionally.

FEBRUARY 9 Spontaneous and exciting, those born on February 9 can be quite productive once they learn how to direct their energy. Lovers of variety, they must be careful not to disperse their energy among too many projects.

FEBRUARY 10 Seeking respect, those born on February 10 work extremely hard to find acceptance. Though they are confident, they often do not gain the respect they want and must learn to be satisfied with teaching their skills to others.

FEBRUARY 11 Improvement is the goal for February 11 people, and they often use their creative energies to better the lives of the people around them. Well intended, they sometimes try to change things that others are not ready to relinquish.

FEBRUARY 12 Protective and strong, February 12 people strive to unify contrasting viewpoints. Good mediators, they tend to work better alone, however, and are prone to disappointment when their plans are not completed to their satisfaction.

FEBRUARY 13 Spontaneous and open, February 13 people enjoy revealing themselves to others and being the center of attention. They can be impulsive, however, and must guard against opening up to the wrong person.

FEBRUARY 14 Those born on February 14 are skilled in the use of language and can make profound statements to prompt both thought and laughter. Usually well intentioned, they need to be aware that their verbal abilities may upset as well as inspire.

FEBRUARY 15 Creative and ingenious, those born on February 15 have an uncanny ability to realize unusual dreams that others would see only as fantasy. Hypersensitive at times, they must learn that sometimes it's best to hide their feelings.

FEBRUARY 16 Valuing spontaneity and flexibility, those born on February 16 are lively and energetic in all that they do. Abrupt and explosive at times, they must learn to respect the views of other people.

FEBRUARY 17 Extremely sensitive from a young age, February 17 people often build a wall around their emotions, making them very strong and determined. This armor makes it difficult for them to be touched, though, and they may lose out on possible friends.

FEBRUARY 18 Adept at seeing the big picture, February 18 people live their lives according to a wide world view, and are good at brushing off small failures. Although their goals are very impressive, they nevertheless must learn to notice the details that will form an important part of their success.

FEBRUARY 19 February 19 people strive to attain distant goals and are good at balancing the practical with the adventurous. Creative and ambitious, they tend to make hasty decisions and need to learn how to control their fantasies.

FEBRUARY 20 Wanting to make an impact, February 20 people try to make their mark on whatever they do, while still being sensitive to the feelings of others. Their need to be accepted leads them to be easily swayed, however, and they should learn to stick to their own beliefs.

FEBRUARY 21 Deeply emotional, those born on February 21 feel that the greatest gift is intimacy with another. Giving and passionate, they must nevertheless be careful not to let their egos get in the way of their relationships.

FEBRUARY 22 Those born on February 22 fight for freedom for everyone and often lose their ego in the quest. Dedicated, they must be careful not to become overly idealistic, for they may fail to see the positive aspects of their society.

FEBRUARY 23 Realistic and convincing, those born on February 23 shine when offering themselves to a suitable position. Helpful people, they can also be overly analytical and must work to control their critical tendencies.

FEBRUARY 24 Overly generous with their energies, February 24 people sacrifice many things in order to further a worthy cause. Committed, they demand a lot in return and may consequently experience frustration and resentment.

FEBRUARY 25 Powerful and impressive, those born on February 25 believe that real happiness is achieved in giving to a higher cause. Eager to give at all times, they must learn to analyze a situation to see whether the receiver is open to their gift.

FEBRUARY 26 Attuned to the vulnerabilities of others, February 26 people understand how to stir up controversy and get people thinking about important issues. Captivating and influential, they must learn to harness their power and be tolerant of those who do not understand them.

FEBRUARY 27 February 27 people use their great knowledge of the world around them to explore all areas of society. Loyal people, they demand a lot of themselves and their partners and may find it difficult to sustain a serious relationship.

FEBRUARY 28 Those born on February 28 are vibrant and expressive individuals who brighten any occasion with their presence. Animated and eager, they must understand that their enthusiasm may sometimes irritate others.

FEBRUARY 29 True to their unusual birthday, those born on February 29 are distinctively youthful and manage to continually avoid serious danger. Prone to extremes, they need work to maintain a moderate and balanced lifestyle.

MARCH 1 Sensitive to their surroundings and appreciative of beauty, those born on March 1 are also ambitious and practical. Usually balanced, they must be careful not to retreat into fantasy when things are not going well.

MARCH 2 Loyal and dependable, those born on March 2 are faithful to people and ideas they admire. Respectful of others, these kind people must be careful not to become obsessed with individuals they do not know well.

MARCH 3 Imaginative but practical, March 3 people enjoy finding a need and using their abilities to fulfill that need. Very giving of themselves, they are often dissatisfied with their own personality and may become overly involved to avoid this discomfort.

MARCH 4 Self-contained and comfortable, those born on March 4 prefer to work alone and have little contact with society. Highly independent and successful, they must take care to cultivate better relationships with others.

MARCH 5 Classic, refined, and creative, the individuals born on March 5 tend to be very productive people. They have a distinct and secretive dark side, however, and must learn to manage this aspect of themselves in order to be happy.

MARCH 6 Attracted to beauty, those born on March 6 find that a subtle force draws them to pleasant people and events. Imaginative, they may be overcome by their fantasies and must work to keep themselves grounded.

MARCH 7 Conceptual individuals, those born on March 7 find great success when they can give form to their abstract ideas. They may feel abandoned and solitary, though, because their innovative minds work quite differently than most people's.

MARCH 8 Although mindful of tradition, those born on March 8 rarely conform to the norms of society. Thoughtful and loving life, they may nonetheless find themselves isolated due to their unusual views.

MARCH 9 Curious and intuitive, March 9 people are concerned with both their immediate surroundings and the far reaches of space. Adventurous, they may be detached from the reality of their situation as they yearn to travel throughout the world.

MARCH 10 Striving to understand themselves and their emotions, those born on March 10 would much prefer to have fun than to earn money or fame. These sensitive and astute people tend to feel things deeply, though, and may become withdrawn when success eludes them.

MARCH 11 The progressive people of March 11 believe that success depends on an understanding of the world around them. Dedicated, they may also be opinionated and must try not to give in to possessive behavior.

MARCH 12 Good at overcoming obstacles, those born on March 12 have a strong sense of themselves. Versatile and able, they often struggle to maintain direction and must work hard to avoid reckless behavior.

MARCH 13 Strong believers in fate, those born on March 13 are accepting of their lives and try to convince others to be the same. Enthusiastic in their beliefs, they need to be more tolerant of those whose opinions differ from theirs.

MARCH 14 Flexible and compassionate, those born on March 14 define themselves in relation to other people. Often complacent, they must learn to commit themselves and to understand that a passive approach is not always best.

MARCH 15 Always looking to rise in their careers, March 15 people are natural leaders who can easily switch professions to succeed. They can be overly competitive, though, and must be aware that working with others is sometimes preferable to working alone.

MARCH 16 Through a combination of creativity and pragmatism, March 16 people are an inspiration to others. Good at compromising, they must learn to be more committed and to stand up for what they believe in.

MARCH 17 The enthusiastic individuals born on March 17 are good communicators who do well working for a cause they believe in. Devoted and idealistic, they must take care that they don't become disconnected from the more pragmatic aspects of life.

MARCH 18 Those born on March 18 have an exquisite sense of timing and are taken with completion and evolution. Often absorbed in their work, they need to learn patience in order to avoid becoming obsessive.

MARCH 19 The persuasive and persistent people of March 19 understand how to use their abilities to realize their dreams. Committed, determined, and successful, they often have to work hard to control their obstinate tendencies.

MARCH 20 Born on the last day of the astrological year, March 20 people often have unusual gifts and strong logic. Interested in the world around them, they can be indecisive and passive and may have to push themselves to start new projects.

The Six Karmic Paths

This section is designed to act as a general guide to your life in the coming years. Through following its general and specific suggestions you will discover the course of action most appropriate for each time period. Each of the following six karmic paths has its own set of values and suggests a highly individual course of action in order to achieve success:

The Way of Emancipation
October 9, 2002–February 27, 2003

The Way of Recharging
February 28–July 18, 2003

The Way of Dropping the Mask
July 19–December 7, 2003

The Way of Emergence
December 8, 2003–April 27, 2004

The Way of Satisfaction
April 28–September 15, 2004

The Way of Confrontation
September 16, 2004–February 4, 2005

The Way of Emancipation: October 9, 2002 – February 27, 2003

Your primary task during this period is to shake off limitations and restrictions—no matter what the cost. This will involve paying more attention to detail and perhaps giving up on some of your far-reaching visions, which may have been standing in the way of your progress for quite some time now. This period favors working in a straightforward, meticulous fashion and refusing to get sidelined or detoured. Only by adopting a highly pragmatic attitude can you liberate yourself from the powerfully determining attitudes which have been holding you back.

You may have to adopt a somewhat anarchic attitude toward life to avoid falling under the spell of rules and prohibitions. This path is concerned more with results than with intentions, requiring that those who tread it be more interested in the outcome of a situation than with the motives before the event. Particularly important will be discarding unnecessary expectations and judgments, even getting rid of a good part of your personal moral code. You may have been held back by self-fulfilling prophecies or old scripts from childhood, which must also be discarded. This will leave you open to almost any new happening and will fill you with a sense of exhilaration and a newfound hope.

It is in the world of personal experience rather than that of book learning that your greatest lessons will be learned. You should not be surprised if you make frequent errors, for you will largely be employing a method of trial and error. After all, in order to learn from your mistakes you must not only make them, but also be aware that they were made. For this reason, developing a heightened awareness and consciousness is tied up with the karma of this path if the individuals on it are to grow spiritually. Those who experience things without realizing that they have experienced them will not proceed as far in their evolution. It is likely that many on this path will seek out challenging and even progressively more dangerous experiences, for it is only in probing these areas that they feel truly alive. It will be extremely important for you to really lay it on the line, perhaps even occasionally risking your well-being or own best interests.

Should you refuse to change and in fact insist on following your grand schemes, you run the very real danger of falling prey to optimism and idealism. For example, refusing to believe the worst about people or failing to dig for underlying motives for their behavior could leave you disillusioned and bewildered at times. On the other hand, a real balance must be found, since if you drop your good thoughts about others completely you could easily fall prey to irony and a pessimism which could bury any good intentions or hope. You must be careful not to pay more attention to how you say something than in what is actually being said, i.e., valuing the medium more highly than the message. Also, the temptation exists to repeat the same negative message again and again rather than just stating it once and then letting it go.

Unfortunately, at this time guaranteeing yourself freedom could be predicated on taking someone else's freedom away. Therefore, this path likely could breed resentment among a social group, particularly those who see you as being terribly selfish. Others surely will react badly if they see anarchistic tendencies emerge in you or if your political leanings swing strongly to the left. In any case, it will be hard for you to spend time with strongly conservative individuals now, but in fact these people could do a lot more to help you maintain a state of balanced mental health than those with rebellious orientations similar to your own. In fact, people who think the same way as you could drag you into a great deal of trouble and generate more conflict in political areas than you care to deal with. The best direction to take is simply to avoid unnecessary or stupid rules rather than urging others to break them.

At this time family relationships could become especially difficult. Major conflicts easily could emerge with one or both of your parents. This is particularly true of those parents who themselves were rebellious in youth, but became progressively more rigid and tyrannical in their later years. By repressing their own children they awaken rebellion in them, thus re-creating models of their own turbulent youth.

A real need for affection emerges on this path, but in friendships and love relationships it may be difficult to accept. Such relationships may become highly contentious, and you must be careful not to let things get out of hand and tear these unions apart. Getting married at this time is not especially recommended, although it could provide stability as long as your intentions are serious and both parties are able to commit completely to each other.

During this period it is best to guarantee yourself as much time to yourself as possible. Hobbies and other leisure-time activities may even come to assume more importance than your main profession. The Way of Emancipation allows you to give the required energy while on the job, so long as your nonprofessional activities can receive full attention. What is absolutely necessary on this karmic path is to seek out ever-new opportunities and horizons, because the hunger for experience in this time period is very great and there is an all-consuming need to learn and to innovate.

An image which symbolizes the Way of Emancipation is that of a captive, perhaps a political prisoner, who escapes again and again after being captured. No walls can hold them, no bars contain them. Perhaps such an individual welcomes limitations and restrictions so that they can be surmounted and outwitted. Ultimately, however, the captive breaks free for good and outgrows such psychological needs for restriction, finding enough real challenge in surpassing the ordinary limitations of everyday life. In this way the captive's anarchy can take the direction of a spiritual quest and a striving for the infinite.

The Way of Recharging: February 28–July 18, 2003

During these months you will find it difficult to resist being rebellious and combative. You will have to work hard to find a steady source of energy. Once this energy source is located, it must be directed toward a variety of goals. This will help you to avoid getting bogged down in fruitless struggles. The Way of Recharging will help us all understand the benefit of not getting fixated on one way of doing things. Too often at this time the tendency is to react vengefully against another person or point of view, instead of ignoring them and formulating an original concept, which could emanate from a highly personal creative source. The metamorphosis demanded by this karmic path can open the eyes of any or all of us to a whole new world of ideas. Such concepts may seem unrelated, but in fact they are guided by a far-seeing plan.

Learning to walk away from a fight or other confrontation is an essential lesson to be learned at this time. Most of this aggression is predicated on a need to struggle, so it may be difficult now to accept that there is an easier way to do things. Since the tendency to become a workaholic frequently surfaces now, you must force yourself to remember that often a brilliant flash of insight or a lucky occurrence can accomplish just as much as unrelenting labor. You have to remember to trust your instincts now and learn to fly by the seat of your pants, and in so doing surrender your need for control to the larger powers of the universe, in effect giving in and going with the flow. Likewise, this is an opportune time to reexamine your worldly aspirations and need for financial reward, which may have to be muted or even dropped for now. What is best is to think less consciously about what is in it for you and give time to interesting partnerships and projects, particularly those which hold out little or no hope for direct remuneration. Paradoxically, it is these very activities which can lead to great spiritual, creative, and in certain cases even material gain.

This is a time when life lessons will often be learned in school settings, whether full- or part-time at a university or community college. Best are educational programs that open up new vistas and discourage premature specialization. Inspirational teachers can reveal a whole wide range of subjects which may be explored at leisure rather than under pressure or threat of failure. Although the temptation is strong on the Way of Recharging to rebel against authority, drop out of school, and start focusing your energy on immediate social advancement or financial gain, you must try to enjoy fully the lack of fixed responsibilities afforded by your student days. Allow your mind to roam freely over a variety of philosophical, technical, and artistic pursuits.

One of the great lessons on this karmic path is coming to understand human values, and consequently dropping the idea of your own superiority, and with it the idea that one person is any better than another. Getting mired down in conceit, sarcasm, ruthlessness, and autocratic tendencies are ever-present dangers. In other cases, overreaching tendencies may lead you to get too diffuse and undirected in your stance, and thus you may begin to drift aimlessly through life or to put off making important decisions.

Yet another possibility is that your autocratic tendencies may lead you into taking a garrulous stance, prodding you to control others by monopolizing the airwaves and not allowing anyone else to speak.

One danger on this path is that you may withdraw from the world by adopting an aloof and unapproachable position. In order to fight this tendency, which will not work in your favor now, it will be necessary to come down off your pedestal and mix more easily, even if superficially, with those you come in contact with. Unfortunately, many people you know will be difficult to reach during these months; some will even be impossible to connect with. But by slowing down, developing patience, and not having such high expectations of others you will eventually be able to get in touch.

In professional matters, your bosses, colleagues, and clients may demand more of you than you are prepared or able to give. In other circumstances, you may give your energy to the wrong people or simply fritter it away in idle pursuits, once you have managed to recharge. Therefore, try to find a fine line between selfishness and altruism once your energies have been replenished on the Way of Recharging.

Because you may inevitably have more frequent but also more superficial human contacts at this time, you must beware promiscuity, carrying with it the possibility that you may be unable to carry on one single long-standing significant relationship. Sexual promiscuity can be downright dangerous and the direct result of your sudden surge in energy. In this way you stand to become the victim of your own newfound interests and powers. Your family could prove the only ones who can exert the necessary control over your wilder side, awaken you to your own best interests, and alert you to pitfalls. Even if you are not particularly close to your family you may need to depend on them heavily from time to time to provide the stability you so desperately require.

It is best at this time to find many different outlets for your boundless energy. On the physical plane, a whole gamut of activities, from vigorous walking or swimming to contact sports or martial arts, is advised. Travel and exploration of all sorts may beckon, but caution must be taken that you do not wear yourself out and weaken your already stressed-out mental state.

All activities that promote stability will ground your nervous energies. If you can find a partner who will help establish a comfortable home and share an interest in the domestic arts, so much the better. Above all, the process of recharging demands that you first learn to empty yourself, perhaps through meditation and reflection.

In this latter respect, being on this karmic path could be likened to a pitcher filled with standing water. In order to be filled with pure, fresh fluid again, the pitcher must be emptied. This simple image typifies your needs and symbolizes the futility of trying to acquire more before you are prepared to give up what you already have. The image also emphasizes the need to surmount possessiveness and control, daring to give up everything in the firm belief that something better will come along to take the place of that which has perhaps already turned flat or stale.

The Way of Dropping the Mask: July 19 – December 7, 2003

During this period, you will be required to give up your need to exert an influence on others in favor of rediscovering your own natural self. Once this is accomplished you may well find that you are even more persuasive and influential than you were before. However, this process of dropping the mask is not an easy one, particularly since it can require denying yourself the rewards of money, fame, and power, or at the very least reorienting yourself toward more personal or spiritual goals. Often a shift of values toward the natural aspects of life will involve a temporary abnegation of or even disgust with worldly matters. On this karmic path nature itself is pictured as an ideal, and along with it an unpretentious lifestyle, diet, and exercise regimens, environmental awareness or activism, and eschewing all forms of pretense and snobbism.

Now is the time to learn to have more fun and take yourself less seriously. This may sound like an easy enough task, but being yourself in a natural fashion is not always the easiest task, particularly for more serious or moral individuals. Letting go of your more conservative side and letting your hair down, particularly in public, is an act which could require breaking down many innate inhibitions. The Way of Dropping the Mask implies a dissolving of a social persona that may have taken years to build up, one which has successfully served as an effective defensive and controlling tool. Giving up a careful approach to life, an attitude which has guaranteed you a certain amount of success in the past, and working to become a more carefree person cannot be accomplished by some without significant stress. Yet, the relief experienced when such a heavy mask finally can be dropped also will be enormously rewarding.

Important life lessons can be learned in both personal and professional spheres during this time period. Although important transformations often are required in career activities, perhaps even necessitating a major change in profession, the beginnings of such changes on this karmic path usually are accomplished first in your private life. Chief among these changes seems to be worrying less about what others think and having the courage to just be yourself. Fear of rejection may have been a strong motivating factor in the past for the use of a charming but controlling nature to assure being accepted by friends, colleagues, and lovers. An ego reorientation which promotes more of an I-don't-care or take-it-or-leave-it attitude is frequently an important step in seeking a more natural approach to life.

One danger in this whole process is that you may overshoot the mark and become overly rebellious. So much relief may accompany your metamorphosis that you may become careless and insulting in social interactions. Unless you learn to put your redirected energies in service of those around you, you run the risk of reveling in dangerously antisocial behavior. Indeed, a short period of time spent indulging in such activities may be necessary before you achieve a more balanced state. On the other hand, some individuals may experience just the opposite difficulty and get mired in arch-conservatism. If you are one of these people, you may get so frustrated over your inability to change that you simply dig in your heels and become unable to move forward in your development.

Family members and friends could become appalled at your behavior, should your path take a more extreme or bizarre turn. Changes in your appearance and conduct may convince them that you are engaged in throwing away all the benefits you have so carefully built up for yourself over the years. Frequently they will assume that a wicked or even slightly deranged person has exerted undue influence here, and blame for your radical transformation may be loaded on this person's shoulders. Usually it is the reverse that has really occurred, however—first the change takes place and then the involvement with an unusual figure follows. In any event, more conservative family members will no doubt feel threatened or even rejected by such behavior.

Your personal relationships may change radically at this time. For example, if your mate is undergoing such changes you could experience great relief and joy when your partner begins to become more natural in his or her approach to life. On the other hand, some partners may feel threatened by this process, particularly if such individuals step out of their relationship and become involved with younger or more vibrant partners. Such stresses usually are weathered more easily in friendships, and adjustments are made with less difficulty. As far as love affairs are concerned, the sensual and sexual pleasures experienced at this time are often a strong incentive for further change, and also serve as a confirmation for the transformations which have already taken place.

Your desires to indulge in all sorts of natural activities run high on the Way of Dropping the Mask. Although wildness may reign initially, it is highly doubtful whether such behavior will be beneficial to you in the long run. At a certain point it may be necessary to ground yourself and again take control of the situation in order to provide the stability necessary in everyday life. After all, fun and pleasure are useless to a person whose personality is wildly unstable—it's just like pouring gasoline on a fire. Thus, imaginative drives may have to be tempered to more practical ones. The most appropriate balance on this path will be between your newly found naturalness and your ability to keep things under control.

An image which describes this karmic path may be that of a soldier who has served dutifully and zealously in the defense of his country. At a certain moment the war is over and he can again return to civilian life. It is necessary to give up the formal uniforms which he has worn and again to wear informal clothing and to adjust to a freer lifestyle. However, coming back to civilian life may not be as easy as it seems. Nonetheless, using the discipline and technical know-how acquired in the military to advantage in civilian life can help him to achieve professional success.

The Way of Emergence: December 8, 2003 – April 27, 2004

The Way of Emergence allows your fullest potential to blossom. You could really surprise yourself during this time period, since you may find yourself emerging from your secret hiding place to take up your post with the important figures in society. Your star may be about to rise high whether you are from an advantaged or disadvantaged background. You can accomplish this through being chosen by an individual or group who will open many doors for you. Once this choice is made, you may find yourself growing into a social persona which was ideally suited to you all along without your realizing it.

The processes just described hinge on being in the right place at the right time. Chance and coincidence can play an important role in your life in general. Even if you are serious by nature and do not generally believe in the paranormal or recognize miracles when they occur, you are fated now to be touched repeatedly by unexpected happenings. You must learn to be open to such events and by surrendering to the dictates of destiny to give up your doubts about the wisdom of the universe.

The primary area of life lessons on the Way of Emergence is in the social arena. It is here that many of your worries can be left behind and your best energies freed up to work, often in the service of others. You also can develop your leadership skills, whether in managing a family or professional group. Another productive pursuit for you would be acting as a consultant or troubleshooter. By identifying with a larger group you could acquire a new form of security and protection which could satisfy needs formerly met only by withdrawing from the world.

Nonetheless, there is the danger during this time period of getting mired down in a depressive or escapist stance. Often neurotic role patterns and addictive tendencies can emerge here, making it even more difficult to undergo the kinds of transformation required by this karmic path. At the opposite end of the spectrum, it also could be possible to go overboard on social involvements, thereby running the risk of giving up your own individuality or skimming superficially over life's surface. Other individuals could adopt a highly critical or inflexible stance. This demanding attitude could ultimately take its toll in the form of stress and a possible breakdown. Preferable to any of the above would be slow organic change and meaningful growth in one's personality and beliefs.

The theme of emergence not only can figure prominently in your own life but in the influence you have on others as well. Quite often such influence does not take place in your role as a teacher but rather as a guide in the school of life. Thus, you may choose to play a role as parent, friend, coach, therapist, or trainer to younger individuals to whom you may be able to point out the way. The most vital lesson you could teach would be to show them how to be true to themselves and to show the world who they really are. In such a role you must beware making highly impressionable individuals unduly attached to you, for it is vitally important for their development to learn from their own experiences. Ultimately you will avoid having to adopt a dictatorial role or allowing yourself to be dragged down by a welter of dependent energies.

Finding your life partner could be in the cards for you now. A dedicated marriage might result, one which includes the raising of children and the broadening of social horizons. Thus, family ties are very important at this time, particularly working on building a cohesive unit that can provide benefits to its members in times of acute need.

On an intimate personal level, the emphasis on this path is less on sexual expression and more on sensuous and affectionate feelings. Such an orientation can bring relief from the strain of intense, passionate demands and not involve any disappointments. You could find yourself less involved in an exclusive relationship during this time and more at the center of a broad circle of friends, or becoming an active member of a social group. Such involvement also can serve as a link to your occupational work, particularly that involving planning and administration.

The kind of lifestyle favored at this time is a wide open, vibrant one with lots of variety and personal challenge. You will find that you bore easily now and that you need constant stimulation in order to be able to give your very best. Your greatest satisfaction could lie in watching the emergence and growth of new life as spring approaches, especially as a gardener, caretaker, parent, property owner, or entrepreneur. However, on this karmic path you must have the wisdom to say no when demands get excessive and to stockpile your resources in order to be able to give more effectively in the future. Health as reflected in diet, exercise, checkups, and treatment will be of more importance than usual. Moreover, rearranging or redecorating your living space along with various domestic activities of all sorts could be crucial to your psychological health and well-being.

An apt image for the Way of Emergence could be an animal emerging from hibernation. As it awakens from its winter sleep, the full glory of spring bursts in on its consciousness and it is quickly transformed into an alert, ambient creature. Having used up its stores of depot fat, it is hungry for a good meal and swiftly sets off in search of nourishment. Awakening to new life and challenge, the animal leaves its dormant state behind and takes its place in the world around it.

The Way of Satisfaction: April 28–September 15, 2004

The Way of Satisfaction demands a lessening of tension and a more relaxed attitude from those who tread its path. Relaxation, easy for some of us, is probably the most difficult goal to achieve at this time. In addition, moral attitudes must be tempered by pragmatism, which asserts the priority of results over intention. What is necessary is to use your intensity at will rather than being its slave. Thus, during this time period pleasurable rewards for hard work will be forthcoming, while at the same time the intense focus which is required can be followed by healthy and enjoyable breaks.

Because your attachment to truth and honesty is so high now, it may be extremely difficult to temper a rigid moral stance. Further, it will be an important lesson to learn flexibility and compromise, and also the necessity for simple daily acts of kindness, as these are more important at this time than any degree of worldly success. Moreover, you will be able to appreciate the importance of emotional fulfillment once you realize what a positive effect it can have on your work. In this respect, sharing love and affection is important along with the periods of uninterrupted time it takes to develop your relationships fully. Although the physical aspects of such relationships are important you must be careful that they do not produce as much pain as pleasure for all concerned. In order to orient yourself more positively you should perhaps first deal effectively with your own self-destructive tendencies.

The arena in which life lessons are inevitably learned on the Way of Satisfaction is interpersonal relationships. On this karmic path you may be so caught up in your work that even acknowledging that you have a meaningful private life in the first place can be significant. A second step could be spending more energy on making social contacts that have little or no bearing on your career. Although you may view such relationships as frivolous at first, your pleasure-loving side will kick in eventually and begin to seduce you away from your work. Given that you can handle the accompanying feelings of conscience and guilt that assail you, you may prove remarkably gifted in the subtle arts of conversation, intimacy, and sexual expression. Third, learning to indulge your sensuous side without falling back into obsessive or compulsive patterns may help you to replace your frustration with true satisfaction.

If you concentrate too much on modifying your hardworking attitudes, you run the risk of giving yourself over to a life of laziness. Another possibility is that by becoming too pragmatic your spiritual development could fall by the wayside. In extreme cases, the risk exists of indulging in somewhat selfish and antisocial behavior once your ethical stance is softened. The trick is to find a way to balance moral and sensuous drives and above all to put a good part of your energies in service of the common good. The temptation for you when you see a chance for real contentment is that you may want to eat your dessert before the meal, and thus expect reward before work. This could result in pursuing pleasure with the same single-minded intensity with which you approached your career, and by playing hard after working hard you may deprive yourself of any real chance for long-lasting relaxation.

In the process of transformation it will be helpful to find others who need you. If you feel wanted, useful, and important your development will progress much more easily. Thus, attracting needy individuals is not necessarily wrong, since even dependencies could lead to a positive outcome through awakening your nurturing side. Your family and friends should have the good sense to back off and rid themselves of jealousy when they see others taking advantage of you (as they see it), since by interfering or being overprotective they may slow down your spiritual growth. Once your nurturing tendencies have kicked in you will invariably find a balance between these and your own personal needs, so that serving others and yourself can be brought into balance.

Obviously, strengthening your social and family ties can have a positive influence on your development during this period. The joys of holiday festivities, marriages and births, educational and recreational involvement, and vacations can all play their part. Since love is the best medicine against your own uptight attitudes, you will benefit enormously from a partner who can give you daily doses of kindness and affection. You will gain a great deal from spending many hours with children, either your own or those of relatives and friends, since a child's laughter and joy may do much to orient you in a positive direction and stimulate your sense of well-being.

Many activities will help you during this period to achieve your goal of satisfaction. Beginning on the physical plane, body work, cooking, jogging, and a sensuous relationship, for example, will serve to ground you. Next, mental and spiritual activities that involve taking classes or meditation to begin with will be useful as long as they do not lead you to regress to workaholic behavior. Living in the country and growing your own food also can bring spiritual fulfillment.

An image which comes to mind to describe this path is that of a hardworking person who undergoes a breakdown as a result of pushing themselves too hard. Forced to spend hours alone away from the professional world they come up against themselves and realize that they have a choice between stressing themselves out and learning to relax and enjoy life. They are able to develop personal goals for the first time and learn the value of love. Once they are able to heal they can make a more intelligent choice of a career and fine-tune the connection between their personal and professional lives.

The Way of Confrontation: September 16, 2004–February 4, 2005

This time period dictates that you will not only be able to develop your powers but also begin to understand how to put them to good use. The Way of Confrontation also demands that you show awareness of how power works and also that you demonstrate the courage to go into battle, often against daunting odds. Laying it on the line, as opposed to just talking about it, is implicit here. Building an imposing nature and challenging your opponent may be required in order to develop your personality effectively during this period. Using a mixture of resolve and willpower, even those of diminutive stature will inspire awe in formidable adversaries. Confrontation also denotes having the strength to be told the truth and take it, without it being diluted or sugar-coated. At some point on this path you must learn that the truth, no matter how much it hurts, is preferable to deceit and illusion.

The Way of Confrontation grants you the opportunity to put your realizations about how power works to good use. Thus, your awareness can become a powerful weapon in your arsenal but must never become an excuse for inaction, unless this is the most effective course. Quite likely a powerful confrontation will force you at some point to assert yourself, and thereby set the process of transformation into motion. Should you back down out of fear or uncertainty at first, you may be able to rethink your difficulties and strengthen your resolve to prove more effective on the next occasion. The core lesson here is to learn that getting bottled up in your head through excessive rationalization may cause disempowerment, and that following your instincts by taking swift and direct action is at certain times the best way. Two talents which you would do well to develop at this time are the art of persuasion and knowing the best time to act, both of which can be enhanced through a wide variety of experience.

Inevitably, the arena in which these lessons are worked out is in one-on-one encounters. Facing a powerful challenger or a series of them may be your inevitable destiny at this time. On the other hand, it may equally well be facing the challenges arising in your career which force you to confront difficulties and invent creative solutions. Overcoming a physical or mental handicap also may confer greater stature and power. Such a process implies that your greatest adversary may be yourself, and even if you are not challenged by your own deficiencies you may learn that mastering your emotions is essential to winning the battle. Thus, the area in which many of your life lessons are to be learned is a psychological one. Winning here can mean greater stability, and through self-control you may raise your personal pride and accompanying self-esteem.

If you succumb to the lure of unbridled power you could cause damage to others and to yourself. By arousing antagonisms through unethical behavior you might bring yourself down. Getting mired down in overly critical or rigid attitudes could keep you from plugging into the process of transformation, which is so essential to your development. In addition, sensuous and lavish tendencies could slow down the process and take the edge off your fighting spirit. As a result, on the Way of Confrontation even the strongest and best-developed elements of your personality can work against you and subvert your efforts.

Others may hastily back off from you if they view you as overly belligerent or fixated on gaining personal power. Therefore it is important at every step of the way on this karmic path to prove your intentions and justify your strivings through a well-defined ethical code which is clear to all. You may realize at this time that you can benefit from giving up power, especially when kindness and love take its place. Placing your trust in God is a way of giving power back to its own true source. Individuals who are power obsessed or control freaks would be best avoided during this period.

It could be that the greatest challenges for you on the Way of Confrontation will arise in your relationships. Learning to compromise could be difficult for you now, since your first instinct may be to fight and not back down. Your choice of partner is particularly crucial to your learning to love. Through participation in a deep and caring relationship, you are likely to learn values of cooperation, empathy, and kindness that will enrich all areas of your life. Such values can also guide your drive toward ambition in your career. In this way, family, friendship, and married life can all function as good moral testing grounds for professional and career endeavors.

What is best on this karmic path is a life in which a healthy balance can be maintained between establishing a strong ego through active assertion and guiding such action with an equally powerful moral and loving stance. In accomplishing this balance, bridges must be built among your personal, social, and professional lives. In all these areas, you must learn to treat people as ends in themselves rather than means to an end if you are to evolve spiritually. Matters of an inspirational nature are particularly good for you, whereas competition feeding on greed and blind ambition should be shunned. Since putting power directly in the service of love is such a high priority now, you will benefit from many forms of human interaction, both personal and service-oriented.

An image comes to mind of a chivalrous knight going to battle in service of high ideals. Having achieved a victory, his weapons are laid at the feet of the loved one and formerly warlike energies placed in the service of gentleness, love, and peace. The strongest drive here is no longer to control or overcome, but to plug into even higher strengths, energies, and forces by surrendering to them. In this manner, the warrior becomes even more powerful than before.

INDEX